# A
# SPIRIT
## FOR THE
## REST OF US

08/09/09

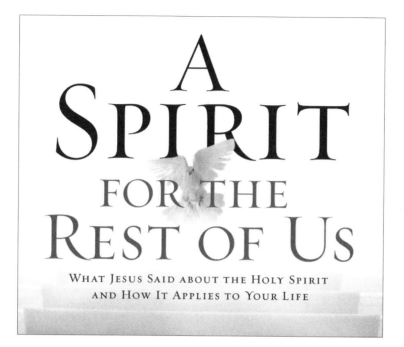

# A SPIRIT
## FOR THE
## REST OF US

WHAT JESUS SAID ABOUT THE HOLY SPIRIT
AND HOW IT APPLIES TO YOUR LIFE

# TIM WOODROOF

# LEAFWOOD
PUBLISHERS

Abilene, Texas

**A SPIRIT FOR THE REST OF US**
*What Jesus Said about the Holy Spirit and How It Applies to Your Life*

LEAFWOOD
P U B L I S H E R S

Copyright 2009 by Tim Woodroof

ISBN 978-0-89112-627-0

Printed in the United States of America

Cover design by Marc Whitaker
Interior text design by Sandy Armstrong

Leafwood Publishers is an imprint of
Abilene Christian University Press.

1648 Campus Court
Abilene, Texas 79601
1-877-816-4455 toll free

For current information about all Leafwood titles, visit our website:
www.leafwoodpublishers.com

09 10 11 12 13 14 / 7 6 5 4 3 2 1

# ACKNOWLEDGEMENTS

Please allow me to thank several people for their kindnesses to me during the writing of the book.

I initially thought through this material while preaching for the Otter Creek Church in Nashville, Tennessee. I am grateful for their patience and for the freedom they gave me to color outside the lines. The writing of this book was also made possible by their financial support as I transitioned out of a preaching role to a new work as writer and church consultant.

I also worked through these ideas at the Abilene Christian University lectureships, and with the Christian Educators' Conference (a dedicated group of ministers—I appreciate them), the Okalona Church of Christ in Louisville, Kentucky, and the Central Church of Christ in Wichita, Kansas. My thanks to each audience for careful listening and enthusiastic responses.

Writing requires quiet and privacy. Lee and Kelley Beaman and Rex and Cathy Harrison provided guest houses for me. And, increasingly, writing requires technological support: my grateful thanks to Kirk Davidson and his computer wizardry.

Several readers made comments on the manuscript—always supportive, often helpful, and sometimes vital. I am grateful to Grady King, Brad Sullivan, Benjamin Neeley, Curt Sparks, and—especially—Jerry Neill, Edward Fudge, Mom, Dad, David, and my sweet Julie. The book wouldn't be the same without their encouraging and insightful partnership.

As I write this, I'm preparing to travel to Beaverton, Oregon, to preach the funeral of a man whose friendship and mentoring have meant the world to me—Ron Stump. He was a great man in God's Kingdom, a greatness measured not in acclaim or wealth but in the pleasure of the Father. I miss you already, Ron.

Finally, a word of thanks to Leonard Allen: for seeing the great need to talk about the Spirit again, for his encouragement of this project, and for his sensitive editing.


Tim Woodroof

# CONTENTS

Chapter One

# A Spirit for the Rest of Us

I have seen church done in the absence of the Spirit of God and it is an arid, ugly thing. Powerless, self-reliant, tradition-bound, fearful of the future—a of church that experiences no living Spirit is not what God intends. It focuses on forms, on ritual, on an obsession with correctness, and is devoid of the transformative vigor that alone produces the image of God and promotes the Kingdom of God. It is a lava tube—a cold and hollow shell formed by a fire that once flowed hot and thick.

I have also seen church done with little *but* Spirit (or at least what is often confused with the Spirit) and it is a frightening, fickle thing. Visceral, abandoned, careless of both past and future—the kind of church that attends to little but signs and wonders is equally not what God intends. It is often impatient with Scripture, suspicious of any authority beyond the Spirit's personal whisperings, hungry for the sensational, and—oddly—devoid of the transformative vigor that promotes holiness and a mature relationship with Christ. It is a river in spate, a torrent breaking out of all channels, a deluge that sweeps away reason and self-control and, eventually, even the gospel itself.

I have seen churches that looked like the Laodicea of old—complacent, content, comfortable—with no expectation the Holy Spirit could break in and do some new thing today. And I have seen churches that looked like Paul's Corinth—a lot of tongues and wonders, a lot of Spirit-talk, but little comprehension of the Cross or the call to maturity or the true priorities of the Spirit. Both sorts of churches are unworthy of the Name and ill-equipped to conduct God's essential Kingdom business.

You and I are caught between the rock of Spirit-denying church and the hard place of Spirit-obsessed church. We are no longer willing to practice a faith in which the Spirit is confined to the words of the Bible, with no living and active presence within us. But neither are we willing to abandon ourselves to the contrived and melodramatic. We long to invite the Spirit into our lives and into our churches. But that invitation is not extended so that we can experience a giddiness of gifts. Rather, we long to experience a supernatural *transformation* that takes broken sinners and grows them into the "fullness of Christ" (Eph 4:13). We need the Spirit; we are hungry for the Spirit; we are eager to seek the Spirit "beyond the sacred page." We suspect there is a relationship with the Spirit more profound than anything we have yet experienced and are quite sure we will not discover it by continuing to keep the Spirit at arm's length. But neither are we ready to stand on a spiritual precipice and leap blindly into the unknown.

We are concerned, on the one hand, that Christ could look at our spiritual walk and accuse us of being lukewarm—neither hot nor cold (Rev 3:16). We certainly don't want him to spit us out or give us up. But, on the other hand, we do not want to go to church with the Corinthians, enduring their frenzied worship and fractured fellowship, missing out on what Paul identifies as the Spirit's *greatest* gifts.

Spirit, yes. But not Spirit at any cost. Not Spirit at the expense of Scripture or the abandonment of reason or the loss of the essential gospel. Spirit, yes. But not *any* Spirit. A *discerned* Spirit … a *tested* Spirit … a *trustable* Spirit.

Is there a Spirit for the rest of us? Something personal and tangible without surrender to the sensational or arrogant? Something that produces real spiritual fruit, not just head-turning signs? Something that offers an experience of God without requiring us to walk through the Pentecostal door?

What, oh what, are the *rest* of us to do?

## The Multi-Channeled Stream

The subject of the Holy Spirit is difficult for many of us. Truth be told, it's been a difficult subject for most people at most times, beginning with Paul's labored attempts to talk about the Spirit with the Corinthians and running all the way to modern musings about whether and how the Holy Spirit works in our lives today.

From the outset, we should admit that the relationship between church and Spirit has always been a multi-channeled stream. For some, the experience of the Spirit rushes full and powerful and overwhelming. For others, the experience is more restrained and subtle. For still others, the experience is minimal, a mere trickle.

As always, there are those who would measure all other Christians by the yardstick of their own experience. If one Christian's walk in the Spirit is not identical to another's, there must be something sadly lacking (or perilously excessive) in that Christian's life before God.

But this diverse experience of the Spirit has been a fact of Christian life from the beginning. Turn to the New Testament and you will find churches that were richly charismatic and miraculously endowed. Tongues, prophecies, healings, revelations—certain churches seemed to experience the mystically miraculous as a matter of course.

Judging from Paul's letters, however, this was not the case with every first-century church. Roman Christians, for example, were very aware of the Spirit and the need to be "led by the Spirit of God" (Rom 8:14). But there is no hint in Paul's letter to the Romans of the miraculous as commonplace. No mention of tongues or healings or special wisdom. No indications of charismatic worship. The Romans were certainly controlled by the Spirit (Rom 8:6), indwelled by the Spirit (Rom 8:9), helped by the Spirit (Rom 8:26), given peace and joy and hope in the Spirit (Rom 14:17; 15:13). But there is no evidence of charismatic fireworks at Rome. Indeed, a quick comparison of the list of "gifts" enjoyed by the churches in Rome and Corinth (Rom 12 and 1 Cor 12) makes clear the differences in their experience of the Spirit. In Corinth the listed gifts are largely extra-normal. In Rome they seem quite ordinary.

In still other New Testament churches—judging again from the letters written to them—an experience of the Spirit does not appear to be as central to their Christian walk. The Spirit is barely mentioned in Paul's letters to the Philippians and Colossians or in Peter's epistles. When he *is* mentioned, references are either to the past (what the Spirit did through the prophets or in the ministry of Jesus) or vague (e.g., "your love in the Spirit"—Col 1:8). James, in his letter, does not mention the Spirit at all.

So the witness of the New Testament appears to suggest that not all churches experienced the Spirit in the same way or to the same degree. The relationship between church and Spirit has been a multi-channeled stream from the beginning.

We see the same thing in the two thousand years of church history stretching between the first century and our own: movements that were radically charismatic; others that focused on unity, holiness, and assurance as the Spirit's true gifts; and yet others where the Spirit played no obvious or central role.

Of course, that same multi-channeled stream is evidenced in the variety of experiences of the Spirit enjoyed by various branches of God's people today: the flood of Pentecostalism, the transforming flow of Methodism or the Nazarenes (for example), or the trickle that is the usual experience of those who share my particular heritage.

## A Trustable Path

If you and I are to discover a trustworthy way to welcome a living Spirit, let me suggest several principles that will be important to that search.

First, it would be wonderful if we could find an approach that allowed Jesus himself to be our guide to the Spirit. Not the raw and confusing experience of the first Christians. Not even the comments and observations of writers who, though inspired, tend to address specific issues involving specific situations in the early church's life. Rather, words about the Spirit from Jesus himself. Guidance from the One who is the source of the Spirit. An introduction to the Spirit from the One who knows him best.

Second, we need an approach to the Spirit that stresses who the Spirit *is*, not just what the Spirit *does*. One of our greatest problems with the Spirit touted by some (though no means all) of the Charismatic/ Pentecostal persuasion is that he seems *strange* to us, a being we do not recognize with an agenda we do not understand. Who is the Holy Spirit? What is his character? What are his values and goals? If we are to open up our lives to him, we need to trust that everything we know about God, everything we have come to love about Jesus, is personified in the Spirit. We need to trust that making ourselves vulnerable to a living Spirit is not going to lead us in some direction *other* than what we committed ourselves to when we signed on as disciples of Christ.

Third, we need an approach to the Spirit that emphasizes the Spirit's most vital work—making us *spiritual*. The Corinthians could speak in tongues; yet they remained "infants in Christ," "worldly," carnal and not spiritual. What good is it to experience the miraculous if we lack the love, joy, peace, patience, kindness, goodness, faithfulness, gentleness, and self control that are the Spirit's most important bequests? Far from celebrating the Corinthians' spectacular feats in the Spirit, Paul mourned an experience of the Spirit that left the Corinthians immature, immoral, and immodest; that left the church divided, conflicted, and unloving. There is a greater work intended by the Spirit than displays of miraculous power. Transformation. Sanctification. Killing the flesh. Conferring the mind of Christ. Unity. Assurance. Presence. It is this greater work that must be emphasized if we are to find an approach to the Spirit that is trustable.

Fourth, it would be best if we could walk into the Spirit's realm without being forced to enter through the door of the supernatural. Face it. If we have to wade through tongues and prophetic utterances and the Spirit striking people dumb or dead in order to get to the Spirit who transforms us, it's going to be a long and difficult journey. Is there an approach to the Spirit that allows us to put the question of the miraculous on hold while we pursue the possibility of presence? Is there a way to reach for a Spirit who indwells us without first having to address the thorny issue of modern-day signs and wonders?

Finally, we desire an approach to the Spirit that fits our present need so well that pursuing such a Spirit is worth whatever effort and risk may be involved. The most important word in that sentence is "need." If you are satisfied with your life as a disciple, if you have all the spiritual power you want, if your life is full of holy fruit, if you walk in confidence and a constant consciousness of God's presence, read no further. This book is not for you. There is no need for those who already have everything they require for life and godliness to bother with an extended quest for the Spirit.

But if, in fact, you are hungry for more, if you long for holy fruit and power for living, if you yearn for greater confidence and a deeper awareness of God's presence, if you've lived with the sense that there must be more to the walk of faith than you currently experience, then you are ready to explore what God's Spirit might do for you.

## A Place Somewhere Between

Somewhere between Spirit-famine and Spirit-excess is a Spirit for the rest of us.

Somewhere between no Spirit and nothing-but-Spirit is a Spirit for the rest of us.

Somewhere between lifeless tradition and slippery slope, between quenching and disorder, between sitting on our hands and rolling in the aisles, there is a Spirit for the rest of us.

Somewhere between mind-without-Spirit and Spirit-without-mind lies the possibility of a Spirit the rest of us can appreciate and experience. Between the anemia of life-without-the-Spirit and the fever of possession-without-transformation there exists that place where we meet the Spirit and know the Spirit and walk in the Spirit in tangible, trustable ways.

Somewhere between the parched land of an undiscovered Spirit and the trackless swamp of abandon to the Spirit lies that slaking spiritual stream from which we drink and are revived. Between rote liturgy and riotous chaos, between the cold cathedral and the over-heated revival tent, between strict rationalism and frothy emotionalism, between con-jugating Greek verbs and babbling in unknown tongues lies that ter-ritory where mind and heart find their shared home and we embrace the Spirit in all his empowering, transforming, convicting, truth-giving presence.

I want to find that place. That place "somewhere between." That place God has reserved for "the rest of us." You may want to find that place too. If so, I invite you to join me on this journey.

Chapter Two

# THE SPIRIT AND THE FINAL DISCOURSE

No wonder they are frightened. Something awful is about to happen. They don't know what. They don't know when. But soon. And terrible.

They can see it written on their Master's face, bearing down on his shoulders. They can smell it in the air, the sour stench of danger. They can feel the pressure of its coming—like a storm approaching.

So they gather this night in dread. It's hard for them to meet each other's eyes. Conversations are subdued. A meal is prepared but no one has much appetite. They pick at their food. They pick at each other. There are no jokes, no lighthearted banter. Their Master is "troubled in spirit," and the disciples match his mood.

Everything is about to change. And none of them wants that.

None but he. He wants it. In ways, he welcomes it. He knows exactly what is about to happen and when. He's known all his life. On this evening, no doubt, he has his own fears to wrestle with, his own dread. After all, the blood to be spilled is his. The agony endured will be his.

But it is *their* agony that consumes him this evening, their fears and uncertainties. Everything is about to change. And he wants their faith to survive the storm.

He's tried to warn them: cryptically at first ("I am going away"); more bluntly later ("I lay down my life"). And they see glimmers of the dangers he faces: "Let us also go [back to Judea], that we may die with him" (John 11:16). The anxieties and sense of dread they bring to this final supper indicate they sense something will happen and soon.

Yet still they seem confused by it all, stunned, like witnesses to a tragedy unfolding before disbelieving eyes. They don't understand about Mary's anointing and its appropriateness to the moment. They don't understand what the triumphant crowds mean and how they will force the Pharisees' hands. They don't understand about Judas.

They don't get it. Even this close to the end, they don't get it. Perhaps they can't *afford* to get it … they have too much at stake.

## Addicted to His Presence

They left everything to follow him—families, friendships, houses, businesses. They trudged after him for three long years, sharing the fatigues of the road and the poverty of nomads, the conflicts in the synagogues, the successes and failures with the crowds. They saw wondrous things in that time: water to wine, temples cleansed, the lame healed, the blind sighted, a dead man called from the tomb. They *heard* wondrous things as well: "I am the bread of life," "I am the resurrection and the life," "I am the way, the truth, and the life."

What they saw and heard changed them. They are different men now, unfitted for fishing boats and tax tables. Their lives have been turned upside down. Jesus has done his damage. They followed him and cannot turn back at this point. "You don't want to leave too, do you?" Jesus asked them once as the fickle crowd leaked away. Peter's reply—"Lord, to whom shall we go?"—is part statement of faith and part lament. They believe Jesus has "words of eternal life." But he has also ruined them for ordinary living. They've grown accustomed to the company of the Holy One of God.

And Jesus knows that also. He intended it. It was the reason he came, the reason he called them. All along, he planned to bind them to himself, addict them to his presence, create a dependency on him from which they would never recover. Not just a need for his words or his wisdom or his wonders—a need for Jesus himself, his closeness, his intimate imminence.

Jesus has taught them that being with him is better than families and friends. He has shown them that being with him is better than Torah and Temple and tradition. He has demonstrated—repeatedly—that when they are with him, they need not go hungry ("I am the bread of life"), they need not fear thief or robber ("I am the good shepherd"), they need not dread death ("I am the resurrection and the life"). They have learned that, so long as Jesus is in the boat, winds and waves cannot prevail.

They count on him. They rely on him. They trust him.

## "I Will Come to You"

But all that is about to change. As Jesus washes their feet, as he breaks bread with them, as he sends Judas off to do his treacherous business, he understands that he has only this final evening to prepare them for life in his *absence* after spending three years persuading them that life in his *presence* is the only life worth living.

He is leaving them. And he has this last conversation—the "Final Discourse" recorded in John 13-16—to help them come to grips with that terrible truth.

> My children, I will be with you only a little longer. You will look for me, and just as I told the Jews, so I tell you now: Where I am going, you cannot come. (John 13:33)
>
> I am going to the Father, where you can see me no longer. (John 16:10)
>
> I came from the Father and entered the world; now I am leaving the world and going back to the Father. (John 16:28)

Over and over. Repeatedly. Without relent. Ten times in the span of three chapters. "I am going away." This is Jesus the truth-teller, stubbornly stabbing a hard truth home. This is Jesus the bad-news prophet, predicting their worst nightmare. Things are about to change. Jesus is leaving. And they can't stop it, they can't change his mind, they can't go with him.

No wonder they are "troubled" and afraid. No wonder they share such foreboding. They are right to be anxious. After all they'd been through, after all they'd sacrificed, Jesus is leaving them. And now they must contemplate a life without his voice, without his touch, without his face.

That, however, is not the whole story. Not by a long shot. As determined as Jesus is to tell his disciples he is going away, he is equally determined to tell them that he is *not* going away, that he will *never* leave them. After the leaving, he wants them to know there is a "coming again":

> I will not leave you as orphans; I will come to you. Before long, the world will not see me anymore, but you will see me. (John 14:18-19)

I am going away and I am coming back to you. (John 14:28)

I will see you again and you will rejoice, and no one will take away your joy. (John 16:22)

Ten times in the same span of chapters. Ten antidotes to the poisonous news of his leaving. Long before General MacArthur said it, Jesus promised, "I shall return."

This paradox, this essential contradiction—"I am going away … I am coming back"—is buried in the heart of the Final Discourse. It is a tension that threatens to tear the Twelve apart: warning and promise … bad news and good … trauma and comfort.

We can excuse the disciples for hearing the word "leaving" and listening to nothing else. But for Jesus, the "leaving" is not the point. It's the "coming back" that is the important part. Jesus wants his disciples to know how they can still be followers in the wake of the Cross. He is desperate for them to grasp how they can continue to cling to him when he is no longer there.

*This* is the overriding message of the Final Discourse. *This* is the fundamental point of everything Jesus has to say. He is not simply cramming in a few final principles before his voice is stilled. He is steeling his disciples for his departure with the repeated and emphatic promise that he is not abandoning them. It will seem that way, no doubt. It will *feel* as if he is dead and gone. But the reality will be very different. Jesus has a plan for them—a plan to remain present with them past the grave.

Sharing that plan is his pressing agenda for this final evening.

## The Spirit

It is in the Final Discourse that Jesus introduces his disciples (and us) to the *Paraclete*—the Holy Spirit the Father is about to send them. He's already said important things about the Spirit in John's Gospel (e.g., the Spirit's role in new birth and worship and life to the full). But he's never used this name before: *Paraclete*. Nor has he ever spoken as frankly and fully on the role of the Spirit in the lives of believers.

He knows his time is short. He knows the disciples need something to sustain them in the days ahead, something to fill the vacuum of his imminent departure. And so he talks about the Spirit. Repeatedly. He keeps coming back to the subject. He never really leaves it. The Spirit will be his presence when he is gone. The Spirit will live in them and walk with them. The Spirit will teach them what they need to know. He will calm their troubled hearts and give them peace. He will testify to the world and encourage their testimony. He will convict the world of guilt. He will continue to reveal the Father. Jesus says more about the Spirit in the course of this one conversation than in all his other teachings combined.

Of all the things Jesus could have told his disciples to prepare them for his leaving, it is the *Spirit* he focuses on. In five sublime *Paraclete* Passages, Jesus introduces them to the "Companion," the "Comforter," explaining when the Spirit will come, what the Spirit will do, how the Spirit will help, and why the Spirit will be their sustaining strength for the remainder of their lives.

He doesn't offer them Torah or the Psalms. He doesn't point them to the faith of people in the past as a means of bolstering their faith in the future. He doesn't draw a parallel between Moses (stuck in the wilderness between Egypt and the Promised Land) and themselves (caught between incarnation and second coming).

He doesn't shore up their self-esteem. He doesn't tell them they have what it takes to tough out the hard days to come. He doesn't ask them to be brave or keep their eye on the ball. He doesn't encourage them to trust their better angels.

Nor does he point them to each other, suggesting that they will need to draw strength and wisdom from one another if they're going to make it in the coming years. Love each other, yes. Wash each other's feet, certainly. But as Jesus prepares to leave them, he knows it will take something stronger than their friendship and mutual support for them to survive and carry on his mission. He offers them the *Spirit* as Companion, not one another.

He doesn't give them the sacraments or the church as the sustaining force of their lives in the future. He doesn't tell them that the New Testament is coming; that if only they can hang on for thirty or forty years, the word of God will be present among them again. He mentions only briefly and cryptically his second coming ("I will come back and take you to be with me"—14:3), but he doesn't imply that the hope of his return will uphold them with the vigor they'll require.

What he offers his disciples on the cusp of his departure is a relation-ship with a living, indwelling, empowering, equipping, convicting, and revealing Spirit; someone who will be for them in the future what he has been for them in the past; someone who will continue his presence and mission, enabling disciples to *experience* his presence and mission forever.

Of all the things Jesus could have talked about this final night, it is the Holy Spirit of God who dominates the conversation. Why?

## And What of Us?

Strangely, we haven't taken the Final Discourse and what Jesus says about the Holy Spirit there very seriously. In fact, we've hardly *heard* what Jesus teaches the Twelve on this last night at all.

We've told ourselves that these words are for the Twelve alone. They were special men, specially chosen and commissioned, with special powers and privileges. We listen with some curiosity to what Jesus tells them about the Spirit. We're grateful that John preserved this Discourse. But we're not sure why he did so. We don't believe these words are actually for us.

In fact, if we want Spirit-words, we're better off going to Acts or the Epistles. (That's what they tell us, anyway.) Better to hear how the Spirit worked in the first-century church. Better to hear what is said about the Spirit to people more like ourselves—those who have not seen and touched; those who, like us, have believed through the Apostles' witness.

Even with them, however, we feel a divide. Our first-century broth-ers experienced spiritual things we could never dream of. We read Acts but cannot identify with the Spirit we find there. We read about the Corinthians and wonder what spiritual planet they came from. We read Paul's words about "living by the Spirit" and "being sealed" with the Spirit and the "fruit" of the Spirit but have little idea what he's really talking about.

I say it is "strange" that we have ignored the Final Discourse, and the Spirit within the Final Discourse, because there are so many compelling reasons for us to listen to this passage afresh. If it is a "trustable path" to a living Spirit we seek, what Jesus teaches in the Final Discourse provides our best route.

First, Jesus himself is our guide to the Spirit in this section of John. In other parts of the New Testament, where other words are spoken about the Spirit, it is Luke or Paul or Peter who does the talking. I certainly believe these writers are inspired and speak for Jesus. I do not think their words about the Spirit are in any way "secondary" or "once removed" from Jesus himself. But I do find it compelling when Jesus speaks in Scripture to any subject. He talks about the Spirit only rarely in the Synoptic Gospels. In John, however, Jesus speaks directly and at length about the Spirit *fifteen* times. And that's important for people who are hungry to hear from Jesus himself on this critical subject.

Second, the Final Discourse places great emphasis on *who the Spirit is*, not just what the Spirit does. He is a Companion, a Helper, a Teacher, a Comforter (see Chapter Six). More than that, as we will see, he is *Jesus* present again and forever in the world. His work is Jesus' work. His name is Jesus' name. He shares Jesus' heart and priorities and character. The Holy Spirit is no stranger, with an odd agenda and an unknown nature. Jesus tells us, in the *Paraclete* Passages, that we can trust the Spirit because we know the Spirit. He is the very essence of Jesus.

Third, what Jesus says in the Final Discourse about the work of the Spirit has little to do with miracles and much to do with making us spiritual. Although Jesus talks about the Spirit at great length in this passage, he never mentions tongues or healing or prophecy or any other supernatural manifestations of the Spirit's gifts. Let me hasten to add that this is not because Jesus disdains such gifts. He, in fact, is the author of them all, blessing his church, through his Holy Spirit, with every good gift that comes from his Father. But Jesus never mentions miraculous gifts in the *Paraclete* Passages. He has other Spirit-filled matters he wants to talk about with his fearful disciples.

Thus, in the Final Discourse, we don't have to wade through the *charismata* to get at the work of the Spirit we crave most: the possibility of presence; an indwelling Spirit who touches our hearts and minds; a Spirit who can make us *spiritual*. It is that "greater work" of the Spirit Jesus addresses in the Final Discourse. That work is still *supernatural*: the Holy Spirit of God offering us companionship, teaching, peace, courage, conviction, and revelation that no physics can explain. It is still God breaking miraculously into our lives and our world to accomplish his sovereign purposes. But (at least in the Final Discourse) that "in-breaking" happens in our hearts and results in maturity and transformation rather than signs and wonders.

Finally, the Spirit Jesus describes and promises in the Final Discourse is so winsome, so fit for our present need, that pursuing him is worth whatever effort and risk may be involved.

The original disciples are not the only ones to wonder what becomes of disciples who can no longer see, hear, and touch their Master. We ask the same question. For us, as for them, Jesus has returned to his Father. For us, as for them, the struggle to be followers in his absence is real and wracking. Just as they did, we yearn for and need an experience of Jesus that goes beyond the mere memory of his words and deeds. The stories recounted in the Gospels are no substitute for companionship with the man himself.

So when Jesus promises *them* he is coming back, when Jesus offers *them* a Spirit by which he intends to be present again, it is only natural that we should crowd around the Twelve and wonder if Jesus might be talking to us as well. Is the promise of "return" only good for the Apostles? Is the offer of teaching and testimony and truth for them alone? Is the promise to "be in" disciples and to make a "home" with disciples only for those who were actually present on the night he made it?

Or might these promises be for us as well?

The finger of Jesus, pointing past his physical presence to a "forever" presence, is the subject of this book. I believe Jesus intended this promise to extend beyond the Twelve to all those who would follow him in years to come. This "presence" is not a limited-time offer or a temporary measure or a phase the church grows out of or something that the birth of the New Testament makes redundant.

It is the birthright of all those who leave everything to follow Jesus. It is the inheritance, security, and hope of all who dare to become his disciples. It is the necessary power made available by our Lord to all those who must soldier on in his absence.

The fact that we have managed to limp along this far without claiming our Spirit-legacy is a testament to God's grace. The fact that we would *remain content to do so* is a testament to how habituated we've become to tepid hopes and temporary victories and tiny lives.

A life without the Spirit, a life without the Presence, is not the life God intends for us. He never meant for those who love him—then or now—to live in abandonment and absence. He has something far better in store for us.

# THE SPIRIT IN SCRIPTURE

Every mountain is climbed twice: first with the mind and then with the body. Long before boots are laced and packs hoisted, climbers plod up a mountain mentally, mapping their route, anticipating difficulties. It is the mental map that makes possible the physical steps to follow.

We stand at the base of Spirit Mountain, staring up at the promising, challenging, potentially dangerous slopes above. How can we climb these spiritual heights? Where lie the sheer cliff-faces and scree-covered approaches? Where are the hidden crevasses? Is there a route up the mountain where the footing is sure? Is there a path that can support our weight and provide us spiritual traction?

We are no longer content to stand below and gaze above. There is something up there, calling to us, a spiritual summit that beckons. We've lived on the plains below long enough to know all about that "dry and weary land where there is no water" (Ps 63:1), where the thirst for God, the longing for him, takes on a visceral urgency. We cannot stay where we are.

Yet we squint up at these spiritual heights with scars on our faces. For there have been other summits that promised fulfillment, security, and intimacy with God. False summits as it turns out; summits that promised but could not deliver. We've been disappointed, climbing the mountains of doctrinal correctness and necessary inference and fidelity to first-century patterns only to find frozen fields that sapped the soul.

Not every beckoning mountain gives access to the presence of God. Not every promising peak takes us to heavenly realms.

The testimony of our religious neighbors to *their* experience of Spirit Mountain is appreciated but, ultimately, less-than-helpful. We listen to tales of their climb, of routes taken, of hardships endured and ecstasies encountered. But we listen with two minds. Part of us rejoices in their attainment, in the planting of their soul-flag on some Spirit-peak. But part of us remains skeptical, questioning whether the route they traveled is the route that is best, or even possible, for the rest of us. We question whether we can put full weight on so subjective a rope.

In the end, you and I need a "published" map, a route up the mountain that has divine credentials. Neither our need nor others' testimony are sufficient as a starting point for our own journey. We turn, as always, to God's Word.

Let's assume that, for people like ourselves, any trustable approach to the Holy Spirit must begin with Scripture. Such an approach may require us to see Scripture through new eyes or to challenge long-accepted teachings with fresh perspectives. But wrestling with what the *Bible* says about the Spirit is where we must start. Not our need for the Spirit—too emotive. Not others' testimony about the Spirit—too subjective. What God tells us about the Spirit. In his Word.

Section One is a survey of what the Bible says about the Spirit. Those with little patience for thoroughness may want to skip this section and go straight for the heart of the book—Section Two. But those who appreciate the broad understanding that only perspective brings and crave the confidence that only thought-rooted-in-Scripture can give will value this overview.

We start (in Chapter Three) with the surprisingly robust treatment of the Holy Spirit in the Old Testament. How did the Spirit work before Christ appeared? What was the experience of Israel with the Spirit?

Chapter Four gives a quick survey of teaching on the Spirit in the Synoptic Gospels (Matthew, Mark, and Luke) and in Acts.

You may be surprised (as I was) to discover what is *not* said about the Spirit in these books.

In Chapter Five we walk through the letters of Paul. Paul has a unique contribution to make to our understanding of the Spirit's work, including most of what we know about an *indwelling* Spirit.

Chapter Six zooms in on the Gospel of John—our ultimate destination—by reviewing what is said about the Spirit in the Fourth Gospel and, particularly, about the *Paraclete*.

Finally, in Chapter Seven, I reproduce for you the text of the Final Discourse (John 13-16) and draw special attention to the *Paraclete* passages.

I am 53 years old. I have preached for over 25 years. Yet, in all that time, I had never done a comprehensive review of the Holy Spirit in Scripture until I decided to write this book. What I found was startling, eye-opening. What I found—simply by looking to Scripture—were the first glimmers of a path to a Spirit for the rest of us.

Chapter Three

# THE SPIRIT IN THE OLD TESTAMENT

You get only two verses into the Bible before the Spirit shows up. "In the beginning God created the heavens and the earth. Now the earth was formless and empty, darkness was over the surface of the deep, and the Spirit of God was hovering over the waters" (Gen 1:1-2).

God and the heavens, the formless earth and the dark deep, are the only things to precede the Spirit in Scripture. The reference to the Spirit is simple and enigmatic. No explanation. No development. It's as if the writer mentions the Spirit "for the record," wanting his presence noted before the world came into existence. God was there. The Spirit of God was there. In the beginning.

He was there again when God created man (breathing into him "the breath of life," a phrase commonly associated with the Spirit—see Job 33:4) and when, later, God pondered what to do with his fallen creatures: "Then the LORD said, 'My Spirit will not contend with man forever, for he is mortal; his days will be a hundred and twenty years'" (Gen 6:3).

The Spirit was present during the days of the Exodus. We see him (symbolically) in the flames of the burning bush (Exod 3:1-6) and in the pillar of cloud and fire (Exod 13:21-22). But he is mentioned explicitly in the ministry of Moses: "I will come down and speak with you there, and I will take of the Spirit that is on you and put the Spirit on them" (Num 11:17).

This is the first reference in Scripture to the Spirit being "on" a specific individual. That the individual is Moses, the most significant figure in the Old Testament, does not surprise us. It does, however, lend weight to the importance of the Spirit's presence in accomplishing God's work.

This Spirit on Moses marks him. The evidence is as plain as the radiance on his face. In the book of Exodus, we learn that "the Lord would speak to Moses face to face" (33:11). Such close communion with God sets Moses aglow:

> When Moses came down from Mount Sinai with the two tablets of the Testimony in his hands, he was not aware that his face was radiant because he had spoken with the LORD. When Aaron and all the Israelites saw Moses, his face was radiant, and they were afraid to come near him.... When Moses finished speaking to them, he put a veil over his face. But whenever he entered the LORD's presence to speak with him, he removed the veil until he came out. And when he came out and told the Israelites what he had been commanded, they saw that his face was radiant. Then Moses would put the veil back over his face until he went in to speak with the LORD. (Exod 34:29-35)

This "radiance" reappears as the "glory" that descends on Sinai and later fills both the Tabernacle and the Temple. It is a frequent sign of God's presence and a common symbol for God's Spirit.[1]

Like Moses, Joshua was anointed with the Spirit (Num 27:18; Deut 34:9). So were the Judges: "the Spirit of the Lord came on Othniel" (Judg 3:10); "Then the Spirit of the Lord came upon Gideon" (Judg 6:34); "Then the Spirit of the Lord came upon Jephthah" (Judg 11:29); and—especially—"the Spirit of the Lord came upon Samson in power" (Judg 14:6).

The first kings of Israel were anointed, not just with oil, but with the Spirit. It happened with Saul ("the Spirit of God came upon him in power"–1 Sam 10:6) and with David ("So Samuel took the horn of oil and anointed David in the presence of his brothers, and from that day on the Spirit of the Lord came upon David in power"–1 Sam 16:13). King David was especially conscious of the Spirit's presence in his life. On his deathbed, David rejoiced that "the Spirit of the Lord spoke through me; his word was on my tongue" (2 Sam 23:2). He credited the Spirit with inspiring him with "the plans of all that the Spirit had put in his mind for the courts of the temple of the LORD and all the surrounding rooms, for the treasuries of the temple of God and for the treasuries for the dedicated things" (1 Chr 28:12).

David depended on God's Spirit to lead him (Ps 143:10); marveled that God's Spirit was everywhere (Ps 139:7); and begged God never to take his Holy Spirit away (Ps 51:11).

The Prophets experienced the presence of God's Spirit. Elijah (1 Kgs 18:12), Isaiah (Isa 48:16), Ezekiel ("the Spirit came into me and raised me to my feet, and I heard him speaking to me," Ezek 2:2), and Micah ("I am filled with power, with the Spirit of the Lord," Mic 3:8)—all felt the quickening and empowering of the Spirit. The author of Nehemiah attributed the work of the prophets (admonishing Israel) to "your Spirit" (Neh 9:30).

But it wasn't just Israel's leaders and holy men who experienced the Spirit's presence. All Israel remembered a God who "set his Holy Spirit among them" (Isa 63:11). All Israel received God's "good Spirit to instruct them" (Neh 9:20) and "were given rest by the Spirit of the Lord" (Isa 63:14). All Israel "rebelled against the Spirit of God" (Ps 106:33) and "grieved his Holy Spirit" (Isa 63:10). And "the whole house of Israel"— dry bones though they were—experienced a national renewal and return because of an encounter with the Spirit:

> I will make breath enter you, and you will come to life. I will attach tendons to you and make flesh come upon you and cover you with skin; I will put breath in you, and you will come to life…. I will put my Spirit in you and you will live, and I will settle you in your own land. (Ezek 37:5-6, 14)

I had no idea there was so much Spirit in the Old Testament. But there he was when I finally looked … everywhere: in the beginning, through the Exodus, with every form of leadership in Israel's history, and experienced palpably and profoundly by Israel as a whole. According to the prophets, however, the best was yet to come.

## The Spirit in the Messianic Age

A widespread and radical experience of the Spirit was to become the distinguishing characteristic of the Messianic Age—that much-anticipated time when the Spirit would be "poured out" in special measure. The Spirit who had been present for God's people since the beginning would be extraordinarily, dramatically present when the "Anointed One" came.

Yes, "the Spirit of the Lord" was to rest on the Messiah himself to an exceptional degree:

> the Spirit of wisdom and of understanding,
> the Spirit of counsel and of power,
> the Spirit of knowledge and of the fear of the LORD. (Isa 11:2)

And, yes, God did promise to "put my Spirit on" his Messiah so that justice could be established upon the earth (Isa 42:1-4) and the "year of the Lord's favor" proclaimed (Isa 61:1ff).

But the defining mark of the Messianic Age would be the availability of the Spirit to *all* people—everyone who put their hope in the Lord and his Anointed. Isaiah, with his grand visions of the Messianic Kingdom, attests to this spate of the Spirit again and again. He looks forward to a time when "the Spirit is poured upon us from on high" (32:15), when God will "pour water on the thirsty land, and streams on the dry ground ... and my Spirit on your offspring" (44:3). On that day, the Spirit of God will gather the Messianic people together (34:16) and gush forth upon them like streams in the desert (35:1-10). (Joel echoes Isaiah's proclamation of a Spirit for "all people." Sons and daughters, male and female, old and young will be filled: everyone who calls upon the name of the Lord—2:28-32.)

And this presence of the Spirit, this watering of the dry land, is to be "forever"; for the Messiah's people, their children, and "their descendants from this time on" (Isa 59:21).

Taken as a whole, the witness of the Old Testament is that the Spirit has *always* been present—with God, with God's creation, and with God's people. From the beginning to the Messianic Age. And not just present: *actively* present ... *vigorously* present. The Spirit creates, gives life, accompanies, anoints, leads, empowers, grants prophetic visions and utterances, and rehydrates dry spiritual bones. The withdrawal of that Presence is a dreaded prospect for ancient Israel. The demonstration of that Presence is a comfort to and affirmation of ancient Israel. And the promise of a greater Presence, the prospect of the Spirit poured out in the Messianic Era, is a hope that fuels Israel through the dark days of the Exile and the lean times of Second Temple Judaism.

## Observations on the Spirit in the Old Testament

With this summary behind us, a few observations are in order. First, and to repeat, the Old Testament portrays an *ever-present Spirit*. The significance of that for us is the recognition that the Holy Spirit is not a "first century" phenomena, an artifact of apostolic Christianity. He is, rather, a "constant." Wherever and whenever God encounters his people, the Spirit has always been there.

Raised as many of us were on cessationist views, this active, present Spirit in the Old Testament comes as a surprise. We cut our teeth on the notion that the time of Jesus and the Apostles was *unique* in regard to the Spirit. Nothing like it before or since. The Spirit was present and vigorously active during the first century. But only then.

In order to cut the Spirit off from our present, we also had to cut the Spirit off from Israel's past. How could we argue for a diminished experience of the Spirit *after* the Messiah when the Spirit was so active and vibrant before he ever arrived? Instead, we ignored the Old Testament's witness to the Spirit. We ignored an essential commonality between experiences of the Spirit in both Testaments: common vocabulary like "power," "poured out," "glory," and "filling" … common manifestations like prophecy and visions. We ignored the evidence that the Spirit conducted God's business with Israel much as he did, later, with the first-century church.

Even a cursory look at the Old Testament evidence, however, leads us to recognize that the Spirit played a far larger role in ancient Israel than we have previously supposed. And if God's Spirit was so available to God's people *then*, why would he not also be available to God's people *now*?

A second observation: Even in the Old Testament, we begin to get an inkling of a distinction between the Spirit's *miraculous* work and his *transformative* work. Certainly, the presence of the Spirit is closely linked to supernatural manifestations like prophecy and revelation; manifestations where people are *conduits* for the Spirit's power and God's words.

Yet there are also hints of a *transformative* work of the Spirit, a work done in hearts and character.

The Spirit, for instance, is closely connected by Old Testament writers with the giving of the Law and the words of the prophets. Both were intended to cause a "change of heart" in Israel, to produce repentance and righteousness. (David, as an example, speaks of the Spirit leading him "to do your will," Ps 143:10). To the degree that revelation was able to accomplish this heart-change in Israel, the change should be seen as a work of God's Spirit.

Ezekiel foresees a day when God will put his Spirit directly into the hearts of Israel—a Spirit who needs no mediation of words and law—and transform them. He laments an Israel who has abandoned God's commands and followed the ways of the surrounding nations. He confesses Israel's sins and offenses. But he then envisions God showing mercy to his people and bringing them back to the Promised Land where, once again, "they will be my people, and I will be their God" (Ezek 11:20). This restoration is only possible, however, because of an outpouring of the Spirit:

> I will sprinkle clean water on you, and you will be clean; I will cleanse you from all your impurities and from all your idols. I will give you a new heart and put a new spirit in you; I will remove from you your heart of stone and give you a heart of flesh. And I will put my Spirit in you and move you to follow my decrees and be careful to keep my laws. (Ezek 36:25-27)

This Spirit "in you" will do something more wondrous than making the sun stand still—he will empower Israel for obedience. He will cleanse and soften and motivate. He will change Israel's heart and stimulate a hunger for the holy.

A third observation: In the Old Testament, the transformative is always miraculous but the miraculous is not always transformative. David's penitence over Bathsheba was prompted by Nathan's prophetic visit. Solomon's famous wisdom was a supernatural gift of God. Whenever Israel acted in obedience to God—especially given her stubborn history—that should be understood as the stuff of miracles, as much a source of wonder as any pillar of fire or stream of water from a rock. Transformation that results in penitence, God-hunger, and holiness is *always* miraculous.

But the miraculous does not always prompt transformation. Consider the seventy elders of Israel who saw the plagues, walked through the Red Sea, and ate the manna and quail; the elders who, in addition, personally experienced a powerful, miraculous filling of the Spirit: "Then the Lord came down in the cloud and spoke with [Moses], and he took of the Spirit that was on him and put the Spirit on the seventy elders. When the Spirit rested on them, they prophesied ..." (Num 11:25).

That extraordinary experience of the Spirit, however, did little to soften hearts or encourage obedience. Not long after, these same elders led a rebellion against Moses (Num 14), threatening to stone him and take the people back to Egypt. It was these elders (among others) God condemned when he said: "Not one of the men who saw my glory and the miraculous signs I performed in Egypt and in the desert but who disobeyed me and tested me ten times—not one of them will ever see the land I promised .... No one who has treated me with contempt will ever see it" (Num 14:22-23). These same men defied Moses again with Korah. They were among the 250 supporters of Korah's attempted coup, the "well-known community leaders who had been appointed members of the council" (Num 16:2). In his anger, God devoured them with fire (Num 16:15).

This is but one instance where people experienced the Spirit's miraculous work yet were not changed. These men actually prophesied by the Spirit's power. But they were not transformed as a result.

The troubling case of Samson presents us with the same paradox. His birth was announced by an angel and accompanied by wonders and signs (Judg 13). More than any of the other judges (in fact, more than all the other judges combined), Samson is described in Scripture as a man who experiences the Spirit of the Lord "in power" (Judg 13:25; 14:6, 19; 15:14). Yet that power is mostly a matter of biceps and pectorals, manifested in feats of physical strength. Samson tears a lion apart with his bare hands. He breaks bonds with ease. He kills enemies by the hundreds. He topples a temple.

The Spirit falls on Samson and the result is super-human physical strength. But Samson is not transformed because of it. To the contrary, he rivals Ahab as the most wicked character in the Bible. There is not a single redemptive quality mentioned in the four chapters devoted to his life (Judg 13-16). Samson is relentlessly portrayed as rebellious, violent, lustful, greedy, vindictive, foolish, and whiny. In the end, he dies by his own hand.

Once again, in the life of Samson, we have wonders without transformation, marvels without character. As we will see, this same disconnect between the miraculous and the transformative repeats itself in the New Testament.

The Spirit, then, is alive and well in the witness of the Old Testament. His fingerprints are all over creation and covenant, Tabernacle and Torah, prophets and kings. He cannot change every heart but, whenever heart-change happens, you can be sure the Spirit has been working. The Spirit is an integral and indispensable part of the life of Israel.

With the coming of the Messiah, however, the Spirit will have an even larger role to play. He will be poured out in fullness. And once he is unleashed into the world, there will be no return to dry ground.

## Chapter Four

# THE SPIRIT IN THE SYNOPTIC GOSPELS AND ACTS

As you might expect of a collection of books describing the Messianic Age, the Spirit plays a prominent role in the New Testament. The word "spirit" (*pneuma*) occurs over 350 times. Twenty-three out of twenty-seven New Testament books raise the subject of God's Spirit (only Philemon, 2nd and 3rd John—exempted by reason of brevity—and James' letter omit any reference). Some New Testament writers seem obsessed with the subject: the word "spirit" occurs over seventy times in Acts!

The New Testament's witness to the Spirit, then, is broad and strong. But, as we will see, it is not always or equally *deep*. This becomes evident when we turn to the Synoptic Gospels—Matthew, Mark, and Luke.

## The Witness of the Synoptic Gospels

The word "spirit" occurs some seventy-five times in the Synoptics (so called because they tend to see—"optic"—things similarly). At first blush, this abundance of references promises a wealth of information for people who want to understand the Spirit better. When you look more closely, however, you discover that precious little of what is said about "spirit" in the Synoptics has much direct application to the lives of disciples.

For one thing, almost half of spirit-references in the Synoptics are to *evil* spirits (fifteen in Mark alone!). Jesus drives them out, rebukes them, gives his disciples authority over them, teaches parables including them, and is accused of being possessed by one himself. Another nine times, the word "spirit" is used to mean *personal attitude* or the *interior self* (e.g., "the spirit is willing, but the body is weak," Matt 26:41).

That leaves only thirty-three direct references to the *Holy Spirit* in the Synoptics. Yet the majority of those speak to the Spirit and the *Messiah* rather than the Spirit and *disciples*. We learn, for instance, that the Messiah is predicted by the Spirit (Matt 22:43; Mark 12:36; Luke 4:18); that he and his forerunner will be filled with the Spirit (Matt 3:16; 4:1; 12:18; Luke 1:15-17, 80; 4:14, 18); that the arrival of the Messiah is prompted by the Spirit (who impregnates Mary—Matt 1:18—and inspires various people to announce the coming birth—Luke 1:41; 2:25); and that Jesus will be proved the Messiah by baptizing with the Holy Spirit (Matt 3:11 and parallels).

What do we actually glean from the Synoptics that might be pertinent to *disciples*? It's good to know that the Spirit can conceive a child in a woman. But since few of us are planning a virgin birth, that information has limited relevance. And it's important to know that the Spirit predicted Jesus' coming and descended on him at baptism. But these were *distinguishing marks* by which the Messiah would be recognized, not experiences offered to all disciples.

When it all boils down, there is relatively little found here about how the Spirit works in the hearts and lives of disciples. This is what we *can* say:

First and foremost, the Synoptics proclaim that disciples have access to the Spirit because of Jesus Christ. He baptizes them with the Spirit, *in* the Spirit. "John answered them all, 'I baptize you with water. But one more powerful than I will come, the thongs of whose sandals I am not worthy to untie. *He will baptize you with the Holy Spirit* and with fire'" (Luke 3:16 and parallels).

John, eager to say "I am not the one," points to Jesus and claims for him the power of Spirit-baptism. John can get people wet. But Jesus can bathe people in the Holy Spirit. We may argue about what, exactly, this means and to whom, specifically, it applies. But this power to baptize with the Spirit is a defining mark of the Messiah's ministry. It is the line in the sand that distinguishes the limits of the Spirit prior to the Messiah from the fullness of the Spirit after the Messiah. The Messiah, dripping with the Spirit, immerses all who come to him with that Spirit. This is certainly true for his first disciples. Is it true for all disciples? For us? That is not a question the Synoptics address.

They do tell us, however, of a God who wants to give his Spirit to those who ask: "If you then, though you are evil, know how to give good gifts to your children, how much more will your Father in heaven give the Holy Spirit to those who ask him!" (Luke 11:13). Jesus portrays here a Heavenly Father who is ready, willing, and eager to pour out his Spirit. He describes God as a gift-giver anxious to bestow his Spirit-gift on those he loves. In this word picture, God does not give grudgingly or against his better judgment. He gives with all the love and generosity a good father feels for his cherished children.

All that remains in the Synoptic gospels, after these meager morsels about the Spirit's interaction with disciples, are a few interesting details. We learn, for instance, that the Spirit can put words in the mouths of disciples when words come hard. In all three Synoptics, Jesus tells the Twelve: "Whenever you are arrested and brought to trial, do not worry beforehand about what to say. Just say whatever is given you at the time, for it is not you speaking, but the Holy Spirit" (Mark 13:11 and parallels).

Again, to whom this promise applies (only the Twelve or others?) is not a question addressed by the Synoptics. (Although the fact that this offer of the Spirit's help is written to Christians who are themselves under attack and subject to persecution may suggest that the promise extended at least to them.)

Another detail: we are warned in the Synoptics about the dangers of blaspheming the Holy Spirit—the unforgiveable sin.

> And so I tell you, every sin and blasphemy will be forgiven men, but the blasphemy against the Spirit will not be forgiven. Anyone who speaks a word against the Son of Man will be forgiven, but anyone who speaks against the Holy Spirit will not be forgiven, either in this age or in the age to come. (Matt 12:31-32 and parallels)

We may not know what such "blasphemy" looks like or how it is accomplished. But we're quite clear we don't want to be guilty of it.

Finally, Mark mentions that "signs" will accompany disciples in their ministry (Mark 16:17-18). Though the Spirit is not mentioned in this passage, it is clear that these signs anticipate a Spirit-filled future.

That's the sum and total of what we learn about the Holy Spirit and believers from the Synoptics: the Spirit is available because of the Messiah; God wants to give him to disciples; he can speak through disciples in trying times; we mustn't speak against him; and signs (prompted by the Spirit?) will go hand-in-hand with discipleship in times to come.

## The Witness of Acts

Acts has more to say about *spirit* than any other book in the New Testament canon. Like the Synoptics, there are references here to *evil spirits* or an individual's *inner spirit*. But these are rare. Most references—fifty-five specific passages—point directly to the *Holy* Spirit. His footprints are all over Luke's story of the earliest church. Unlike the Synoptics, however, and as you would expect given the different focus of this book, Acts testifies to the work of the Spirit in the *lives of believers* rather than in the ministry of Jesus.

Listen, for instance, to the variety of ways Luke (the author of Acts) describes the advent of the Spirit for disciples. Disciples are *baptized in* the Spirit (Acts 1:5, 8; 2:4ff; 11:15-16) and *filled with* the Spirit (2:38; 4:31; 9:17; 13:9). They *receive* the Spirit (1:8; 2:38; 8:15, 17; 10:47) and are *given* the Spirit (5:32; 8:18; 15:8). The Spirit *comes on* disciples (1:8; 10:44; 11:15; 19:6) and is *poured out* upon them (2:17; 10:45). The breadth of vocabulary is striking.

Luke uses this *vocabulary of fullness* some thirty times in Acts, repeatedly and emphatically proclaiming that these first Christians were Spirit-endowed. He may not tell us much about individual disciples like Stephen or Philip or Cornelius or Barnabas or Agabus, but he wants us to know they were all filled with the Holy Spirit. He may not spend time describing the first church's worship liturgy or sacramental practices, but he goes into long and loving detail about the Spirit falling at Pentecost, again at Cornelius' house, and repeatedly as the Apostles go out to "the ends of the earth."

The result of this *fullness* was a very tangible experience of the Spirit for the disciples. They *saw* the Spirit's presence (Acts 2:3, 33), *felt* his power (4:31), and *heard* his voice (8:29; 10:19; 13:2; 21:11). They could recognize him in others (6:3-5), sense his encouragement and support

(4:8, 31; 9:31; 13:9), and listen to his specific guidance and commissioning (8:29; 13:2-4; 16:6-7).

And, also as a result of this *fullness*, the first believers enjoyed a consistent experience of the miraculous. The testimony throughout Acts to this close connection between the Spirit and the supernatural is frequent and unambiguous.

At Pentecost, there was a loud sound "from heaven," the Spirit fell, tongues of flame appeared, believers spoke in other languages, and Peter bore witness to a crucified man brought back to life. The church witnessed "many wonders and miraculous signs" (2:43). No wonder they were all "filled with awe."

A cripple was healed at the temple gate, Peter preached the Messiah to the gathered crowd, the Council of Elders were "astonished" at the courage and boldness of the Apostles, the church gathered to pray and felt the building shake as they were filled with the Spirit (3:1ff, 11ff; 4:13, 31). No wonder "much grace was upon them all."

Ananias and Sapphira were accused of lying to the Holy Spirit and struck dead for their deception (5:1ff). No wonder "great fear seized the whole church."

"The apostles performed many miraculous signs and wonders among the people" (5:12). The sick were healed and evil spirits cast out (5:15-16). Angels appeared to release the Apostles from jail (5:17ff). Of course "they never stopped teaching and proclaiming the good news." With all these wonders taking place, would you?

Philip performed miraculous signs in Samaria (including exorcisms and healings). When the crowds saw the miracles, "there was great joy in the city" (8:5-8). I understand why. Later, the Spirit directed Philip to meet a man on a desert road. He preached to and baptized the Eunuch. And then he was (suddenly) "beamed" to a city fifteen miles away. No wonder he "traveled about, preaching the gospel," thrilled to be part of something so ... well ... thrilling (8:36-40).

Paul received a vision on the Damascus Road (Acts 9). He heard the divine voice. He was told to go into the city and wait. His sight was taken away. Ananias was also given a vision. He was specifically instructed to find Paul and heal his blindness. It doesn't surprise me that, in such a context, Ananias did as he was told, or that Paul was marked by the vision and subsequent healing, or that he accepted Christ's commission to the Gentiles.

Do I need to remind you of Tabitha raised from the dead (9:40), or Peter's vision of the sheet and the unclean animals (10:9ff), or the falling of the Spirit on Cornelius (10:44-46), or Peter's release from prison by an angel (12:6-10), or Herod struck dead by God (12:23)? Do we need to revisit the Spirit "calling" Barnabas and Saul to mission work (13:2), or Saul's blinding of Elymas the sorcerer (13:11), or the healing of the cripple at Lystra (14:10), or the vision of the Macedonian Man (16:6ff) and the healing of the slave girl at Philippi (16:18), or the miracles in Ephesus (19:11-12), or the rescue from the shipwreck (ch. 27)?

Wherever the Spirit shows up in Acts, something supernatural breaks out. The Spirit falls and people speak in tongues. The Spirit enters and people prophesy. The Spirit empowers healings, physically "teleports" disciples, grants visions, speaks directly and directively to the church, and "compels" or "prevents" specific actions (Acts 16:6-7; 20:22). In the most extreme (and disturbing) case recorded by Luke, the Spirit strikes people dead.

In Acts, the Spirit is persistently, relentlessly miraculous.

That is the extent of what we learn about the Holy Spirit and believers from Acts: the Spirit is poured out on followers of Jesus Messiah; they experience that Spirit in very tangible ways; the Spirit works miracles for and through them.

## Observations on the Spirit in the Synoptics and Acts

In light of this review, a few observations can be made about the witness of the Synoptics and Acts to the Spirit.

Observation #1: Acts would seem to be a more relevant source of information about the *Spirit and disciples* than the Synoptics. There simply isn't much said by Matthew, Mark, and Luke on the subject of the Spirit's role in believers' lives. Certainly, we should glean what *is* there. But a theology of the Spirit's work in God's people based solely on the Synoptics would be a very slim volume.

Acts, on the other hand, speaks to the subject of the Spirit and disciples with great frequency. There is a Spirit-seam here that should be mined afresh: a fullness of the Spirit available for disciples; a tangible

Spirit who can be readily experienced; and a miraculous Spirit who works through disciples. Whether this Spirit *remains* available in this way is not a question Luke addresses directly in his account of the early church. It is, in fact, a question that has provoked considerable controversy through the centuries, including our own time. The power of Luke's story demands that we ask and continue to ask that question, even if the answer proves difficult or elusive.

Observation #2: There is a great deal we *don't* learn about the Spirit from the Synoptics and Acts. There is nothing in these writings about who the Spirit is or his indwelling presence in believers. Nothing about the Spirit's transforming or sanctifying work. Nothing about the Spirit's forming of character or changing of hearts. Nothing about killing the sinful nature and prompting new life or shaping morality and relationships and communion with God.

The Synoptics hardly address the Spirit's interaction with disciples at all. The disciples watch the Spirit work through Jesus. They receive an offer of the Spirit for the future. But the Synoptics say nothing about how the disciples experienced the Spirit for themselves. (John insists, in fact, that the disciples could not receive the Spirit until after the death and resurrection of Jesus—7:39; 20:22.)

It is not unfair to state, then, that—in the Synoptics—disciples were *witnesses* to the Spirit, even *students* of the Spirit. But the Spirit had no *presence* in the disciples and left behind no *residue* in their lives. He was promised to them in the Synoptics, but not delivered.

Acts is a different matter. The promised Spirit comes. He baptizes the disciples. He works on and through them. The Spirit in Acts changes what disciples *do*, what they *decide* about certain matters, how they *act* in particular situations. The Spirit empowers believers to speak boldly and well, causes them to heal and prophesy, calls them to certain ministries or places.

And yet, it must be noted that Acts says little about the Spirit maturing disciples or convicting them of sin or teaching them to love holiness. The Spirit-themes so prominent in Paul's letters are largely absent in Acts. No words about the Spirit's role in putting to death the old man, controlling the minds and appetites of believers, or prompting growth into the likeness of Christ. I am not saying hearts do not change in Acts or that people don't deepen in the Lord. They do. Saul becomes Paul, after all! I am simply saying that Acts never portrays the Spirit in such a way that we would *expect* character changes as the natural and intended effect of the Spirit's presence in the lives of believers. If all we had was Acts, we would know much about the Spirit's signs and wonders but little about the Spirit's work of maturing and sanctifying.

Thus, the same thing can be said of Acts as was said of the Synoptics: disciples are *witnesses* to the Spirit, *students* of the Spirit. Even more in Acts, they are also *conduits* for the Spirit, *channels* through whom the Spirit demonstrates his presence and power and to whom he communicates his will. But Acts simply does not address an *interior* work of the Spirit, breaking the power of sin and creating new, Christ-like lives. The book is focused on the church and its beginnings, not on individuals and their spiritual development.

Observation #3: As in the Old Testament, so in the Synoptics and Acts, we trip over the truth that an experience of the miraculous is not always transformative. The Pharisees witnessed Jesus' miracles, but refused to come to faith (Matt 9:32-34). Capernaum saw miracles that would have made Sodom weep, yet remained unmoved (Matt 11:23). Jesus went home to people who knew his life and heard reports about his miracles, and discovered a lynch mob (Luke 4:14ff). And, of course, there is the troubling case of Judas, who witnessed all the healings and wonders, who—presumably—cast out a demon or two himself on Jesus' authority. But his heart remained hard. The signs made no dent in him. In the end, he decided it was better to have betrayed and lost than never to have betrayed at all.

We find the same truth in Acts. The Pharisees continue their resistance in spite of more healings. Ananias and Sapphira saw the signs and wonders performed by the Apostles, but it did not cure their greed or prevent them from lying to the Holy Spirit (Acts 5:1ff). Simon was "astonished by the great signs and miracles he saw" (Acts 8:13), but he still tried to buy spiritual power with filthy mammon. Paul visited Corinth and established his most charismatic church; but spiritual gifts did not translate there into spiritual people.

We could keep going, but perhaps these examples will suffice. Miracles don't necessarily change hearts.

Observation #4: There are obvious differences between the experience of the Spirit by disciples in the Synoptics and Acts and the experience of the Spirit that is my common lot. These differences may limit how teachings about the Spirit found there apply to my life now.

Hold on a minute, some will say. Our contemporary experience of the Spirit *should* be the same as the ancients. "The Spirit should be just as present, just as vigorous and miraculously active, now as then!" they will say. "The problem is with us. We must be quenching the Spirit, preventing the Spirit, in some way. We need to repent and redouble our efforts to experience the wonders of Acts for ourselves."

That may be true. But I still insist that there are obvious differences between now and then when it comes to the sphere of the Spirit.

Take the matter of evil spirits, for instance. In the Synoptics, they were so thick that even confused, doubting, "little faith" disciples stumbled over them at every turn. They inhabited children, raving lunatics, and helpless women. They spoke out loud, witnessing and begging for mercy. They fled their preferred, human victims and entered animal hosts. On almost every page of the Synoptics, Jesus meets and casts out an evil spirit.

But that's not my common experience of the spiritual world. I can't remember the last time I ran into an evil spirit—and I think I *would* remember something like that. Perhaps I am so spiritually blind that I can't see an evil spirit when it's staring me right in the face. Maybe I have quenched the Spirit so thoroughly that I am oblivious to obvious spiritual forces and entities. Before I succumb to spiritual self-contempt, however, it's at least worth asking whether there might be an actual and significant difference between Jesus' day and my own (or, for that matter, between Palestine and other places in the first century world where the gospel took root without mention of evil spirits). Could it be that a different world-view, a different understanding of causality, or a different level of access by the forces of evil to other times and places explains the absence of evil spirits in our present experience? Must we insist that, since evil spirits were a reality then and there, they must be a reality here and now?

If this difference is a function of changing times rather than stubborn hearts, that means we have to read the Synoptics and Acts differently.

What they tell us about spiritual realities during the ministry of Jesus may spark our curiosity but may *not* prove much help for handling spiritual realities of our own.

I raise this example to segue into another, more troubling problem. I find a similar "difference" in the way the Spirit behaves then and now. There is an "intrusiveness" to the Spirit in Acts that seems thoroughly alien to us. These days we struggle mightily to seek the Spirit, find the Spirit, and engage the Spirit. But in Acts, the Spirit is inescapable. Disciples are baptized in, filled up with, or overcome by the Spirit at every turn. They bump into the Spirit unexpectedly, without request, in surprising and unanticipated ways. The Spirit simply and sovereignly falls, pours, fills, directs, prevents, and warns—without the early Christians so much as lifting a spiritual finger!

Far from requiring invitation, the Spirit in Acts operates in invasive and irresistible[1] ways. He needs neither permission nor encouragement. He is *there*, a fact of first-century Christian life, whether invited or not. In truth, his presence is often inconvenient (his "falling" on Cornelius posed significant challenges for the Jerusalem church—Acts 11:2-3), sometimes scandalous ("These men are not drunk, as you suppose …"—Acts 2:15), and, on occasion, dreaded ("Great fear seized the whole church …" after the Spirit's handling of Ananias and Sapphira—Acts 5:11). The Spirit described in Acts seems little concerned with whether disciples *want* his presence. He never asks them. Rather, his concern is to *be present*, whether wanted or not.

This difference between the first-century experience of the Spirit and our own has been the source of much puzzlement. Even the most charismatic streams of modern Christianity must prescribe specific, intensive regimens in order to induce a discernable experience of the Spirit: cleansing, prayer, fasting, reading, extensive instruction, prolonged meditation, and torturous "seeking." It seems the Spirit must be *cajoled* into appearing, *coerced* into a tangible presence, in these latter days. And yet, in the first century, the Spirit was aggressively seeking out Christians, not the other way around.

I can't explain this difference, but I can recognize it. The disciples of Acts are ambushed by the Spirit while I am left to chase after him, pleading for the least little blessing. Why? I don't know. But surely it's worth considering that Acts may not be the best yardstick for measuring an experience of the Spirit today. Instead of pining for the Jerusalem Spirit—constantly disappointed with ourselves and baffled by God—perhaps we would do better to ask how God's Spirit wants to work with us today, stubbornly believing that he still does. He may not act now as he did then. But perhaps he has a plan to do the same thing differently.

These differences give me the courage to question whether there might be one more. The Spirit in the Synoptics and Acts is always miraculous. Matthew, Mark, and Luke know no other "working" of the Spirit than the supernatural. Whether it be visions and voices or healings and tongues, their Spirit always makes his presence known in extra-ordinary ways.

But that, once again, is not my common experience—or the experience of the people I go to church with. Perhaps it should be. One day it may be. But for now, it is not.

And so I ask: Must the Spirit *always* be accompanied by miraculous manifestations (as Acts suggests)? Does the *absence* of the miraculous necessarily mean the absence of the Spirit? Is the presence of the miraculous the exclusive measure of a valid spiritual experience?

Maybe. But whatever answers we apply to such questions, I can only confess that the Spirit *isn't* elbowing his miraculous way into the experience of the church I know. Wonders *aren't* breaking out all over. Perhaps the Spirit works that way in other churches and in the experience of other Christians. Good for them. But it isn't happening here, to me and mine. I'm not *resistant* to that experience. I have no doubts that such an experience is possible today. But this is not how God has chosen to interact with me.

Some would use this confession to discount my walk in the Spirit. Under the glare of their criticism, I am tempted to spiritual insecurity. Hearing their stories, I sometimes suffer from Spirit-envy. But in spite of that, I cling to the hope that it is possible to confess my different experience without immediately falling on a spiritual sword.[2] Perhaps God has something else, something *other*, for me to experience as a result of the Spirit's work. Perhaps the Spirit has a different agenda to accomplish in the lives of people like me—in the lives of "the rest of us."

To get at that "other," we'll have to leave the Synoptics and Acts with their evil-spirits-I've-never-seen and their intrusive-Spirit-I've-never-met and their miracles-I-keep-missing. We have to sift through what is left in Scripture to see if we can find something that resonates with what we *do* experience of the Spirit. We're going to land, eventually, in the gospel of John, finding there a portrait of the Spirit that is deeply familiar and that fits us far better than Acts.

Before John, however, we need to make one more stop ... a brief detour into the letters of Paul. I think you might be encouraged by what we find there.

## Chapter Five

# THE SPIRIT IN THE WRITINGS OF PAUL

Paul uses the word "Spirit" more than any other New Testament writer—125 times in the thirteen letters attributed to him. Unlike the Synoptics, almost all of Paul's Spirit-references are to the work of the Spirit in the lives of believers. And unlike either the Synoptics or Acts, Paul moves beyond noting the Spirit's miraculous manifestations to offering an understanding of the Spirit as the transformer of human hearts.

Without question, Paul does witness to the miraculous. He insists, for instance, that his preaching and teaching were not only accompanied but made effective by "a demonstration of the Spirit's power" (1 Cor 2:4).

> I will not venture to speak of anything except what Christ has accomplished through me in leading the Gentiles to obey God by what I have said and done—by the power of signs and miracles, through the power of the Spirit. So from Jerusalem all the way around to Illyricum, I have fully proclaimed the gospel of Christ. (Rom 15:18-19)

> For we know, brothers loved by God, that he has chosen you, because our gospel came to you not simply with words, but also with power, with the Holy Spirit and with deep conviction. (1 Thess 1:4-5)

> The things that mark an apostle—signs, wonders and miracles—were done among you [by me] with great perseverance. (2 Cor 12:12)

In these verses, Paul reminds his readers (and informs us) that he came preaching not just with Spirit-words but with Spirit-signs.

Paul is charismatically gifted. He speaks in tongues ("more than all of you," 1 Cor 14:18), heals (e.g., Acts 14:8-10), casts out demons (Acts 16:16-18), prophesies (Acts 27:21-26), and sees visions (2 Cor 12:1-4). He is adamant that his commission to the Gentiles and the gospel he preached were conveyed by supernatural, not natural, means (Gal 1:11-17). Where he goes on mission journeys, what he does, even how long he stays are all dictated by direct revelation of God's Spirit (Acts 13:2; 16:6-7; 18:9-11; 20:22).

Moreover, Paul ministers and writes to Christians who themselves are charismatically gifted. The Corinthians (of course) experience a wide range of miraculous spiritual gifts (tongues, healing, prophecy, and words of "wisdom" and "knowledge," to name but a few). Writing to the Galatians, Paul recognizes that "God gives you his Spirit and works miracles among you" (3:5). Timothy has a "gift of God" which Paul forbids him to "neglect" but, rather, urges him to "fan into flame" (1 Tim 4:14; 2 Tim 1:6). When disciples lack charismatic gifts, Paul lays hands on them to correct the deficiency (Acts 19:6; 2 Tim 1:6). He does not want his converts to "be ignorant" of the Spirit's gifts (1 Cor 12:1). To the contrary, he encourages them to "eagerly desire spiritual gifts" and to "excel in gifts" (1 Cor 14:1, 12).

So far, Paul is another example of what we've already seen in Acts: preaching accompanied by signs; the exercise of charismatic gifts; and the encouragement of those gifts in others. Where Paul goes next, however, treads new ground. A *sign-giving-Spirit* is as far as the Synoptics and Acts venture. But not Paul. There is a great deal more on the subject of the Spirit Paul wants to talk about. When he's done with miracles, he's only getting warmed up. And it is to that "more" we must now turn.

## The Spirit "in you"

Paul introduces a preposition into his discussion of the Spirit that is absent in the writings we've already surveyed: "in." Paul does talk about *receiving* the Spirit and *being given* the Spirit and having the Spirit *poured out*—just as Acts and the Synoptics do. But while these other writings describe the Spirit "on" believers and "with" believers, and believers acting "by" and "through" the Spirit, they never speak of the Spirit "in" believers.

Yet this particular preposition is the one Paul characteristically uses when writing about the Spirit and disciples:

> You, however, are controlled not by the sinful nature but by the Spirit, if *the Spirit of God lives in you*. And if anyone does not have the Spirit of Christ, he does not belong to Christ. But if *Christ is in you*, your body is dead because of sin, yet your spirit is alive because of righteousness. And if the Spirit of him who raised Jesus from the dead *is living in you*, he who raised Christ from the dead will also give life to your mortal bodies through *his Spirit, who lives in you*. (Rom 8:9-11)

> Do you not know that your body is a temple of the *Holy Spirit, who is in you*, whom you have received from God? (1 Cor 6:19)

> Now it is God who makes both us and you stand firm in Christ. He anointed us, set his seal of ownership on us, and put *his Spirit in our hearts* … (2 Cor 1:21-22)

> Because you are sons, God sent *the Spirit of his Son into our hearts* … (Gal 4:6)

> I pray that out of his glorious riches he may strengthen you with power through *his Spirit in your inner being*, so that *Christ may dwell in your hearts* through faith. (Eph 3:16)

> Guard the good deposit that was entrusted to you—guard it with the help of *the Holy Spirit who lives in us*. (2 Tim 1:14)

This Spirit "in you," "living in you," "in your hearts," "in your inner being," resident in the bodies and minds of disciples, is a radical development from the signs-oriented Spirit of the Synoptics and Acts. Yes, Paul experiences the supernatural gifting of the Spirit. But he also experiences something else—an indwelling Spirit who is shaping his heart. Yes, the Spirit prompts tongues and prophecies. But he prompts something more—the mind of Christ and the life of God.

With that tiny preposition "in," Paul introduces the possibility of a Spirit so intimate, so personal, that disciples are touched at the level of heart and soul, mind and character, traits and personality. Whatever else the Spirit may do, Paul understands that the Spirit has an *internal* work to accomplish, a work that takes place *inside* disciples, in their "nature," affecting their appetites and desires, shaping their attitudes and emotions.

This understanding of the Spirit living "in" disciples is foundational for Paul. It colors almost everything he says—from his teachings on gifts, through his instructions about ethical living, to his views on the church.[1] The Spirit indwells. And for Paul, that is a difference that makes all the difference.

Take, for instance, what Paul has to say about the *teaching role* of the Spirit. One of the prime functions of the Spirit (in Paul's mind) is to instruct believers: revealing God's will, teaching God's way, and training God's life. But the Spirit doesn't teach in ordinary ways. He isn't confined to words and PowerPoint presentations. Because the Spirit *indwells* us, he has access not just to our eyes and ears, but to our thoughts and motives, our temptations and emotions. His teaching is "deeper" than any other we have ever experienced. And that makes his instruction uniquely powerful and transformative.

Paul prays, for example, that God will give the Ephesians "the Spirit of wisdom and revelation, so that you may know him better" (Eph 1:17). But his prayer is not for a *lecturing* Spirit who inculcates systematic theology or more facts about the Faith. Rather, the prayer is for a *revealing* Spirit who enlightens "the eyes of your heart" and fosters hope and power (1:18-19). Precisely because this Spirit indwells, his teaching impact is greater than merely informing the mind. He guides the way to intimacy with God. He reveals spiritual perspectives and forms a godly mindset. He turns facts into wisdom. He teaches head and heart, soul and spirit. He mentors motives and desires.[2] He can do this because he indwells and has direct access to our "inner being."

A second passage that makes the same point is that cryptic, strangely compelling paragraph in which Paul connects the Spirit's ability to teach "God's secret wisdom" and "the deep things of God" to the fact that he lives "in" believers. It is a passage worth quoting at length:

> The Spirit searches all things, even the deep things of God. For who among men knows the thoughts of a man except the man's spirit within him? In the same way no one knows the thoughts of God except the Spirit of God. We have not received

the spirit of the world but the Spirit who is from God, that we may understand what God has freely given us. This is what we speak, not in words taught us by human wisdom but in words taught by the Spirit, expressing spiritual truths in spiritual words....

> "For who has known the mind of the Lord
>   that he may instruct him?"
> But we have the mind of Christ. (1 Cor 2:10-16)

Only God's Spirit can know God's thoughts. To know God's thoughts requires an infusion of God's Spirit. And that is precisely what God has made available to believers: his Spirit in them, giving them access to his "deep things." Who has "known the mind of the Lord," Paul asks? We have! We do! God has put his Spirit in us. And because his Spirit indwells believers, we have "the mind of Christ," we can know "the deep things of God."

All this is good and needed: the Spirit "in" believers ... the possibility of an intimate Spirit ... the Spirit teaching and touching us in our "inner being." But it is what Paul does next with the Spirit "in you" that is truly revolutionary.

## The Spirit and Transformation

Because the Spirit lives "in" us and has such intimate access to the deepest parts of our being, Paul believes the Spirit is able to perform a truly miraculous work: healing our broken lives and restoring in us the image of God. Paul directs most of his words about the Spirit to talking about the Spirit's role in *changing hearts*. It is a subject he finds endlessly fascinating and ultimately important.

It is Paul who leads us beyond a *present* Spirit and a *supernatural* Spirit to a Spirit capable of *transforming* the "self." Certainly, there are hints of this capacity in the Old Testament writings (as we have noticed)—a Spirit who creates new hearts and prompts holy living. But it is left to Paul to develop what this transformational work actually looks like in the lives of God's people.

Paul understands (more than most) just how broken humanity is, how much damage sin has done to the children of Adam. He knows that something more radical than a new law and more dramatic than new wonders is required to undo the curse of Adam. People need heart surgery; hearts healed from the hurts of Eden; new hearts with a fresh hunger for things that are holy.

Rules don't change hearts. Words—even *God's* words—can't accomplish what is most needed in us. Signs can lead the heart to water, but they cannot make it drink.

Enter the indwelling Spirit. According to Paul, healing the human heart and transforming our human nature are the Spirit's best and greatest works. Paul envisions an entirely new way of living made possible by the Spirit "in" us, a life that is radically different from the brokenness of life "in Adam" and the impotence of life "in the flesh." This new life is characterized by holiness, God-hunger, Christ-likeness, and true righteousness. It is the life God intended for us all along—the image-of-God-life he created us to live from the beginning. It is a life so different, so "other," it can only be fueled by the supernatural power of the Holy Spirit.

This Spirit-life *begins* when God saves us, "through the washing of rebirth and renewal by the Holy Spirit" (Titus 3:5). This washing[3] leaves believers "sanctified," holy, and righteous before God; not because of anything we have done, but due entirely to the sovereign decision of God:

> From the beginning, God chose you to be saved through *the sanctifying work of the Spirit* … (2 Thess 2:16)
>
> [God made me a minister] so that the Gentiles might become an offering acceptable to God, *sanctified by the Holy Spirit.* (Rom 15:16)
>
> You were washed, *you were sanctified*, you were justified in the name of the Lord Jesus Christ and *by the Spirit* of our God. (1 Cor 6:11)

Already, though, Paul is pointing to something more—not just a change of our *status* in the mind of God, but a change of our *character*. Paul hints in these passages of an *ongoing* salvation—salvation from the penalty of sin, yes: but also salvation from the power of sin, the dominion of sin, the slavery of sin.

For a salvation *that* great, something more than an initial washing is required. Paul believes the Spirit to be a surgeon, cutting away at the old nature of sin and grafting into us a new nature, a new self. There is a "circumcision of the heart," he writes (Rom 2:29), that only the Spirit can perform. Not the law. Not religious ritual. Not our most determined efforts. Nothing less than the knife of God's Spirit, a circumcision of *character* performed by the Spirit, is required for heart-change to occur.

The notion of a cutting and killing work of God's Spirit appears repeatedly in Paul's letters. The Spirit sets believers "free from the law of sin and death" (Rom 8:2), puts "to death the misdeeds of the body" (Rom 8:13), and teaches disciples to "put off the old self" (Eph 4:22). Through the Spirit, we die to the "old way of the written code" (Rom 7:6) and the desires of the sinful nature (Gal 5:16-17).

But Paul's Spirit does not just "cut off"; he also "puts on." It is due to the power and teaching of the Spirit that we are able to put on "the new self, created to be like God in true righteousness and holiness" (Eph 4:24). It is because the Spirit has allowed us to "set our minds on things above" that we are empowered to "put on the new self, which is being renewed in knowledge in the image of its Creator" (Col 3:10). It is the Spirit's control that makes it possible for us to be "living sacrifices, holy and pleasing to God … transformed by the renewing of your mind" (Rom 12:1-2).

Paul's "Spirit in you" is thus a transforming Spirit, sanctifying believers first by washing them, then teaching them, and then cutting off the old self to make room for the new. Paul's "Spirit in you" changes our status with God, then our minds and attitudes, and then our very natures.

This transformative power is, for Paul, the Spirit's greatest and most miraculous ability. He talks about it—revels in it—in every one of his major letters. Consider the following examples.

## The Spirit and Transformation in Paul's Writings

The Spirit who transforms is a major theme in the letter to the Romans, particularly in chapters 7 and 8. Paul, in chapter 7, thoroughly depresses us with his depiction of those who are left to their own devices for living holy lives. ("I am sold as a slave to sin. What I hate, I do. Sin is living in me. I want to do good, but I can't manage it. I keep doing evil. I am a most wretched man!")

But Paul does not intend to leave us to our own devices. His depiction of humanity-without-Spirit in chapter 7 gives way to the depiction of humanity-with-Spirit in chapter 8. And what a difference!

> So now there is no condemnation for those who belong to Christ Jesus. And because you belong to him, the power of the life-giving Spirit has freed you from the power of sin that leads to death…. We no longer follow our sinful nature but instead follow the Spirit.
>
> Those who are dominated by the sinful nature think about sinful things, but those who are controlled by the Holy Spirit think about things that please the Spirit. So letting your sinful nature control your mind leads to death. But letting the Spirit control your mind leads to life and peace…. (Rom 8:1-6—NLT)

"Who will rescue me from this body of death," Paul asks? Christ will! How will he do this? Through the gift of his transforming Spirit! It is the Spirit who sets us free from the law of sin and death. It is by the Spirit we now live. Our minds are set on what the Spirit desires. The Spirit controls us (8:9). The Spirit makes us alive to righteousness (8:10). We put to death the misdeeds of the body by the power of the Spirit (8:13). We are children of God, led by the Spirit of God (8:14).

Far from normalizing chapter 7 as the sad but inevitable experience of Christian living in this broken world, Paul introduces us to the "Spirit of life," inviting us to move into and live out of the spiritual realities of chapter 8. The indwelling Spirit changes everything. And, most of all, he changes *us*.

The transforming Spirit is also an important and recurring theme in Paul's correspondence with the Corinthians. The Corinthians are convinced they are spiritual (*pneumatikoi*) because they are gifted. They believe they have arrived, spiritually, because they can speak in tongues.

Paul begs to differ. He points to a laundry list of problems in the Corinthian church (like sexual immorality, factions, arrogance, lawsuits, idolatry, divisions, and resurrection heresies—to name a few) and dares to tell these spiritually gifted, miraculously endowed brothers:

I could not address you as spiritual but as worldly—mere infants in Christ. I gave you milk, not solid food, for you were not yet ready for it. Indeed, you are still not ready. You are still worldly. For since there is jealousy and quarreling among you, are you not still worldly? Are you not acting like mere men? (1 Cor 3:1-3)

They ask him questions about spiritual gifts, eager to know more. Paul answers briefly (1 Cor 12:1-11), but he is far more interested in teaching them about a transforming Spirit whose gifts are meant to change their attitudes towards each other (1 Cor 12:12-31) and lead them on to the "greater gift" of love (1 Cor 12:31-13:3). What good are tongues and prophecy when the Corinthian church is fractured by factions and pride? What good are spiritual gifts that don't make you spiritual?

By the time he writes 2 Corinthians, Paul is at the end of a long and difficult struggle for the character of this church. The Corinthians are finally showing signs of coming around to Paul's point of view. Paul rejoices that, after hard letters and painful visits, comfort is finally breaking out in Corinth (2 Cor 1:3-7).

Barely past the greeting, Paul sets out to redefine what it means to be "spiritual." It means trusting Paul's motives, even when they do not understand his behavior (2 Cor 1:12-24). It means responding to his correction with penitence (2:1-4). It means forgiving those who have opposed Paul in the past (2:5-11). It means ministering to each other and the world with integrity and competence (2:14-3:6).

Most of all, though, it means *being transformed*. Paul explains that even the ministry of Moses—a ministry that brought condemnation and death—left a mark: it set Moses' face aglow. Our ministry—a ministry of the Spirit that brings life and righteousness—also leaves a mark, one that will never fade. (See 2 Cor 3:7-11)

Now the Lord is the Spirit, and where the Spirit of the Lord is, there is freedom. And we, who with unveiled faces all reflect the Lord's glory, are being transformed into his likeness with ever-increasing glory, which comes from the Lord, who is the Spirit. (2 Cor 3:17-18)

This is not an easy passage, but the point seems clear enough. As we freely, boldly, fully gaze at the glory of Christ, the Spirit acts upon our hearts to transform us into the likeness of the One we worship. It may take some time. It may happen in stages. But transformation does happen. It is, according to Paul, the defining characteristic of the Spirit within us.

The subject of a transforming Spirit comes up yet again when Paul writes to the Galatians. He is afraid they have fallen for a "different gospel" (Gal 1:6). He is worried that, "after beginning with the Spirit," they have decided to rely on themselves instead (3:3).

For four chapters Paul wanders between expressions of astonishment, biographical testimony, and musings on Old Testament stories. By the fifth chapter, Paul decides to get down to business. In his best apostolic voice, he tells the Galatians that the salvation they seek doesn't come through getting it right but through Christ (5:2). Justification before God is rooted in grace, not their keeping of the law (5:4). And—especially—the righteousness they hope for can never be accomplished by circumcision but only by waiting on the transforming Spirit (5:5).

At this point, Paul launches into ten verses that should be tattooed on the right forearm of every believer:

> So I say, live by the Spirit, and you will not gratify the desires of the sinful nature. For the sinful nature desires what is contrary to the Spirit, and the Spirit what is contrary to the sinful nature. They are in conflict with each other, so that you do not do what you want. But if you are led by the Spirit, you are not under law.
>
> The acts of the sinful nature are obvious: sexual immorality, impurity and debauchery; idolatry and witchcraft; hatred, discord, jealously, fits of rage, selfish ambition, dissensions, factions and envy, drunkenness, orgies, and the like. I warn you, as I did before, that those who live like this will not inherit the kingdom of God.
>
> But the fruit of the Spirit is love, joy, peace, patience, kindness, goodness, faithfulness, gentleness and self-control. Against such things there is no law. Those who belong to Christ Jesus have crucified the sinful nature with its passions and desires.

Since we live by the Spirit, let us keep in step with the Spirit.
(Gal 5:16-25)

Okay. It would make a rather lengthy tattoo. But what themes! Here
again are ideas raised in Romans: the tension between flesh and Spirit;
the victory of Spirit over flesh; living by the Spirit, being led by the Spirit,
acting under the Spirit's control. Here again is Paul's confidence that
we can be transformed by the Spirit, freed from the desires of the sinful
nature to follow the desires of the Spirit.

But there is something new here as well: the Spirit's fruit. Delectable
evidence of the Spirit's presence in our lives. The transformative results of
the Spirit within us. Paul expects that those who live by the Spirit, who
are led by the Spirit, will behave in radically different ways: not lust but
love; not rage but joy; not discord but peace; not selfish ambition but
kindness; etc. He anticipates that believers will "keep in step with the
Spirit" and that this lock-step has specific and powerful implications for
the way believers live.

The Galatians want the right fruit. They just refuse to bark up the
right tree. They keep climbing the bough of themselves, looking for fruit
they are not capable of bearing. Paul assures them that, if only they will
return to the Spirit and his transforming ways, they can find the "righteousness for which we hope."

All these passages, all these letters, attest to Paul's conviction that the
Spirit dwells in believers and that his most important work is transforming our hearts. There are references in these letters to the Spirit's miraculous works. But they are relatively rare and brief. What Paul cannot stop
talking about is the miracle of a Spirit who saves believers from the power
of sin and empowers sinners to live faithful lives. Whatever else Paul's
churches experience as Christians, Paul encourages them to encounter
the Spirit who transforms.

## Observations on the Spirit and Paul

Before we put Paul's teaching on the Spirit to rest, a few observations are in order.

First, it is Paul who introduces us to an indwelling Spirit who transforms our hearts. Paul fills in what otherwise would be an incredibly

broad and frustratingly deep gap between the Spirit's release into the world and disciples changed into the image of God. It is because of Paul's writings that we have some awareness of the Spirit "in" us, of the Spirit's ability to touch us intimately, of a transforming work that begins with washing and continues in "circumcision of the heart." It is due to Paul that we learn the Spirit gives power over sin, the ability to live righteously, and the capacity to bear the image of Christ. While the Synoptics focus on the ministry of Jesus and Acts on the growth of the church, Paul focuses on the maturation of God's people into God's image. As a result, we find in Paul a treasure-store of teaching about the Spirit's transforming work.

Second, what we know of Paul reinforces the distinction between the miraculous and transformative works of the Spirit we've seen elsewhere. There are wonders and there are heart-changes, miracle gifts and the new self. Nor are these two works of the Spirit necessarily connected. Experiencing the miraculous does not always prompt transformation (the Corinthians as an example). Circumcision of the heart does not first require an encounter with signs and wonders (the Roman Christians seem to bear this out). What relationship these two spheres of the Spirit's work have to each other is not clear to me. Paul affirms them both as legitimate expressions of the Spirit's presence. But he also demonstrates a decided preference.

Third (and perhaps controversially), it is the *transforming* part of the Spirit's work that most interests Paul. If you stripped Acts and 1 Corinthians out of the New Testament, we would know next to nothing about a charismatic Paul or charismatic churches. I do not say that to disparage or downplay the *charismata*. I say it only to point out that when Paul is speaking (rather than Luke) and when Paul is not correcting charismatic excesses in Corinth, he says little about miraculous manifestations and much about a Spirit who transforms. I suspect this is because, in Paul's thinking, Spirit-signs prompt faith while the interior work of the Spirit matures it. And since his letters are primarily *maturing* documents, he places greater emphasis there on the heart-work of the Spirit.

Even when Paul does take up miraculous gifts (as in 1 Corinthians), he moves quickly to transformative matters. Not that the miraculous embarrasses Paul. He remains an advocate for the supernatural. But he seems pretty motivated to move beyond signs and wonders to the wonder of a Spirit who transforms the broken, stubborn, willful human heart.

Fourth (and more controversial still), there is a clear pecking order to the spiritual gifts in Paul's writings. Tongues are for personal encouragement and have no place in the assembly unless there is an interpreter who can "edify the church" (1 Cor 14:5, 27-28). Prophecy, while better, must still be limited to "two or three" and should only be done "for the strengthening of the church" (1 Cor 14:26). Speaking in the context of spiritual gifts like tongues and prophecy, miracles and healings, Paul can still point to "greater gifts" and a more "excellent way" (1 Cor 12:31) made available by the Holy Spirit:

> If I speak in the tongues of men and of angels, but have not love, I am only a resounding gong or a clanging cymbal.... Love never fails. But where there are prophecies, they will cease; where there are tongues, they will be stilled; where there is knowledge, it will pass away. For we know in part and we prophesy in part, but when perfection comes, the imperfect disappears. (1 Cor 13:1-10)

I don't have to accept the exegetical backflips often attempted to explain the meaning of "perfect" or specify when certain gifts ceased to appreciate that Paul is making a distinction here between gifts of partial and temporary importance and gifts of ultimate and lasting import. The Spirit who changes hearts makes it possible for us to love as Paul describes in this wonderful chapter. The ability to love in Christ-like ways is the Spirit's greatest gift, his highest expression of spiritual maturity. Love makes gifts like tongues and prophecies pale in comparison. Paul encourages the Corinthians to "eagerly desire spiritual gifts." But he insists that they "follow the way of love," whatever other gifting they may receive (1 Cor 14:1). For Paul, the miraculous gifts are optional to the Christian life; the transforming gift is not.

The Gospel of John echoes many of the themes about the Spirit found in the Old Testament, the Synoptics, and Acts of the Apostles. But what John says about the Spirit sounds most like Paul. As we will see, John is equally fascinated by a Spirit "in us," a Spirit who makes his home with us. Like Paul, John champions a Spirit who teaches and reveals and comforts. Most of all, John joins Paul in placing emphasis squarely on a Spirit who transforms. The Spirit who indwells makes a difference in our lives and in our walk as disciples—a needed and necessary difference.

It is to John's witness about the Spirit we turn now.

## Chapter Six

# THE PARACLETE IN JOHN

The Gospel of John provides a unique opportunity for us to learn about the Holy Spirit. John says things about the Spirit—and says them *in a way*—that can be heard and appreciated by people who are hungry for the Spirit but want to be discerning in their approach.

Not that John says a great deal about the Spirit. There are only twenty one Spirit-references in the entire book (compared, remember, to some seventy in Acts). But, in this instance, we really do have a case of quality over quantity. The little John says is well-worth hearing.

It's worth hearing because, unlike the Synoptic Gospels, most of what is said about the Spirit in John is directly applicable to *disciples*. It's worth hearing because, unlike Acts and very like Paul, what is said about the Spirit is focused on the *transforming* work of God's Spirit in our lives. And most of all—as we will see—it is worth hearing because John directly quotes what *Jesus* says and thinks on the subject.

John strips the work of the Spirit down to bare essentials—who the Spirit is, what the Spirit does in the world, how the Spirit works on the hearts of believers—and places those essentials on the lips of Jesus. If we do not understand everything there is to know about the Spirit after reading his Gospel, we at least have a good foundation, a *trustable* foundation, on which to build a relationship with the Spirit.

## John and the Synoptics

A few of the Spirit-references found in John are reminiscent of things we've already seen in the Synoptics.

There are a couple of instances, for example, where the word "spirit" is used to speak of a human rather than divine spirit, an inner being or "self." (John, for example, describes Jesus as "deeply moved in spirit.") This use of "spirit" (with a little "s") has its Synoptic equivalents.

John, like his fellow Gospel writers, stresses the importance of the Spirit at the beginning of Jesus' ministry. He has the Baptist report:

> I saw the Spirit of God come down from heaven as a dove and remain on him. I would not have known him, except that the one who sent me to baptize with water told me, "the man on whom you see the Spirit come down and remain is he who will baptize with the Holy Spirit." I have seen and I testify that this is the Son of God. (John 1:32-34)

This Spirit "coming down" was a critical part of identifying Jesus, pointing to the "Lamb of God," the "Son of God," the One who "takes away the sins of the world," and the One who "will baptize with the Holy Spirit."

We also find in John (in one of only two comments made about the Spirit in John's voice) an assuring promise: "For the one whom God has sent speaks the words of God, for God gives the Spirit without limit" (John 3:34). Here, like the other Gospel writers, John connects Jesus to the Messianic Age—a time when God would pour out his Spirit on all flesh. It's easy to hear in this statement an echo of Luke's portrait of a Father "who gives the Holy Spirit to those who ask him" (Luke 11:13).

Finally, John (like the Synoptics) talks about the Spirit in the context of Jesus' miraculous ministry. John 1-12 is often titled "The Book of Signs." In these chapters, John builds his story of Jesus around seven miracles: water to wine, healing an official's son, healing a lame man, bread for the crowds, walking on water, opening the eyes of the blind man, and raising the dead.[1] Everything we learn about the Spirit in John is learned in the wider context of Jesus' miraculous ministry.

Thus, John does a few things we've seen the Synoptic writers do: begin Jesus' ministry with the Spirit; promise Jesus would baptize with the Spirit; assure readers that God would be giving the Holy Spirit; and talk about the Spirit in the context of Jesus' miraculous and sign-filled ministry.

On the other hand, there are a few things the Synoptics talk about frequently that John entirely ignores. While they see evil spirits around every corner and under every rock, John says nothing at all on that subject. There are no exorcisms in John, no mandate given to the disciples to cast out demons. Nor does John, so intent on talking about signs in the ministry of Jesus, say anything about signs accompanying the disciples. Jesus performs wonders in this Gospel, but the disciples never do.

## The Spirit in the Voice of Jesus

John testifies to signs throughout his Gospel as proof that Jesus is who he claims to be. But he also drops teachings about the Spirit like breadcrumbs—as though he wants his readers to follow him to some greater destination. That greater destination is somewhere readers of the Synoptic Gospels have never been before, for the rest of John's teaching on the Spirit leads in a different and strikingly original direction.

This may be due (in part) to the fact that John consistently places words about the Spirit on the lips of Jesus. In the Synoptics, Spirit-sayings come from angels or Old Testament quotes or the Gospel writers themselves (reporting specific events). But Jesus says "Spirit" only five times in Matthew, three times in both Mark and Luke.[2]

In John, however, the great majority of times the Spirit is mentioned, Jesus is doing the mentioning. He speaks directly and personally about the Spirit *fifteen* times—often at great length and depth. In other words, when the Spirit comes up in John, the letters are likely to be in red. This is something unique to the Fourth Gospel … and uniquely precious.

The first time Jesus raises the subject of the Spirit is in his long conversation with Nicodemus. They have met "at night" and Nicodemus wants to talk about new birth:

> In reply Jesus declared, "I tell you the truth, no one can see the kingdom of God unless he is born again."
>
> "How can a man be born when he is old?" Nicodemus asked. "Surely he cannot enter a second time into his mother's womb to be born!"
>
> Jesus answered, "I tell you the truth, no one can enter the kingdom of God unless he is born of water and the Spirit. Flesh

gives birth to flesh, but the Spirit gives birth to spirit. You should not be surprised at my saying, 'You must be born again.' The wind blows wherever it pleases. You hear its sound, but you cannot tell where it comes from or where it is going. So it is with everyone born of the Spirit." (John 3:3-8)

There is a great deal to process here: "born again," the divide between flesh and Spirit, the mysterious and sovereign nature of the Spirit "blowing" where he pleases. Nicodemus has to work hard to keep up. What is striking for our purposes, however, is how different this is from anything we've heard in the Synoptics. Not *contrary* to Matthew, Mark, and Luke, but certainly novel and more detailed. And certainly important information for disciples to have as they learn to walk in the Spirit.

It is also striking how much more these ideas sound like Paul than the other Gospel writers. Paul draws a connection between the Spirit and new birth (Gal 4:29; Titus 3:5), a new "self" (Eph 4:23-24; Col 3:10-11), that sounds very much like "You must be born again." He makes the same distinction between flesh and Spirit (e.g., Romans 8). He also has a vast appreciation of the mysterious nature of the Spirit (Eph 3:2-5; Rom 8:26-27; 1Cor 2:6ff). John's treatment of the Spirit has a lot more in common with Paul than with Luke and the others.

Jesus brings up the subject of the Spirit again while standing with a woman by a well in Samaria.

> Believe me, woman, a time is coming when you will worship the Father neither on this mountain nor in Jerusalem. You Samaritans worship what you do not know; we worship what we do know for salvation is from the Jews. Yet a time is coming and has now come when the true worshipers will worship the Father in Spirit and truth, for they are the kind of worshipers the Father seeks. God is spirit, and his worshipers must worship in spirit and in truth. (John 4:23-24)

She wants to talk about well-water and buckets and worship-traditions. Jesus prefers to talk about missing husbands and life-style and true worship. Worship, says Jesus to the woman, must be "in Spirit and truth." It is not defined by place or tradition. It is defined by the heart of the worshiper.

Again, there is nothing like this in the Synoptic Gospels. And, again, this sounds a great deal like Paul ("It is we who worship by the Spirit of God"—Phil 3:3).

When Jesus feeds the crowds (John 6:1-15), they clamor for more. But Jesus knows they want bread for their stomachs, not nourishment for their souls. They'll eat, but they will not believe. They crave his loaves and fish but not his words. Jesus tells them what they should be hungry for: "The Spirit gives life; the flesh counts for nothing. The words I have spoken to you are spirit and they are life" (John 6:63). Like Nicodemus and the Samaritan woman, the crowds are stuck at the level of the flesh. Jesus keeps trying to lift their eyes to the Spirit plane. The *Spirit* is where eternal life is found, not lunch. "Live above this world," Jesus seems to say. "Live for more than this world."

The same plea is found in the Synoptic Gospels (e.g., "Store up for yourselves treasures in heaven"—Matt 6:19ff). But only in John's Gospel is this plea linked directly to the Spirit. And in Paul. "Those who live according the flesh have their minds set on what the flesh desires. Those who live according to the Spirit have their minds set on what the Spirit desires" (Rom 8:5).

## The Spirit in the Final Discourse

Already, Jesus has said some wonderful and original things about the Spirit in John's Gospel: the Spirit "without limit"; the Spirit and new birth; the Spirit and worship; the Spirit and life.

But as the Gospel of John reaches its climax—and especially when we come to the Final Discourse—Jesus steps up to a whole new level. His teaching about the Spirit becomes frequent and compacted. In chapters 14-16 (the heart of the discourse), Jesus talks directly about the Spirit in five extended passages. Because the Spirit is named "the *Paraclete*" in these passages, they are known collectively as "the *Paraclete* Passages." Jesus says more about the Spirit here than in all the rest of his teaching combined.

If the first half of John provides breadcrumbs about the Spirit for us to follow, what Jesus says about the Spirit in "The Final Discourse" is surely the destination to which those crumbs lead.

The purpose of this book is to look at the *Paraclete* Passages in detail, to hear what Jesus promises to the disciples, and to consider what those promises might mean for us. Jesus says that the Spirit is coming; the Spirit will live in the disciples and be Christ's presence for them; the Spirit will help the disciples live informed, obedient, well-equipped lives; the Spirit will witness to and help the disciples witness to the world; the Spirit will convict the world of guilt; and the Spirit will continue to reveal the Father to believers.

These are important promises, with important implications for all who want to follow Jesus. As we will see, what we find in the Final Discourse are teachings never broached in the Synoptic Gospels or Acts: a Spirit who indwells; a Spirit who transforms and matures; a Spirit who touches broken hearts and minds as well as ailing bodies. Jesus talks repeatedly in this Discourse about the Spirit "in" you (just as Paul does).

As he talks, Jesus introduces us to a *person*. The Spirit is not just a force or a power. He has an identity, a personality.

And he has a name.

## The Paraclete

"What's in a name?" asked Shakespeare. "That which we call a rose by any other name would smell as sweet."[3] Perhaps that is true. Still, names are important, even if they don't affect the way roses smell.

At the heart of the Final Discourse are five passages where Jesus speaks of the Holy Spirit. In each (each save the last), he calls the Spirit the *Paraclete*—the only instance in the New Testament when the Spirit is called this and the only place in the New Testament (except once in 1 John) where the word *Paraclete* occurs at all. Because the word is rare (even in secular Greek), it is hard to define precisely. Yet *this* is the particular word Jesus used when referring to the Spirit. The word meant something, conveyed something, that had significance to Jesus and (presumably) to the disciples he addressed. Rare or not, then, it is important to understand as best we can what the word means.

Jesus actually refers to the Spirit by other terms in these chapters—the Spirit of Truth, the Holy Spirit—and a variety of descriptors: the One the Father gives (or sends), the One Jesus sends, the One who will be with the disciples forever. But *Paraclete* is his most consistent and distinctive name for the Spirit.

A Spirit by any other name might also smell as sweet. Still, if Jesus thought enough of the name *Paraclete* to use it so persistently for the Spirit, I'd like to know more about what that name means.

The reason I am about to drag you, Dear Reader, through the etymological swamps is because I want you to know the name of the one Jesus has given us to be our Companion on life's journey. Enough of that depersonalizing "It." Enough avoiding a living Spirit with talk about "influence" and "attitude" and "spiritual frame of mind." No more "Holy Ghost."

The Spirit is a being, a person.

And, according to Jesus, his name is *Paraclete*.

## Para-who?

[Warning: technical jargon ahead!]

*Paraclete* is actually the anglicized form of the original Greek word *parakletos*. It is a *transliteration* (to use the formal term) rather than a *translation*. Because the meaning of this Greek word is obscure (and the focus of no little scholarly debate), some translations actually avoid the word entirely rather than commit themselves to a particular English noun.[4]

Even when they decide to translate, however, there isn't much agreement among scholars as to which word renders the meaning best. In fact, translations are all over the map. The variety of options in English Bibles (Advocate,[5] Comforter,[6] Companion, Counselor,[7] Helper,[8] Friend,[9] Intercessor,[10] and—regrettably—Strengthener[11]) and the frequency of marginal notes suggesting even *more* alternatives, gives us some indication as to how long and hard translators have grappled with this term.

A clue to the meaning of *Paraclete* comes by looking at the two words from which it is formed: *para* and *kaleo*. *Para* is a preposition meaning "beside" or "along with." *Kaleo* means "to call." Putting these two words together suggests a meaning for *Paraclete* of "one who is called beside or summoned."

As it turns out, this meaning has considerable merit. In secular Greek, the word *Paraclete* most often takes this very sense when it shows up in legal contexts. When it does, it refers to what we moderns would call a "lawyer": a legal advocate who speaks in another's defense.

Professional, paid lawyers did not exist at the time of the New Testament. (They were a later invention of the Romans—the same folks who brought us blood sports and world domination.) Instead, a family member or friend would be "called" to serve as spokesman, standing with the defendant to argue his case before a judge and jury. This "friend" was known as a *Paraclete.*

Jesus could be borrowing this term to describe the Spirit as one who stands beside us, who speaks up for and defends us, who vouches for us in the divine court. This is the background for *Paraclete* that recommends translations like "Advocate" and "Intercessor."

The problem with drawing a definition for *Paraclete* from a legal context is that there is nothing very "lawyerly" about the work of the Spirit described by Jesus in John's Final Discourse.[12] There is no hint of divine courts or judges and juries or the Spirit speaking up in the defense of believers in this passage.

The idea of the Spirit as someone who is "on our side," who "stands beside" us through thick and thin, is certainly appropriate—especially when we understand more about how Jesus describes the Spirit's work in the Final Discourse. But the legal context just doesn't work. Not in John. Thus, to use a translation like "Advocate" may push us too far in a direction John never intended.[13]

There is a verb form of this word (*parakaleo*) that is much more common in the New Testament and in the Greek world of the first century. Paul uses this word, for instance, when he wants to *urge* (Rom 12:1) or *encourage* (1 Thess 2:12) or even *plead with* (Phil 4:2) his readers. It is the word used in passages that speak of *comfort* ("who *comforts* us in all our troubles"—2 Cor 1:4) or *exhortation* ("Do not rebuke an older man harshly, but *exhort* him as if he were your father"—1 Tim 5:1).

The common thread between these various translations of *parakaleo* is of someone speaking into the lives of others—often powerfully—in order to achieve a positive effect. If you read this meaning back into the name Jesus uses for the Holy Spirit, it's easy to see how we got translations like "Comforter," "Helper," "Friend," or "Counselor." The *Paraclete* is the one who comes from the Father to encourage us, to comfort and console us, to advise and strengthen us. He speaks into our lives—often powerfully—in order to achieve a positive effect.

With this meaning, you still get overtones of someone who "is at our side," who stands up and speaks up for us (which is a good thing). But there is the added nuance of one who not only speaks *for* us, but one who speaks *to* us. Jesus may well be saying that the Spirit is not just our "defender," he is also our supporter and advisor, someone who whispers wise counsel to us.

Regrettably, none of the English words that try to convey these ideas really seems up to the task. They are either lacking in breadth and power or carry significant baggage for English speakers. To translate *Paraclete* as "Helper" makes the Spirit sound like an errand boy and carries unfortunate overtones of servant status and lower class. "Friend" seems overly familiar (in the same category with God as "Daddy"). "Counselor" brings up associations like "marriage counselor" or "financial counselor," associations that contaminate rather than enlighten. D. A. Carson regrets that, "In today's ears, 'Comforter' sounds either like a quilt or like a do-gooder at a wake, and for most speakers of English should be abandoned."[14] "Strengthener" (shudder) reminds one of hair products.

Each of these terms reflects an aspect of the actual work of the *Paraclete* described here.[15] Jesus paints the Spirit as someone who lives with and in disciples, teaching them who they are and what God wants them to do, revealing ever more of God to them. He portrays the Spirit—whatever we name him—as someone who helps, comes to aid and assist, offers encouragement and consolation, and gives guidance and wisdom. He is friend, mentor, parent, teacher, spouse, role-model, older and wiser sage, partner, workmate, and foxhole buddy—all rolled into one.

It's just that no single English word seems capable of carrying all that load.

Thus, Herman Ridderbos writes:

> "'Paraclete'—we may conclude—here has a specific meaning that can hardly be conveyed in one word in our language (and many others) but of which the dominant idea is of someone who offers assistance in a situation in which help is needed."[16]

And Andreas Köstenberger concludes:

> Perhaps "helping presence" captures the import of the term better than any other ... for the following reasons: (1) this is what

Jesus was while with the disciples; (2) this encompasses the various functions laid out for the Spirit in John 14-16; (3) this transcends (but may include) the legal context of the term. . . .[17]

Here, then, are the meanings that lie behind the Greek word *Paraclete:*

| | | | |
|---|---|---|---|
| Advocate | Counselor | Intercessor | Supporter |
| Comforter | Helper | Encourager | Advisor |
| Companion | Friend | Exhorter | Consoler |
| Guide | Helping Presence | | |

One who is called beside or summoned
One who speaks up for us
One who speaks into our lives to achieve a positive effect
One who offers assistance in a situation where help is needed

For purposes of this book, I cannot bring myself to settle for any one English term. So I will simply keep the original word *Paraclete* (italicized whenever it occurs) and ask you—the reader—to keep in mind the layers and nuances encompassed by the word.

## The Name that Smells as Sweet

Jesus is leaving his disciples. He promises to send someone in his place, someone who will help his disciples *be* his disciples after he has gone.

Essentially, he promises himself in other form.

As we will see, the *Paraclete* will not be a "Jesus substitute" ... some kind of "Jesus lite." Rather, the *Paraclete* will be the hands and face and voice of Jesus, his actual presence and the means by which he will continue to commune with the disciples.

The Final Discourse bears witness to this Helping Presence, available to all who love Jesus, sent by the Father to walk with believers along the way. According to Jesus, the *Paraclete* will keep the disciples alive to God. He will make them effective in their living and work. He will help them in their mission. And his presence, as we will see, will last "forever."

These promises raise all manner of questions, like: Why is this Spirit so necessary? How does he work? Is this same Spirit for us? We will spend the rest of this book pursuing such questions.

For the moment, I simply ask you to consider how the *name* we use for the Spirit will affect the way the Spirit *smells* to us. In a religious context where "Spirit" might as well be called "Bible Study" or "Careful Exegesis" or "Proper Hermeneutic," the bloom is certainly off the rose. Any discussion of the Spirit that bogs us down in historical-critical methodology and the conjugation of Greek verbs is bound to fail the sniff test.

At the other extreme, there are religious contexts where "Spirit" might as well be named "Stranger" or "Unknown Quantity" or "Perpetrator of the Odd and Offbeat" or "Handy Excuse for Egregious Behavior" or "Justification for Getting My Own Way." Names like these will always smell fishy no matter how much essence-of-rose you sprinkle on them!

When we talk, however, about a Spirit named *Paraclete*, there is a certain fragrance that fills the air. You catch a whiff of the aroma of Christ. You inhale the breath of God and smell the rich perfume of life.

The Spirit as *Paraclete* smells sweet indeed. I want to inhale that Spirit with every breath I take. I want his scent in my life and on my heart. I need his heady perfume.

I suspect you do too.

Chapter Seven

# THE TEXT OF THE
# FINAL DISCOURSE

Below is the text of the Final Discourse from John. I include this passage in its entirety because I believe it is important for readers of this book to root their reading in the key text that forms the basis of the book. We will be wading in and out of this passage through the pages to follow.

There is debate in the literature about what verses actually constitute the Final Discourse. Some don't begin the Discourse until Judas leaves the room (13:30). Others want to extend the Discourse through the prayer recorded in John 17.

I have chosen to let the fundamental dynamics of this conversation—the Last Meal, the Upper Room, Jesus interacting with his disciples—set the boundaries for the Final Discourse. Thus, because the evening begins as chapter 13 opens, I start the discourse there. And because Jesus is addressing his Father rather than the disciples in chapter 17, I end the discourse before the High Priestly Prayer.

Please spend some time immersed in this passage. Wash yourself with its words. Scrub its themes and messages into the pores of your soul. Jesus has something important to say to the Twelve on this final night. If my reading is correct, he has something important to say to us as well. Imagine Jesus speaking over the heads of his Apostles to all the other disciples through all the ages to follow who listen to this conversation by means of John's testimony.

I've included the chapter and verse markings in this passage only to help you navigate more easily. And I've marked the *Paraclete* Passages so you cannot miss them in italics.

**13** [1]It was just before the Passover Feast. Jesus knew that the time had come for him to leave this world and go to the Father. Having loved his own who were in the world, he now showed them the full extent of his love.

[2]The evening meal was being served, and the devil had already prompted Judas Iscariot, son of Simon, to betray Jesus. [3]Jesus knew that the Father had put all things under his power, and that he had come from God and was returning to God; [4]so he got up from the meal, took off his outer clothing, and wrapped a towel around his waist. [5]After that, he poured water into a basin and began to wash his disciples' feet, drying them with the towel that was wrapped around him.

[6]He came to Simon Peter, who said to him, "Lord, are you going to wash my feet?"

[7]Jesus replied, "You do not realize now what I am doing, but later you will understand."

[8]"No," said Peter, "you shall never wash my feet." Jesus answered, "Unless I wash you, you have no part with me."

[9]"Then, Lord," Simon Peter replied, "not just my feet but my hands and my head as well!"

[10]Jesus answered, "A person who has had a bath needs only to wash his feet; his whole body is clean. And you are clean, though not every one of you." [11]For he knew who was going to betray him, and that was why he said not every one was clean.

[12]When he had finished washing their feet, he put on his clothes and returned to his place. "Do you understand what I have done for you?" he asked them. [13]"You call me 'Teacher' and 'Lord,' and rightly so, for that is what I am. [14]Now that I, your Lord and Teacher, have washed your feet, you also should wash one another's feet. [15]I have set you an example that you should do as I have done for you. [16]I tell you the truth, no servant is greater than his master, nor is a messenger greater than the one who sent him. [17]Now that you know these things, you will be blessed if you do them.

[18]"I am not referring to all of you; I know those I have chosen. But this is to fulfill the scripture: 'He who shares my bread has lifted up his heel against me.'

¹⁹"I am telling you now before it happens, so that when it does happen you will believe that I am He. ²⁰I tell you the truth, whoever accepts anyone I send accepts me; and whoever accepts me accepts the one who sent me."

²¹After he had said this, Jesus was troubled in spirit and testified, "I tell you the truth, one of you is going to betray me."

²²His disciples stared at one another, at a loss to know which of them he meant. ²³One of them, the disciple whom Jesus loved, was reclining next to him. ²⁴Simon Peter motioned to this disciple and said, "Ask him which one he means."

²⁵Leaning back against Jesus, he asked him, "Lord, who is it?"

²⁶Jesus answered, "It is the one to whom I will give this piece of bread when I have dipped it in the dish." Then, dipping the piece of bread, he gave it to Judas Iscariot, son of Simon. ²⁷As soon as Judas took the bread, Satan entered into him.

"What you are about to do, do quickly," Jesus told him, ²⁸but no one at the meal understood why Jesus said this to him. ²⁹Since Judas had charge of the money, some thought Jesus was telling him to buy what was needed for the Feast, or to give something to the poor. ³⁰As soon as Judas had taken the bread, he went out. And it was night.

³¹When he was gone, Jesus said, "Now is the Son of Man glorified and God is glorified in him. ³²If God is glorified in him, God will glorify the Son in himself, and will glorify him at once.

³³"My children, I will be with you only a little longer. You will look for me, and just as I told the Jews, so I tell you now: Where I am going, you cannot come.

³⁴"A new command I give you: Love one another. As I have loved you, so you must love one another. ³⁵By this all men will know that you are my disciples, if you love one another."

³⁶Simon Peter asked him, "Lord, where are you going?" Jesus replied, "Where I am going, you cannot follow now, but you will follow later."

³⁷Peter asked, "Lord, why can't I follow you now? I will lay down my life for you."

³⁸Then Jesus answered, "Will you really lay down your life for me? I tell you the truth, before the rooster crows, you will disown me three times!

**14** [1]"Do not let your hearts be troubled. Trust in God; trust also in me. [2]In my Father's house are many rooms; if it were not so, I would have told you. I am going there to prepare a place for you. [3]And if I go and prepare a place for you, I will come back and take you to be with me that you also may be where I am. [4]You know the way to the place where I am going."

[5]Thomas said to him, "Lord, we don't know where you are going, so how can we know the way?"

[6]Jesus answered, "I am the way and the truth and the life. No one comes to the Father except through me. [7]If you really knew me, you would know my Father as well. From now on, you do know him and have seen him."

[8]Philip said, "Lord, show us the Father and that will be enough for us."

[9]Jesus answered: "Don't you know me, Philip, even after I have been among you such a long time? Anyone who has seen me has seen the Father. How can you say, 'Show us the Father'? [10]Don't you believe that I am in the Father, and that the Father is in me? The words I say to you are not just my own. Rather, it is the Father, living in me, who is doing his work. [11]Believe me when I say that I am in the Father and the Father is in me; or at least believe on the evidence of the miracles themselves. [12]I tell you the truth, anyone who has faith in me will do what I have been doing. He will do even greater things than these, because I am going to the Father. [13]And I will do whatever you ask in my name, so that the Son may bring glory to the Father. [14]You may ask me for anything in my name, and I will do it.

[15]"If you love me, you will obey what I command. [16]*And I will ask the Father, and he will give you another Paraclete to be with you forever—* [17]*the Spirit of truth. The world cannot accept him, because it neither sees him nor knows him. But you know him, for he lives with you and will be in you.* [18]I will not leave you as orphans; I will come to you. [19]Before long, the world will not see me anymore, but you will see me. Because I live, you also will live. [20]On that day you will realize that I am in my Father, and you are in me, and I am in you. [21]Whoever has my commands and obeys them, he is the one who loves me. He who loves me will be loved by my Father, and I too will love him and show myself to him."

[22]Then Judas (not Judas Iscariot) said, "But, Lord, why do you intend to show yourself to us and not to the world?"

[23]Jesus replied, "If anyone loves me, he will obey my teaching. My Father will love him, and we will come to him and make our home with him. [24]He who does not love me will not obey my teaching. These words you hear are not my own; they belong to the Father who sent me.

[25]"All this I have spoken while still with you. [26]*But the Paraclete, the Holy Spirit, whom the Father will send in my name, will teach you all things and will remind you of everything I have said to you.* [27]Peace I leave with you; my peace I give you. I do not give to you as the world gives. Do not let your hearts be troubled and do not be afraid.

[28]"You heard me say, 'I am going away and I am coming back to you.' If you loved me, you would be glad that I am going to the Father, for the Father is greater than I. [29]I have told you now before it happens, so that when it does happen you will believe. [30]I will not speak with you much longer, for the prince of this world is coming. He has no hold on me, [31]but the world must learn that I love the Father and that I do exactly what my Father has commanded me.

"Come now; let us leave.

**15** [1]"I am the true vine, and my Father is the gardener. [2]He cuts off every branch in me that bears no fruit, while every branch that does bear fruit he prunes so that it will be even more fruitful. [3]You are already clean because of the word I have spoken to you. [4]Remain in me, and I will remain in you. No branch can bear fruit by itself; it must remain in the vine. Neither can you bear fruit unless you remain in me.

[5]"I am the vine; you are the branches. If a man remains in me and I in him, he will bear much fruit; apart from me you can do nothing. [6]If anyone does not remain in me, he is like a branch that is thrown away and withers; such branches are picked up, thrown into the fire and burned. [7]If you remain in me and my words remain in you, ask whatever you wish, and it will be given you. [8]This is to my Father's glory, that you bear much fruit, showing yourselves to be my disciples.

[9]"As the Father has loved me, so have I loved you. Now remain in my love. [10]If you obey my commands, you will remain in my love, just as I have obeyed my Father's commands and remain in his love. [11]I have told you this so that my joy may be in you and that your joy may be complete. [12]My command is this: Love each other as I have loved you. [13]Greater love has no one than this, that he lay down his life for his

friends. [14]You are my friends if you do what I command. [15]I no longer call you servants, because a servant does not know his master's business. Instead, I have called you friends, for everything that I learned from my Father I have made known to you. [16]You did not choose me, but I chose you and appointed you to go and bear fruit—fruit that will last. Then the Father will give you whatever you ask in my name. [17]This is my command: Love each other.

[18]"If the world hates you, keep in mind that it hated me first. [19]If you belonged to the world, it would love you as its own. As it is, you do not belong to the world, but I have chosen you out of the world. That is why the world hates you. [20]Remember the words I spoke to you: 'No servant is greater than his master.' If they persecuted me, they will persecute you also. If they obeyed my teaching, they will obey yours also. [21]They will treat you this way because of my name, for they do not know the One who sent me. [22]If I had not come and spoken to them, they would not be guilty of sin. Now, however, they have no excuse for their sin. [23]He who hates me hates my Father as well. [24]If I had not done among them what no one else did, they would not be guilty of sin. But now they have seen these miracles, and yet they have hated both me and my Father. [25]But this is to fulfill what is written in their Law: 'They hated me without reason.'

[26]"When the Paraclete comes, whom I will send to you from the Father, the Spirit of truth who goes out from the Father, he will testify about me. [27]And you also must testify, for you have been with me from the beginning.

**16** [1]"All this I have told you so that you will not go astray. [2]They will put you out of the synagogue; in fact, a time is coming when anyone who kills you will think he is offering a service to God. [3]They will do such things because they have not known the Father or me. [4]I have told you this, so that when the time comes you will remember that I warned you. I did not tell you this at first because I was with you.

[5]"Now I am going to him who sent me, yet none of you asks me, 'Where are you going?' [6]Because I have said these things, you are filled with grief. [7]But I tell you the truth: It is for your good that I am going away. Unless I go away, the Paraclete will not come to you; but if I go, I will send him to you. [8]When he comes, he will convict the world of guilt in regard to

*sin and righteousness and judgment:* [9]*in regard to sin, because men do not believe in me;* [10]*in regard to righteousness, because I am going to the Father, where you can see me no longer;* [11]*and in regard to judgment, because the prince of this world now stands condemned.*

[12]"I have much more to say to you, more than you can now bear. [13]*But when he, the Spirit of truth, comes, he will guide you into all truth. He will not speak on his own; he will speak only what he hears, and he will tell you what is yet to come.* [14]*He will bring glory to me by taking from what is mine and making it known to you.* [15]*All that belongs to the Father is mine. That is why I said the Spirit will take from what is mine and make it known to you.*

[16]"In a little while you will see me no more, and then after a little while you will see me."

[17]Some of his disciples said to one another, "What does he mean by saying, 'In a little while you will see me no more, and then after a little while you will see me,' and 'Because I am going to the Father'?" [18]They kept asking, "What does he mean by 'a little while'? We don't understand what he is saying."

[19]Jesus saw that they wanted to ask him about this, so he said to them, "Are you asking one another what I meant when I said, 'In a little while you will see me no more, and then after a little while you will see me'? [20]I tell you the truth, you will weep and mourn while the world rejoices. You will grieve, but your grief will turn to joy. [21]A woman giving birth to a child has pain because her time has come; but when her baby is born she forgets the anguish because of her joy that a child is born into the world. [22]So with you: Now is your time of grief, but I will see you again and you will rejoice, and no one will take away your joy. [23]In that day you will no longer ask me anything. I tell you the truth, my Father will give you whatever you ask in my name. [24]Until now you have not asked for anything in my name. Ask and you will receive, and your joy will be complete.

[25]"Though I have been speaking figuratively, a time is coming when I will no longer use this kind of language but will tell you plainly about my Father. [26]In that day you will ask in my name. I am not saying that I will ask the Father on your behalf. [27]No, the Father himself loves you because you have loved me and have believed that I came from God. [28]I

came from the Father and entered the world; now I am leaving the world and going back to the Father."

[29]Then Jesus' disciples said, "Now you are speaking clearly and without figures of speech. [30]Now we can see that you know all things and that you do not even need to have anyone ask you questions. This makes us believe that you came from God."

[31]"You believe at last!" Jesus answered. [32]"But a time is coming, and has come, when you will be scattered, each to his own home. You will leave me all alone. Yet I am not alone, for my Father is with me."

[33]"I have told you these things, so that in me you may have peace. In this world you will have trouble. But take heart! I have overcome the world."

# THE SPIRIT IN THE FINAL DISCOURSE

From the moment Jesus called them from tax tables and fishing nets, the disciples stuck close to their Master. They were with him at the Wedding Feast, when he cleared the temple, as he talked with the Samaritan woman, in the wilderness with the crowds. They never ventured far from Jesus, nor he from them. There were rare occasions when he withdrew to pray. Once, he sent them out to preach on their own. But, for the most part, Master and followers were inseparable.

It was the one constant of Jesus' ministry. Whatever else happened, whatever uncertainties they had to navigate, the disciples knew Jesus was *there*. They steered by his Star. From the beginning, he was their fixed and certain point as they sailed the chartless seas of Messianic ministry and their own new calling.

But no more. On the night he is betrayed, Jesus has to watch his disciples run aground on the unexpected rock of his imminent departure.

It is at this point Jesus introduces his disciples to the *Paraclete*. In a series of five passages, Jesus equips his disciples for a life without his physical presence by pointing them to the ministry of the Spirit who will continue his work. The chapters of Section Two take up each of these passages in turn.

Chapter Eight looks at the First *Paraclete* Passage (John 14:16-17) and the "promise of presence" it contains. Through the Spirit, the disciples will continue to experience a relationship with Jesus. Because of the Spirit, they will continue to "see" Jesus and "live" with him. The Spirit will become Jesus' forever presence with his disciples.

Chapter Nine focuses on the Second *Paraclete* Passage (John 14:26) and its "promise of teaching." The disciples have a mission to accomplish. Jesus assures them that the Spirit will guide and instruct them as they continue the vital work he began in the world.

Chapter Ten examines the Third *Paraclete* Passage (John 15:26-27) and it's "promise of witness." Part of the mission given to the disciples involves testifying about Jesus before a hostile world. Jesus wants them to know they will not be alone in that work—the Spirit will testify with and through them.

In Chapter Eleven we look at the Fourth *Paraclete* Passage (John 16:7-11) and its "promise of conviction." In a world so full of sin, disciples can feel lonely and oh-so-inadequate. There is no need. God is still at work in his world, acting through his Spirit to convict his broken creatures of their sin and their need for him.

Then in Chapter Twelve we study the Fifth *Paraclete* Passage (John 16:12-15) and the "promise of revelation." Jesus has so much more to say about his Father. But the disciples cannot bear it. So he offers them the Spirit who will reveal the Father in portions they can swallow. The Spirit, knowing their limits, reveals what they need to know of God as they are capable of receiving it.

Section Two is the heart of this book. This is where we do the hard digging in turning to Scripture to discover the treasure that lies buried there: Jesus' promises about the Holy Spirit. In Section Two we stick mainly to what Jesus tells the Twelve about the Spirit. In the following Section we'll apply what he tells them to ourselves and our particular circumstances.

Chapter Eight

# THE PROMISE OF PRESENCE

(JOHN 14:16-23)

No wonder they feel abandoned. Jesus is going away. He's just told them so. He is leaving and they cannot go with him.

Into their foreboding, Jesus pours every reassuring word he can lay his hands on. Many of these reassuring words point to the *Paraclete*. And the first of these reassuring *Paraclete*-words promises both a future for the disciples in the wake of the Cross and the presence of Jesus as they meet that future.

Jesus begins by talking to the Twelve about who the Spirit *is,* his nature and identity.

> 14:16And I will ask the Father, and he will give you another *Paraclete* to be with you forever—17the Spirit of truth. The world cannot accept him, because it neither sees him nor knows him. But you know him, for he lives with you and will be in you. 18I will not leave you as orphans; I will come to you.

## Jesus Is God

John 14, from beginning to end, addresses identity questions. It opens with the question, "Who is the Father?" Jesus answers by making an astounding claim: "I am the way and the truth and the life. No one comes to the Father except through me. If you really knew me, you would know my Father as well. From now on, you do know him and have seen him" (John 14:6-7). He has made such claims before. In fact, these claims have been a source of major conflict with the religious authorities. The Pharisees were driven to murderous rage when, early in his ministry, they heard him "calling God his own Father, making himself equal with God" (John 5:18). They picked up stones to throw at him again when he made the bald statement, "Before Abraham was born, I AM" (John 8:58—a clear echo of God's self-defining statement to Moses: "Tell the Israelites, 'I AM has sent me to you'"—Exod 3:14). Yet again, they reached for rocks when Jesus proclaimed, "I and the Father are one" (John 10:30).

But now, alone with his disciples, Jesus strings together a series of claims linking himself directly to God—not as a prophet or a teacher but as the living incarnation of Deity, God in the flesh, the visible revelation of the invisible God. Since he *is* God, to know Jesus is to know God; to see Jesus is to see God.

When Philip misses the point and asks Jesus to "show us the Father," Jesus repeats himself and elaborates on the theme just to be clear.

> Don't you know me, Philip, even after I have been among you such a long time? Anyone who has seen me has seen the Father. How can you say, 'Show us the Father'? Don't you believe that I am in the Father, and that the Father is in me? The words I say to you are not just my own. Rather, it is the Father, living in me, who is doing his work. Believe me when I say that I am in the Father and the Father is in me ... (John 14:9-11).

He *has* shown them the Father. He has revealed God by disclosing himself! Jesus is God in flesh-form. Jesus and the Father are living in each other; they are the same in nature and character. Jesus speaks the words of God and does the work of God. The Father and the Son are *one*.

Jesus answers Philip's request in a way that unmistakably identifies the Father with himself. God is no stranger to the disciples. He is not hidden and unknown. Jesus reveals God to the disciples by letting them get to know *him*.

## Jesus Is Spirit

In a similar way John 14 also asks the question, "Who is the Spirit?" In answering that question, Jesus uses the same strategy, doing with the Spirit what he's done with the Father: pointing to himself.

"And I will ask the Father, and he will give you another *Paraclete* to be with you forever—the Spirit of truth" (John 14:16-17a).

In this initial broaching of the Spirit subject, Jesus introduces the Spirit as the *Paraclete*. We've already looked at this term and seen that it carries a number of different and important overtones. For now, remember that the dominant idea behind *Paraclete* is "someone who offers assistance in a situation in which help is needed."[1]

Jesus promises that God will send "someone to help" the disciples as soon as he himself leaves. And a good thing too. For if ever a group of men *needed* help, it was the disciples on the eve of Calvary. They needed help coping with and understanding the Cross. They needed help wrapping their minds around resurrection. They needed help knowing what to do next and how to continue their mission and where to find courage and power. So Jesus promises that his Father will send them the *Paraclete*, a Helper and Companion for the dark days ahead.

Notice, however, that this *Paraclete* is "another." The Spirit isn't the only Helper the disciples have known. There was an original.

In truth the disciples have needed help from the first moment they met Jesus. All along, they needed constant and tangible assistance: to make sense of what they saw and heard, to understand the parables, to rescue them and encourage them and empower them, to grasp who Jesus was and what they'd gotten themselves into. For the past three years, Jesus himself has provided that assistance. *He* has been their *Paraclete*, their Helper and Companion.

Now Jesus points to *another Paraclete*: someone who will provide for the disciples in the future what Jesus has provided for them in the past; the Holy Spirit.[2] This is the first hint in John's Gospel as to the identity of the Spirit: he and Jesus share exactly the same work.

There is more. Jesus describes the Spirit as "the Spirit of Truth."[3] Jesus himself is intimately connected to truth in this Gospel. John tells us that Jesus is "full of truth" and that "truth came through Jesus Christ" (1:14, 17). Jesus calls himself "a man of truth," who tells the truth and teaches the truth (7:18; 8:31-32, 40). In fact, in this very chapter, Jesus has already named himself "the way, *the truth*, and the life" (14:6). Now, he names the Spirit "Truth" (14:17). The Spirit and Jesus share this defining characteristic.

It is what he says next, however, that forces the Twelve (and those of us who read John's testimony) to recognize that Jesus isn't just *comparing* the Spirit to himself—he is *identifying* the Spirit *with* himself. The Spirit is Jesus in indwelling form. "The world cannot accept him, because it neither sees him nor knows him. But you know him, for he lives with you and will be in you" (John 14:17). To the world, the Spirit will be an unknown and unknowable stranger. But that's not the case with the disciples, as Jesus makes clear in this astonishing statement. "You *know* him," Jesus insists.

But how can that be? Jesus has no more than introduced them to this *Paraclete* (these are, according to John, the first words he's spoken to them on the subject), yet he claims that the disciples already know the one he's talking about. How can he say this when the Spirit "had not been given, since Jesus had not yet been glorified" (John 7:39) and could not come to the disciples until Jesus went away (John 16:7)? The Twelve have not even met the *Paraclete*, much less spent time getting to know him. How can Jesus make such a claim?

The clue comes in what follows. "For he lives with you," Jesus says, "and will live in you." Or as the *New Living Testament* puts it: "He lives with you *now* and *later* will be in you" (emphasis added). What an odd statement! The Spirit "lives with" (or abides, dwells in the present) and the Spirit "will live in" (later on, in time to come).

It is at this point we begin to suspect that—in the mind of Jesus— the Spirit is not just *like* him, the Spirit in some sense *is* him. Jesus is the Spirit living with them presently. The Spirit will be Jesus living with them later. Jesus identifies himself so closely with the Spirit that he can be the Spirit's presence in the here-and-now just as the Spirit will be his presence in the there-and-then.[4]

"He lives with you," states Jesus, as if to say, "Anyone who has seen me has seen the Spirit."

"He will live in you," states Jesus, as if to say, "If you really know me, you will know my Spirit as well."

Like Jesus and the Father, Jesus and the Spirit are one. As Jesus reveals the Father, so he reveals the Spirit. Those who have known Jesus have known both Father and Spirit.

## I Will Come to You

This careful linking of the Spirit to the Christ is neither accidental nor incidental. It is *foundational* to understanding everything Jesus says about the Spirit in the Final Discourse: what the Spirit teaches, why the Spirit witnesses, what the Spirit accomplishes in the world and in disciples.

It is foundational to understanding what Jesus says here in the First *Paraclete* Passage. Because of this essential unity between himself and the Spirit, Jesus is able to forge a continuing and intimate link between himself and his disciples. Yes, Jesus is going away. There is a cross in his near future. And a tomb. And an ascension. Where he is going the disciples cannot come. Yet he is not abandoning the disciples. Far from it!

> [18]I will not leave you as orphans; I will come to you. [19]Before long, the world will not see me anymore, but you will see me. Because I live, you also will live. [20]On that day you will realize that I am in my Father, and you are in me, and I am in you. [21]… He who loves me will be loved by my Father, and I too will love him and show myself to him … [23]and we will come to him and make our home with him. (John 14:18-23)

Is Jesus talking about the resurrection here? There are many who think so. Jesus has been talking about the *Paraclete* (in verses 16 and 17). But now he makes a shift, warning his disciples that he is going away (dying), that he's coming back (the resurrection), and that they will see him again (the appearances).

But reading these verses like this causes real difficulties. How does the resurrection not leave the disciples as "orphans" when Jesus' resurrection appearances will be infrequent, brief, and painfully temporary?[5] Forty days past the empty tomb is the ascension, when Jesus will leave the earth for good. Are a few fleeting glimpses of a risen Christ enough to rescue the disciples from the status of "orphans"?

And what do resurrection appearances have to do with the disciples' dawning awareness that "I am in my Father, and you are in me, and I am in you"?

Jesus is not changing the subject. He is still talking about the *Paraclete* even though the pronoun has changed from "him" to "me." Jesus is going away (returning to the Father), but he is coming back (in the form of the Spirit) and they will "see" him again (through the Spirit's indwelling presence).[6]

The promise here is stunning. The *Paraclete* is coming soon to the disciples. They will *see* him and *know* him. He will live with them and be in them. And that Spirit will be the very essence of Jesus, present with his disciples again. It isn't just the Spirit they will see; it is Jesus himself. He will be in them. He will show himself to them. He will make his home with them. Through the indwelling Spirit.

The reason the world won't "see" Jesus (v. 19) is because unredeemed hearts are incapable of hosting the Holy Spirit. Only the disciples "see" Jesus because only they experience a Spirit who takes up residence in them and becomes Christ's tangible presence for them.[7] Along with the Spirit's indwelling, the disciples will discover that a new communion with Jesus is possible ("you in me and I in you").[8]

## But, Lord ...

In this first Paraclete Passage, Jesus introduces the Spirit to his disciples by pointing to himself. To have the Spirit is to have Jesus. Far from abandoning them, Jesus is returning to live with them in another form ... a forever form.

The fact that the disciples are confused by all of this is understandable. It's confusing to us! How can Jesus "go away" and "remain" at the same time? How can Jesus "leave" and "be present" simultaneously? It's enough to give disciples (then and now) a headache.[9]

That, of course, is the nature of "mystery"—something precious wrapped in something perplexing, a package that is bigger than we are. But perhaps at this point, resolving the riddle is less important than the simple promise of Christ's continued presence. The disciples don't have to live without Jesus. They aren't stranded on the island of this world, cut off from their Master. Jesus will remain with them, remain in them, through the indwelling presence of the Holy Spirit.

Did they grasp all this on that final evening, when so much remained unclear and uncertain? Probably not. But they would grasp it eventually. And when they did, this promise and this presence would prove to be a source of great comfort and great power to them.

**What We Learn about the Holy Spirit
in the First *Paraclete* Passage**

1. The Spirit is "another *Paraclete*" … the Spirit is the very essence of Jesus.
2. When Jesus returns to the Father, he will ask God to send the Spirit.
3. The Father will accede to this request … he will give the Spirit to the disciples.
4. The Spirit will be with the disciples forever.
5. The Spirit (like Jesus) will be "the Truth."
6. The world cannot see, know, or accept the Spirit.
7. The disciples will see and know this Spirit.
8. The Spirit will live "in" the disciples.
9. "I will come to you …"; "Before long …"; "you will see me …"; "On that day …"; "I will show myself …"; "We will come to him …"; and "we will make our home with him …" – all refer to the coming of the Holy Spirit.

## And What of Us?

These were wonderful promises for the Twelve to hear. But are they "wonderful" for us? Do they have any application or pertinence to our lives?

It turns out that modern disciples have much in common with ancient ones. Their fears are ours. Their needs are ours. Their situation is strikingly similar to our own. We too have made a commitment to follow Jesus. We've left behind a great deal in order to become his disciples. We've heard his words and been changed by them, and now find ourselves unfit for ordinary living.

Like the Apostles, who will spend most of their lives ministering in a post-Easter world, we also live out our commitment to Jesus at a time and in a world from which Jesus is physically absent. Like them, we are tempted to feel abandoned, lonely, and lost. We miss our Master. We wish we could be with him. We long to "walk and talk" with the One who has turned our lives upside down.

Jesus has gone to the Father and we have been left behind—just like the Twelve. Yes, we have the gospel stories—echoes of our Lord's words and deeds. Yes, we have the New Testament—witness to the faith of the first disciples and guide for our own faith. These are good. These are necessary. But are they sufficient?

In reality we find ourselves very much in need of the same thing the Twelve were given in order to deal with a departed Jesus: we need the hope that there is, in fact, a continuing experience of Jesus available to us. Not just a book—a presence. Not just stories—a person. Not just ancient words of wisdom—a forever companion.

And so we find ourselves wondering whether the words spoken in this first *Paraclete* Passage (by Jesus to the Twelve) might extend to those who believe in Jesus through their testimony. Is this promise meant only for the original audience? Did it apply to the first readers of John's gospel, sixty years after the events of this evening? Might it be meant for us who read these words of hope two thousand years after that fateful night?

Yes. These words are for us as much as for them. The promises are ours, not just theirs. I believe that.

Believing it, of course, does not make it true. Whether the promise is for all disciples—not just Peter and James—remains an open question we will address later in this book. For now I simply ask you to consider, "What if it *is* true?" What if this promise is for you and me?

There are several ways this opening *Paraclete* Passage has immediate impact and relevance for believers today. First, it requires us to dust off and grapple with that ancient doctrine of the Trinity. It is difficult to comprehend how we can even read John 14, much less glean the important lessons about the Spirit revealed there, without a conviction that God is one-in-three—that Father, Son, and Spirit are distinct expressions of, different forms of, a single divine nature.

We don't mind being "binitarian"—God in two persons. We can confess that Jesus reveals the Father; that he is the full expression of the Father's character, attributes, and purposes; that he shows us the Father's heart and mind. We can confess that Jesus is God in the flesh. And so, when John asks in chapter 14, "Who is God?" we can accept the answer, "Anyone who has seen me has seen the Father."

But John uses the exact same approach to address the question, "Who is the Spirit?" The Spirit is Jesus. To know Jesus is to know the Spirit. To have the Spirit is to have Jesus, and—by extension—to have the Father as well. For John there is an essential oneness between Father, Son, and Spirit that permits Jesus to accurately and completely "make known" the other persons of the Trinity.

If the promise is for us, it means there is an experience of the living and indwelling Spirit available for you and me today. We can have a Companion, a Champion, a Helper along the way. We don't have to struggle through life on our own, under our own power, by our own bootstraps. Hungering for God's Spirit, yearning for his Spirit, is not a sign of immaturity or spiritual thrill-seeking; it is, to the contrary, evidence of faithfulness, a response of trust in the promises of God.

If what Jesus promises here is for us, it means the Spirit we pursue is no stranger. We don't have to reach for something unknown and unexpected. If Jesus and the Spirit are one, the Spirit we seek looks, sounds, acts, and works like Jesus. Which is a critical step for any trustable approach to the Spirit. So long as the Spirit is unfamiliar to us, with an unknown agenda and unpredictable ways, we will always be on our guard against him. But when we recognize in the Spirit the face of Jesus, when we grasp that the Spirit continues the ministry and message and methods of Jesus, then we have the basis for a relationship with the Spirit we can trust.

Finally, this promise means that even we "latter day" disciples can experience—through the Spirit—the presence of Jesus. Most of us have wished (be honest now!) that we could have "been there"; seen with our own eyes; walked and talked with the Living Christ. But if Jesus and the Spirit are one, Jesus walks and talks with us through the indwelling *Paraclete*. In part, the *Paraclete* makes this possible (as we will see in the next chapter) by bringing Jesus' earthly ministry to life again ("he will remind you of everything I have said"—14:26). But an indwelling Spirit also suggests the possibility of an intimate relationship with Jesus that is "beyond the sacred page." It means the same living relationship that sustained the Apostles is available to sustain us. It means a "personal relationship" with Jesus Christ is not just an Evangelical catch-phrase, but a very real, very privileged, and very necessary experience. Building this relationship between Jesus and his followers is the Spirit's prime work.

I confess to you that I want this kind of relationship with Jesus. I want it so badly, I need it so desperately that I can no longer afford to ignore the Spirit or live a form of religion that is devoid of his presence. I want Jesus in me. I want to be in Jesus. I want to see Jesus. I want him to show himself to me.

And so I gladly welcome the Spirit into my heart and life, whatever the uncertainties and risks. For with the coming of the Spirit comes the abiding presence of Jesus Christ—in me, with me, for me, through me.

## Chapter Nine

# THE PROMISE OF TEACHING

## (JOHN 14:25-27)

No wonder they are confused. You can almost see them scratching their heads and shrugging their shoulders at each other. What is Jesus talking about? What do all these words about a "*Paraclete*" mean?

There were so many things Jesus said and did during the course of his ministry they did not understand. Their confusion in the Upper Room on the final night is simply the latest instance of their consistent failure to keep up with their Master.

"Destroy this temple, and I will raise it again in three days" went right over their heads (2:19-22). Why he would speak with a Samaritan woman was beyond them (4:27). They did not comprehend the bread for the crowds (5:1-14) or the ghost on the water (6:16-21). They did not realize what had happened to Lazarus nor why Jesus was so eager to return to dangerous Judea (11:12-13). They did not see the deeper meaning in Mary's anointing (12:1-8) or the Triumphal Entry (12:12-19). They could not grasp why Jesus would wash their feet or what the dipped bread might portend (13).

That's how little they understood about events in the past. But consider what was about to take place in the fifty-day stretch between Passover and Pentecost. Think of the effort required to make sense of the Cross and resurrection; the emotional whipsaw between transcendent ecstasy (in the resurrection appearances) and existential doubt (through the dark days between); the difficulty of conceiving that Jesus expected them—a ragtag band of nobodies—to change the world.

Now pour on top of this massive mix of spiritual obtuseness, stubborn misperception, and sensory overload the challenges of the next few years: a radical redefinition of "Messiah" and "Kingdom" and "Israel"; the unexpected shape of the "gospel" they would preach; the role of "faith" and "grace" in God's plan; the mandate of "church"; the inclusion of the Gentiles; the concepts of redemption, reconciliation, sanctification, transformation, and becoming all things to all men.

So much to grasp. So many lessons to learn. A world to turn upside down. Lives to turn inside out. And Jesus, their Teacher, is leaving them—just when they need him most.[1]

They do not know what lies ahead, of course. And that is a mercy. For the thought of Jesus' leaving is crippling enough this night. Soon, though, they will grapple with how to continue his ministry in his absence. Even then, they won't understand that merely "continuing" isn't the issue. Compared to what lies ahead, their work so far has been child's play. They have been toddlers, terrifying themselves with swing-sets and teeter-tots, while ahead of them looms an Everest of challenge. They will throw themselves at those challenges for the next sixty years. Paul climbs this route. Peter dies on that sheer face. The Galatians will lose their way just there. The Corinthians get stuck on that false summit.

And yet climb they must. How will they find their way from the Upper Room to Judea, Samaria, and the ends of the earth? Who will show them where to go and how to act and what to say? Who can teach them what they need to know? Jesus has been their Teacher to this point. That's what they called him: "Teacher." But Jesus is leaving. He cannot take them where they need to go next. Who will be their "Teacher" now?

Peter?

John?

## The Mission

In the first *Paraclete* Passage (John 14:16-23), Jesus speaks from the context of his imminent departure: "I am going away." But he washes down this bitter medicine with the promise of *another Paraclete*—his presence with them in other form.

Now, however, the context is changing. The emphasis is shifting from the bad news of Jesus' departure to the daunting prospect that there remains a mission for the Twelve to accomplish after their Master has left the building.

> 14:21Whoever has my commands and obeys them, he is the one who loves me. He who loves me will be loved by my Father, and I too will love him and show myself to him … 23If anyone loves me, he will obey my teaching. My Father will love him, and we will come to him and make our home with him. 24He who does not love me will not obey my teaching. These words you hear are not my own; they belong to the Father who sent me… 26But the *Paraclete*, the Holy Spirit, whom the Father will send in my name, will teach you all things and will remind you of everything I have said to you.

Verses 21-24 serve as a transition between the first and second *Paraclete* Passages. On the one hand, they point back to the *promise of presence*: "I will show myself …. We will make our home …." On the other hand, they point forward to the *promise of teaching* in the second statement—help to understand, to know what to say and do, to learn their role in the work to come, and to find comfort and peace in doing that work.

The "teaching" or "commands" of Jesus are mentioned repeatedly in these verses, as is the need for disciples to be obedient. But Jesus means something bigger by "obey" than the specifics of his ethical and religious instruction. There are marching orders embedded in these words. What Jesus has been doing, they must do. What Jesus has been teaching, they must teach. The authorities who once defied Jesus are all theirs now. They must deal with the crowds. They must answer the questions and meet the needs and minister to the hurting horde.

He is addressing the larger issue of *mission.*

That mission is on his mind is evident because Jesus keeps returning to the subject in this Final Discourse. The disciples are "messengers" whom Jesus will send into the world (13:16, 19-20). He anticipates they will do "what I have been doing" (14:12). He expects them to "bear much fruit" (15:2, 4, 5, 8). He knows their work will not be easy: the world will hate them because they carry Jesus' name (15:21) and his words (15:20). Still, he calls them to "testify" to what they have seen and heard (15:27).[2]

But it isn't simply repetition that demands we see mission in this Second *Paraclete* Passage; it is *timing* as well. Mission crops up here because passing on the mission is a top priority as Jesus prepares to leave. He has carried the mission thus far. But he is going away. Now it is time for the disciples to take up that mission and continue it in his absence.[3]

There is, however, a large sense in which describing the mission is begging the question. All well and good for Jesus to say *what* he wants the disciples to do. But *how*, oh *how*, does he expect them to do it?

## The Father Will Send

Every morning for three years the disciples have greeted the morning and broken fast, rolled up their blankets, kicked out the fire, and set off for the next adventure. But always Jesus has led the way.

Every day, in temple courts and on hillsides, the crowds have gathered for words and wonders, wisdom and signs. But, always, the words belonged to Jesus; he has been the focus, the Center. Whenever the lame and blind cried out for healing, it was always Jesus who responded and touched them.

He set the agenda. He knew the script. He burned with the mission.

The disciples never worried themselves about such matters—they simply followed wherever Jesus led. But they need to worry now. For, within hours, Jesus will leave the mission in their trembling hands. In the morning their Master will be hanging on a cross and their world will be in tatters. He will no longer be present to order their days and guide their actions. No more will they hear him say, "Go into the city" or "Take off the grave clothes" or "Open your eyes and look at the fields"—all the specific instructions that disciples receive from their Teacher.

He is leaving; they are staying. His work is "finished"; their work has just begun. His mission is now theirs. But how should they proceed? What should they say and do? Who will show them the way into the future?

Eventually, Jesus expects his disciples to shake off the trauma of the Cross and the shock of the resurrection. When they do, he expects them to continue his vital mission in the world. It will be a mission conditioned by his goals and agenda, even if conducted in his absence. Still, the Twelve will not be left to their own devices in their attempts to "obey Jesus' teaching."

As a resource, to help them accomplish their mission, Jesus offers the Spirit:

> "But the *Paraclete*, the Holy Spirit, whom the Father will send in my name, will teach you all things and will remind you of everything I have said to you" (John 14:26).

It's just one verse. Thirty small words. But don't let its lack-of-size fool you. There is an important message here about the Spirit and his role in equipping disciples for their mission.[4] That message is poured into a dense passage, packed with meaning.

Notice how careful Jesus is—again—to link the Spirit to himself. For the second time, he calls the Spirit "*Paraclete*"—reminding the disciples that the Spirit continues the helping role Jesus has provided thus far. He gives this *Paraclete* a name—*Holy* Spirit—that mirrors a name Jesus himself wore: "the Holy One of God" (John 6:69). And, just as Jesus came from the Father, so the Spirit is sent from the Father. Same function; same name; same source: three points of contact between Jesus and the Spirit in the space of a dozen words.[5]

## Another Teacher

But Jesus does more than identify the Spirit with himself in this passage. For the first time, Jesus addresses the subject of the Spirit's *work*. And he does so in a way that helps the disciples see a glimmer of how they can obey Jesus' commands and continue his mission even after he is gone.

This second *Paraclete* Passage tells us of a *teaching* function for the Spirit, a function that will help the disciples hear the words of Jesus, live obediently to those words, and honor them as words from the Father. The Spirit is not just the continuing presence of Jesus for the disciples (as important as that function is). He is also the means by which Jesus continues to teach his disciples, the instrument by which the disciples keep hearing and heeding their Master.

"[He] will teach you all things and will remind you of everything I have said to you." Like Jesus, the Spirit is *Teacher*. His teaching involves, at the most basic level, a "reminder" of everything Jesus taught. The disciples, as we've already noted, were not particularly good students while Jesus was with them in the flesh. They misunderstood, distorted, forgot, or were oblivious to much of what Jesus told them. He was constantly chiding them for their hard hearts and deaf ears. So, and without doubt, they need the Spirit's reminder of "everything I have said to you."

But is this a promise only for *remembrance*? Might there also be an *enlightening* function to the Spirit's teaching? I would suggest this is not just a promise of Spirit-improved memory—spiritual steroids for enfeebled recall. Implicit in this pledge is an assurance that what the disciples remember, they will also comprehend. Better. More completely. The Spirit will remind; but he will also explain and expound. He will deepen the disciples' understanding and give them insight. He will bestow wisdom. He will take the teachings of Jesus and apply them in relevant ways to believers' new lives and changed circumstances.[6]

That Jesus is making this broader point becomes clear when he tells his disciples that the Spirit will teach them "all things." Let's recognize a bit of hyperbole here. This is not a promise that disciples of Jesus, through the teaching work of the Holy Spirit, become omniscient. The Spirit doesn't teach quantum physics and fractal equations.

In fact, the "all things" the Spirit teaches is connected to and controlled by the phrase "everything I have said to you." The Spirit teaches everything that flows from and is a consequence of Jesus' life and ministry: the greater meaning of his words; the calling, mission, and message of disciples; what disciples' priorities should be, what their values are "in the Lord"; and everything else related to living as believers between the Cross and the Second Coming.[7]

An example of this teaching role of the Spirit is provided by John himself. In the early part of his gospel, John recounts a conflict with the religious leaders, when Jesus challenged, "Destroy this temple, and I will raise it in three days" (John 2:19). In an aside (2:21-22), John admits the disciples did not realize at the time what Jesus was talking about. Only later, after Jesus was raised from the dead, did the disciples "recall" these words and comprehend their deeper meaning.

According to the promise of the Second *Paraclete* Passage, this "recollection" was made possible by the work of the Holy Spirit. It was the Spirit who revealed what Jesus really meant by "destroy this temple ...."

And it was the Spirit who permitted that insight to result in deeper faith: "Then they believed the Scripture and the words that Jesus had spoken."

## My Peace I Give You

It is this promise of a teaching Spirit that gives the words to follow their meaning.

"Peace I leave with you; my peace I give you. I do not give to you as the world gives. Do not let your hearts be troubled and do not be afraid" (John 14:27).

When Jesus speaks these words to the Twelve, their hearts *are* troubled. They *are* afraid. And it's going to take something more than soothing platitudes to make their anxieties and fears go away. It's going to take the kind of empowering, equipping, teaching Spirit Jesus has just promised to give the disciples the sense of confidence and courage they will need to keep going. One of the reasons Jesus is so eager for them to receive the *Paraclete* is that, as a result of the *Paraclete's* teaching ministry, they will discover a lasting, deep, and pervasive peace.

Jesus is not changing the subject when he introduces the notion of "peace." The reason he can offer peace to the disciples is *because* the Spirit is coming. When he gives them the Spirit, he is giving them peace. It is through the Spirit's work that their hearts will be calmed and their fears relieved.

Are the disciples worried about tomorrow (as they certainly are in the context of the Final Discourse)? The Spirit will calm and compose them by teaching them what to do. Are the disciples about to face difficult circumstances and a hostile world? The Spirit will build their confidence and bolster their courage by telling them what to say. Are the disciples tempted to discouragement and timidity and loss of hope? The Spirit will step in to encourage and embolden and strengthen their faith.

The New Testament frequently testifies to this *affective* aspect of the Spirit's teaching in believers. When "filled with the Spirit," disciples experienced boldness and courage (see Acts 4:8, 13, 31; 6:5-10 and 7:55; 13:9-10); they felt love and joy and hope (see Acts 13:52; Rom 5:5; 14:17; 15:13, 30; 1 Thess 1:6); they discovered fresh confidence and

**What We Learn about the Holy Spirit
in the Second *Paraclete* Passage**

1. Besides "*Paraclete*," and "Spirit of truth," this *other* is designated "Holy Spirit."
2. The Father will send the *Paraclete* to the disciples.
3. The Father will send the *Paraclete* "in the name" of Jesus.
4. The Spirit will teach the disciples "all things."
5. The Spirit will remind the disciples of everything Jesus said to them.
6. The result of the Spirit's presence will be peace ... and the absence of troubled hearts and fear.

renewed vigor (Acts 9:31; Rom 8:16-17; 2 Cor 1:21-22). But, above all, the ministry of the Spirit brought "peace" to troubled disciples (Rom 8:6; 14:17; 15:13; Gal 5:22; Eph 4:3).

This affective aspect of the Spirit's teaching should not be overlooked or underestimated. Yes, the Spirit instructs the "head," sharing certain "content" with the disciples: a reminder of Jesus' words; a clarity about what Jesus meant and how his principles apply to their lives. But the Spirit also instructs the "heart," shaping emotions and showing disciples how to react calmly in difficult or uncertain situations. Both kinds of lessons—head and heart—are important for living the disciple's life, and both require their own kind of teaching.

This is precisely the sort of "teaching" Jesus did, of course. Sometimes he addressed his disciples' *thoughts*: with the principles found in the Sermon on the Mount, for example. But he also addressed their *emotions*—fear, anger, worry, insecurity, resentment, joy, pride, ambition—teaching them how to order their inner worlds.

In fact, within the span of the Final Discourse, Jesus does both. There are things he needs his disciples to *know*: the time has come; he is going away; the *Paraclete* is coming. But there are also things he needs his disciples to *feel*: love, hope, trust, calm, joy ... and peace.

The teachings of the Spirit will be directed at both the mind *and* the heart. Which is exactly what you would expect of a *Paraclete*.

## And What of Us?

Again, these were wonderful promises for the Apostles to hear. But are they wonderful for us? Does the promise of a teaching Spirit, who instructs both mind and heart, extend to disciples who weren't in that upper room?

We certainly share the Twelve's condition. Like them, we fail to grasp much of what Jesus teaches. We too are oblivious, forgetful, and spiritually dull. Like them, we crave the practical instruction, the specific direction, that the presence of Jesus could supply. We know we have a mission to accomplish, a grand calling to turn the world upside down. But in the face of that challenge, we feel small and ill-equipped and woefully inadequate. Like them, our hearts are troubled, our fears have grown large.

In a word, we desperately need the very thing Jesus offers the Twelve on that final night: his continuing presence to lead and instruct; his direction and teaching whatever situations arise; his insight into deeper things; his wisdom about living in a fallen world. We need the confidence that comes from knowing what to do, the boldness that comes from knowing what to say, and the peace that comes from understanding what is happening.

We need a Teacher who can touch our minds, showing us what the gospel means in the face of changing circumstances and new challenges. But we also need a Comforter who can touch our hearts, soothing our wounded spirits and fractured feelings.

Such a need makes us impatient with those who point so relentlessly (and exclusively) to the Bible as our sole source of spiritual instruction. Certainly there is teaching to be found there: reminders of what Jesus said and did; principles and propositions and policies. But a book—however revered—is a far cry from the kind of intimate, personal, practical, moment-by-moment teaching offered by Jesus in the form of the *Paraclete*. Our broken hearts require something stronger than words on a page to equip us to take up the mission of Christ and accomplish his goals in this world. Is "something stronger" available to us?

I hope so. I believe so. If Jesus is making promises about the *Paraclete* that extend beyond that single place and time, this offer of a teaching Spirit—showing, instructing, calming, encouraging—is for me. And for you. We are not alone. We have not been abandoned. Jesus is alive and present with us—through the Spirit. He continues to teach and direct us—through the Spirit. He calms our troubled hearts, he soothes our fears, through the Spirit.

Again, I confess freely that I want that. I want that kind of presence, that kind of teaching, that kind of comfort and assurance and encouragement. I want help to be obedient, wisdom to know what obedience means in these difficult times, companionship in the struggle, consolation for my failures. I want the *Paraclete*, not just the verbal echo of the Spirit's teaching that resonates in Scripture.

And so I gladly welcome the Spirit into my heart and life, whatever the uncertainties and risks. For if the Spirit comes, he comes in Jesus' name, doing Jesus' work, bearing Jesus' words, teaching the things of Jesus, enabling obedience to Jesus, shaping minds and hearts for the mission of Jesus. If that Spirit is still available to me, I want all of him I can get.

## Chapter Ten

# THE PROMISE OF TESTIMONY

## (JOHN 15:26-27)

No wonder they are terrified. For three years, they've watched Jesus stand up for truth and speak out for God. Yet, from the beginning, he has been challenged and criticized and condemned. He tells the truth and people call him a blasphemer. He talks of God and people pick up stones. He heals sick people, yet some who witness the miracles walk away plotting how they might kill him.

In the hours to come, the disciples will get a crash course in the dangers of telling the truth. They will watch as Jesus is arrested, flogged, spit on, and nailed to a cross. They'll watch as leading citizens line up to revile, ridicule, and vent their venom. They'll watch as religious folk look on the dying Jesus without a shred of pity or compassion.

The disciples know their master is being killed, not because he is a traitor or thief or murderer, but simply because he loves the light. What lesson could they possibly learn from all this—what has happened to Jesus in the past, what will happen to him next—other than the hard lesson that people who tell the truth about God are hated and hounded, that people who tell the truth about the sin of the world get nailed to crosses, that people who testify to God as powerfully as Jesus did should expect to be thanked with pain and death.

Yet, in this Final Discourse, Jesus commissions the disciples to do the same provocative work he has been doing: "And you also must testify, for you have been with me from the beginning" (John 15:27). They will be the truth-tellers from now on. In his absence, they must speak words the world does not want to hear.

Already during this long evening Jesus has said difficult things to the Twelve. He is going away—and that alarms them. He wants them to continue his mission—and that worries them. Now he says they must testify. Seeing something of the cost of such testimony for their Master, this commissioning terrifies them. Even before Jesus announces, "If they persecuted me, they will persecute you also" (John 15:20), they know instinctively that continuing his mission will mean sharing his fate.

Perhaps for the first time in this Final Discourse, Jesus says something they comprehend. To be his disciple is a dangerous thing. To align themselves with him will be painful and costly. They can understand that. They are soon to understand it better.

## What's Not to Like about Jesus?

It must have perplexed the disciples that the Jesus they knew and loved should be the object of such violent opposition from others.

What was not to like about him? He was kind and compassionate and wise. He taught such wonderful things: love your neighbor, love your enemy, love God. He was that rarest of treasures, a truly good man. He healed sick children, for goodness sake! How can you dislike someone who heals sick children?

And yet there were people who did not like Jesus. Nor was it a matter of simple disapproval. They hated him. They despised him. They wanted him dead. Had the disciples asked these people the reason for their enmity, they would have heard all manner of answers: "He doesn't keep the traditions; he threatens the stability of God's people; he plays fast and loose with Torah."

Jesus has a different answer to their question. It is an answer he needs the disciples to hear and understand. For this answer explains what they are soon to experience themselves.

> 15:21 ... They do not know the One who sent me. 22If I had not come and spoken to them, they would not be guilty of sin. Now, however, they have no excuse for their sin. 23He who hates me hates my Father as well. 24If I had not done among them

what no one else did, they would not be guilty of sin. But now they have seen these miracles, and yet they have hated both me and my Father. [25]But this is to fulfill what is written in their Law: 'They hated me without reason.'

The hatred directed towards Jesus isn't about religious orthodoxy or practice; it has nothing to do with traditions or interpretations of the Law, whatever rationalizations the authorities use to justify their opposition. The reasons for their hatred run far deeper. The problem, as Jesus sees it, is literally "theological"—a problem with "knowing God." He knows his Father and his opponents do not. He loves his Father and they do not. When he shows them God, they are deeply repulsed; though not by what Jesus reveals of God so much as by what that revelation says about *them*. Jesus shows them the Father and they see their own sin and brokenness and shame. They see themselves with a clarity (and a humiliation) that is unbearable. And the result? Denial. Justifications and excuses. A rationalization so vehement and violent it looks like hatred.

Not everyone reacts that way, of course. There are some who respond to this revelation with gratitude and obedience. It is the reason Jesus came preaching—to reach those few. It is the reason he commissions the disciples to testify—some will listen.

But those who don't listen, who can't hear, will hate the message and hate the messenger. And their hatred will be "without reason" (John 15:25). Their hatred will be a blind, cold, raging thing that needs no reasons to sustain it.

## They Will Hate You

Jesus has borne the brunt of that hatred so far. The authorities have been content to direct their frustration and anger at him. Oh, they've questioned his disciples on occasion. But they've reserved the heat of their hostility for the Master himself.

Now, though, Jesus is going away. Will the heat he generated go away as well? Will the glut of violence to come satisfy the authorities?

Not at all. For Jesus intends to be the gift that keeps on giving. Now that he has come and testified, the world will never be the same. The light has come into the world (see John 1:1-4). And even if some show a marked preference for the darkness, the light will continue to shine in the lives of those who have received Jesus. The light—the hated light—will shine long after Jesus is gone.

Part of the point of this Final Discourse is that the disciples must not hide their light. They must shine with Jesus' words and work and mission. He is depending on them to keep his irritating presence alive in the world. He is counting on them to "testify" for and about him.

That means, of course, that the world's hatred is about to turn—full force—on the Twelve.

> 15:18If the world hates you, keep in mind that it hated me first. 19If you belonged to the world, it would love you as its own. As it is, you do not belong to the world, but I have chosen you out of the world. That is why the world hates you. 20Remember the words I spoke to you: 'No servant is greater than his master.' If they persecuted me, they will persecute you also. If they obeyed my teaching, they will obey yours also. 21They will treat you this way because of my name...
>
> 16:1All this I have told you so that you will not go astray. 2They will put you out of the synagogue; in fact, a time is coming when anyone who kills you will think he is offering a service to God. 3They will do such things because they have not known the Father or me. 4I have told you this, so that when the time comes you will remember that I warned you. I did not tell you this at first because I was with you.

Jesus takes up a good portion of the Final Discourse warning the disciples about what is to come. "You must testify. But the world won't like it." He goes into graphic detail (perhaps more than the Twelve want!) about what they should expect in the future. The world will hate them. The world will persecute them. They will be turned out of the synagogue. They will be hunted and killed.

"But don't take it personally," Jesus tells them. "It's not about you. It's about me. And, ultimately, it is about my Father."

Had you been there, you could have cut the silence with a knife. The disciples don't want to hear this. Jesus is touching their greatest fear, their most persistent terror. This is the stuff that makes them want to run away, cower in some upper room, hide from the hostile world that hates them.

You can almost hear Peter thinking, "Thanks for the encouragement, Master. Any more comforting words before we dismiss?"

## The Spirit Will Testify about Me

Actually, Jesus does have something comforting to offer. They won't feel the comfort now. It will take them awhile to discover how great a comfort Jesus is about to bestow. He cannot take back their commission to witness. He cannot change the hostile and violent reactions of the world. What he can do, what he will do, is make sure that they do not bear witness by themselves.

> [15:26]When the *Paraclete* comes, whom I will send to you from the Father, the Spirit of truth who goes out from the Father, he will testify about me. [27]And you also must testify, for you have been with me from the beginning.

This is now the third time Jesus has raised the subject of the *Paraclete* with his disciples. First, he announces he is going away; the disciples are broken-hearted; so he offers them the *Paraclete*. Then it dawns on the disciples they must make their way into the future without Jesus' tangible guidance; they are overwhelmed; so he offers them the *Paraclete*. Now Jesus tells them they must testify, though at great cost; they are terrified; so, once more, he offers them the *Paraclete*.[1]

Again, it is striking how Jesus continues to use language linking the Spirit to himself: references to the role (*Paraclete*), the source (Father), and the name (Truth) they both share in common; a claim that Jesus himself will send the Spirit; an assertion that Jesus will be constantly on the Spirit's lips.

The spotlight in these verses, however, focuses squarely on the matter of *testimony*. In the context of the world's hostility—as Jesus readies himself to die for the truth, as he warns the Twelve that their time is coming—the whole idea of testimony becomes difficult. What can possibly overcome the world's reflexive rejection? If the world answers every witness with venom and violence, how can witness be sustained? If Jesus was unable to win over the world, what hope is there for the Twelve to do so?

It is in the context of such unspoken questions that Jesus brings up the *Paraclete* once again. There is a Companion coming into the world, he assures his disciples, whose mission will be to testify to Jesus. He will speak the truth he receives from the Father about the Father's Son.

There are a few matters implied in Jesus' teaching about the testimony of the Spirit that are important to note. First is the matter of the testimony itself. "Testimony" (or "witness"—both are translations of the same Greek word *martureo*) is a central concept for John, occurring 31 times in his gospel. The fundamental assertion of John's gospel is that Jesus is the Christ, the Son of God. To prove that point, John brings to his story a number of "witnesses" who "testify" to Jesus: John the Baptist (1:7, 34); a woman by a well (4:39-42); the miracles (5:36; 20:30-31); Scripture (5:39); God the Father (5:32, 37; 8:18); and even Jesus himself (3:31-32; 8:14; 18:37). The Spirit is simply the latest in a long list of witnesses who testify in John. But the character of the Spirit's testimony is consistent with the rest: Jesus is the light, the Christ, the Son, the One. The Spirit comes to affirm that Jesus is precisely who he claims to be.[2]

It is clear from the context (John 15:18-25) that the Spirit's testimony is directed to the *world*—the hostile, unbelieving, God-hating world. The Spirit will stand up in the world to insist that Jesus is the Son of God and that his words are true. Disciples need the Spirit to remind them and teach them all things (John 14:26). But a lost world needs the Spirit to *testify*, revealing Jesus and confronting darkness with light.

Since this *Paraclete* will stay "forever" (John 14:16), it can be assumed that his testifying work will go on "forever." The world may kill Jesus' flesh. The world can kill Jesus' followers. But the world will never kill Jesus' Spirit. It cannot still the Spirit's voice. It cannot stifle the Spirit's witness. Here is a testimony to Jesus that no threat can frighten and no violence squelch. It is a "forever" testimony that cannot be touched by the world's opposition.

Finally, there is a certain *independence* to the Spirit's testimony that needs to be appreciated. The Spirit has his own testifying work to do, a work that doesn't depend on us. He has his own voice in this world that speaks whether we manage to witness or not. There is something awe-inspiring about imagining the Spirit—in holy counterpoint to Satan's roaring lion, seeking souls to devour (1 Pet 5:8)—ranging through the world in search of souls to save.

In the next chapter we will hear Jesus describe the Spirit as busily convicting a hard-hearted world. For now, think also of a Spirit hard at work using all of life's ups and downs—joys, tragedies, beauty, illness, mirth, griefs, regrets—to prod and poke people and pull them inexorably towards their Father. Think of a Spirit working through art and literature, music and nature, to make people conscious once again of their forgotten God and their own spiritual hunger. Think of a Spirit acting as holy matchmaker, introducing redeeming relationships into dry and desiccated lives.

There are examples in Scripture of the Spirit working in just these ways: the Ethiopian Eunuch, led by the Spirit to ponder Isaiah long before Philip hitched a ride on his chariot (Acts 8:26-39); Cornelius who was seen and loved by God and prompted by the Spirit before Peter ever came on the scene to preach the gospel to him (Acts 10:1-9); Saul, who experienced the Spirit's "goads" and kicked against them until overwhelmed on the Damascus Road (Acts 26:14); an Athenian named Dionysius who "happened" to serve on the Athenian council and "happened" to be present when a stranger named Paul addressed the Areopagus and "happened" to be open to the idea of resurrection when he heard about it (Acts 17:32-34). All of these were people to whom the Spirit testified, bearing witness to their need for a Savior.

## And You Also Must Testify

There is more here, however, than a promise that the Holy Spirit will speak up for Jesus. There is also (pregnant within these words) the promise that the Spirit will help the disciples speak up.

It is no accident that Jesus ties the testimony of the Spirit so closely to the testimony of the disciples. Only a period separates the two ideas. "When the *Paraclete* comes … *he will testify* about me. And *you also must testify*, for you have been with me from the beginning." The testimony of the Spirit and the testimony of the disciples are linked. Both testimonies are needed, pointing to Jesus. Both witnesses are valued, knowing Jesus as they do. Each witness supports and enhances the other. Each witness plays his necessary part.[3]

The disciples, however, do not have permission to sit back and leave the testifying work to God's Spirit. They can't abandon that responsibility to someone who won't bleed. Yes, the Spirit testifies. But so also must disciples.

What Jesus promises in these verses is that God will be at work in the world long after the Cross, in places far removed from Jerusalem, through the testimony of his Spirit and through the testimony of his people . Just as the Spirit is sent out as a witness into the world, so the disciples will be sent out as witnesses. Their testimony must support his.

This careful linking of the Spirit's testimony with human testimony, however, suggests an even closer relationship between the Spirit and witnessing disciples. The Spirit does more than witness *with* … the Spirit witnesses *through*. He plays a vital role in nurturing the disciples' witness; bestowing boldness, courage, power, wisdom, and (sometimes) the very words the disciples will use to testify.[4] The disciples may feel inadequate for this witnessing task. In many ways, they *are* inadequate. But Jesus assures them with this Third *Paraclete* Passage that they are not alone. Every time they point their trembling fingers towards Jesus, every time they lift their quivering voices in witness, the Spirit will be speaking as well—through them—fueling their testimony with a power beyond themselves.[5]

This thought must have been a comfort to the Twelve. What a relief to learn they do not carry the testimonial burden alone! What a relief to know the Spirit will stand with them, adding his voice to theirs, and speak through them, amplifying their voices with his power![6]

Never the most intrepid band, the disciples took courage from this promise. For, judging by what follows, they set about their witnessing task with unusual zeal. Andrew took his testimony to Asia Minor and

---

**What We Learn about the Holy Spirit
in the Third *Paraclete* Passage**

1. The *Paraclete* will be sent by Jesus.
2. The *Paraclete* will come from the Father.
3. The *Paraclete* is the "Spirit of Truth."
4. The Spirit goes out from the Father.
5. The Spirit will testify about Jesus.
6. The Spirit will help us to testify.

Greece, and was beaten half to death and then crucified in an effort to shut him up. Bartholomew witnessed in Mesopotamia, Persia, and the area around the Black Sea; he would not be silenced until flayed to death by whipping. James the brother of John preached throughout Judea and Syria, making such a nuisance of himself that finally Herod beheaded him in Jerusalem. Thaddeus and Simon teamed up to carry the gospel to Syria and Persia; one was beheaded, the other sawn in half to stifle their testimony. Peter, the denier, affirmed his Lord in Jerusalem, Syria, and Rome, culminating his witness on a cross at the order of Nero. Philip told the story of Jesus in Asia Minor and was scourged, starved, and (finally) crucified for his efforts. Thomas made it all the way to India with his testimony; he stood before a wall and was impaled with spears rather than abandon his message. Matthew witnessed in Africa and was run through with a sword somewhere in Ethiopia.[7]

Only John escaped a martyr's death, though it wasn't for lack of trying. He was as much a witness as any of them. The gospel we have from his hand is the tangible residue of his testimony (John 20:30-31). But Jesus protected him, apparently, granting him a long life and a peaceful end. "If I want him to remain alive until I return, what is that to you?" (John 21:22).

## And What of Us?

Once again, we find ourselves oddly attuned to the Twelve's condition that fateful night. We know that the task of testifying has been passed on to us now. We realize that God is looking to us, just as he looked to them, to stand up for Jesus and speak up for truth.

We understand that, if we take our mission seriously, the hatred of the world will turn on us. Not crosses, perhaps. Not racks and thumbscrews. But something we fear as much: ridicule and rejection and irrelevancy.

Like the Apostles, we wonder if we are adequate to our task. Will we find the courage to give voice to our convictions? Will we find the wisdom to witness effectively? Is it even possible to be an effective witness? If Jesus tried and could not break through, if the Apostles tried and could not break through, what hope is there for our feeble and fear-filled efforts?

No wonder, then, we long to believe that Jesus' promise of a testifying Spirit is for us as much as for them. What if the Holy Spirit is witnessing still? What if he continues to speak to a God-deaf world: apart from us as an independent witness; partnered with us to encourage and empower our own witness? What if we are not alone? What if winning the world is not all up to us?

It is in the hope of a *testifying* Spirit that I open my heart and life to the *Paraclete*, whatever the uncertainties and risks. For if that Spirit is meant to be a reality for us today, I believe he can help us do the essential work of testifying to the Christ who has given us life that is both rich and eternal.

## Chapter Eleven

# THE PROMISE OF CONVICTION

## (JOHN 16:5-11)

No wonder they feel inadequate. Just outside this upper room waits a broken world: lost and hostile. Jesus has already spoken of its enmity, its hatred, its intent to persecute and kill.

To that world, and in spite of hostility and persecution, the disciples must testify. Yes, it is terrifying to tell the truth to people who don't want to hear it. Yes, it is dangerous to tweak the beast's tail. Thankfully, theirs is not the only voice speaking up for truth—Jesus promises that the Spirit of truth will also testify (John 15:26-27).

But it takes more than testimony to change a world. Testimony alone only makes the world angry, only increases its resistance. Testimony must be *believed* before it can be effective. Testimony must *convict* for truth to make a difference.

The disciples can testify. They can speak truth to a hard-hearted world. But they cannot make the heart vulnerable. They cannot break the world's heart. They cannot convince and convict and make contrite. Something more powerful than the disciple's testimony is needed for that. Someone more powerful than Peter or James must do that killing work.

Lord, thy most pointed pleasure take
And stab my spirit broad awake.
Or, Lord, if too obdurate I,

Choose thou, before that spirit die,
A piercing pain, a killing sin,
And to my dead heart run them in.[1]

## The Spirit and the World

John's Gospel is deeply torn about the world.

On the one hand, God loves the world (3:16). He sends his Son to save the world (3:17). Jesus comes to give life and light to the world (6:33; 8:12). He preaches so that the world will believe (12:46). He dies to take away the sin of the world (1:29).

On the other hand, Jesus is certainly not *of* the world (8:23). The world does not recognize Jesus when he arrives (1:10) and does not rush to his light (3:19). Instead, the world hates him (7:7) and rejoices at his death (16:20). Jesus must drive out the "Prince of this world" (12:31) and "overcome" the world (16:33).

We see this same tension in John between the world and disciples. Disciples do not "belong to the world" because Jesus has chosen them out of it (15:19). They will have "trouble" in the world (16:33), be hated by the world (17:14), and need protection from the world (17:15). Jesus calls disciples to despise their life in this world (12:25).

And yet that same world is the mission-field and focus of disciples, the sphere of their primary activity. Jesus, who calls disciples out of the world, also sends them back into the world "so that the world may believe" (17:18-23). Like their Master, disciples don't have the luxury of abandoning the world; they must lay down their lives for it.

We find (surprise, surprise) exactly the same tension between the world and the Holy Spirit. There is a sense in which the Spirit has nothing to do with the world, nor the world with the Spirit. The world does not accept the Spirit, cannot "see" or "know" the Spirit (14:17). The Spirit is for disciples, indwelling and empowering, teaching and encouraging them.

Once again, however, John insists there are two sides to every coin. The Spirit who is promised to the disciples also has a work to do in the world. Not an indwelling work. Not a transforming work. But an important work nonetheless.

The first hint of this world-work came in the Third *Paraclete* Passage: the Spirit *testifies*, the Spirit of truth speaks up for the truth. In doing so, it is the *world* he addresses, not disciples. He stands *with* disciples in the testifying process. He gives courage *to* disciples as they testify. But his testimony (like theirs) is directed at the world.

It is in the Fourth *Paraclete* Passage, however, that the full force of the Spirit's work in the world is felt. What happens when the Spirit and disciples testify? There is a work that must take place at that point which only the Spirit is capable of doing: cutting open the world's chest, placing his hands on the world's heart, and running into that dead heart some killing sin.

## Better for You ...

16:5Now I am going to him who sent me, yet none of you asks me, 'Where are you going?' 6Because I have said these things, you are filled with grief. 7But I tell you the truth: It is for your good that I am going away. Unless I go away, the *Paraclete* will not come to you; but if I go, I will send him to you.

At first blush, "It is for your good that I am going away" sounds like one of those patently untrue statements (on a par with "This is going to hurt me more than you"). The disciples are disappointed, worried, and scared out of their minds. They don't want Jesus to go. They'd give anything for him to stay. And this is the reason he gives? He's leaving "for their good"?

Even at two thousand years removed, it sounds thin.

Yet, though the disciples may find these words hard to swallow, Jesus believes them with all his heart. He knows there is something better than him-in-the-flesh. He knows the disciples will be stronger, more effective, when he gets out of the way so the *Paraclete* can come.[2]

All the promises Jesus makes during the course of this night cannot be kept until he leaves and the Spirit comes: the Spirit who will be their "forever" Companion; the Spirit who will allow them to experience Jesus' presence whenever, wherever, and whatever; the Spirit who will teach them everything they need to know; the Spirit who will calm their troubled hearts and grant them peace; the Spirit who will testify to the world and give disciples courage to testify. It is better Jesus go so the Spirit can begin his needed work.

But it's more than that. Frankly, there are things the Spirit can do that Jesus cannot. There are things the Spirit can do *better* than Jesus. Jesus needs to go so the Spirit can do "even greater works than these" (John 14:12).

That is a hard truth to accept. It is difficult for us to believe there is anything Jesus can't do. We don't often consider that Jesus had limits during his earthly existence. In fact, we don't often use the words "Jesus" and "limits" in the same sentence. It's a little odd to imagine that the One who raised the dead and calmed the storm would suffer any constraints at all.

But the fact that Jesus was "incarnate"—in the flesh—placed very real boundaries on his ministry and power. Some of those boundaries were *physical*. He could only teach people who heard his voice. He couldn't be two places at one time—preaching to crowds in Jerusalem (for instance) while feeding crowds in Galilee at the same moment. He couldn't accompany his disciples everywhere, through every trial, in every challenge—there was only one of him and many of them.[3]

Some of Jesus' limits involved *time*. He only had three years for his ministry—from the beginning, he knew when and how his ministry would end. Even the time he did have was limited by his need to eat and sleep, by the demands of travel, by the religious calendar, by daylight and darkness hours.

Most of the limits Jesus lived with, however, belonged to his *listeners*. When stomachs rumbled, Jesus had to provide bread rather than wisdom. When hearts were hard, Jesus could not break through to make people believe. When the disciples were dull and tired, he could not make them grasp what he was trying to say.[4] When faith was lacking, Jesus could not open minds or work miracles.

But the *Paraclete* will know no such limits. He will not be bounded by flesh. He can be everywhere at once, on duty at all times. He needs no rest, no refueling, no recovery, no recharge. Distance means nothing to him. He speaks with a voice that does not depend on air molecules and ear drums to be heard. He can enter the soul of a person, any number of persons, and reside there—a permanent, living presence in many believers at once. He can encourage without restriction, he can calm without words or touch, he can teach without hurry, he can stay with disciples forever.

And working with the limits of the human heart will be his stock-in-trade. He can soften hard hearts. He can open deaf ears. He can minister to wounded souls. He can imbue courage and hope. Most of all, as we are about to see, he knows how to prompt the kind of godly grief that leads to repentance.

Jesus is telling the truth: it really *is* for their good that he goes away. The Spirit has work to do that even Jesus can't accomplish. Like John the Baptist before him, Jesus points beyond himself to the One who is to come, as if to say, "He must become greater; I must become less."

## He Will Convict the World

One of the "greater works" done by the Spirit is a constant, persistent, enduring conviction[5] of the world's guilt. "When he comes, he will convict the world of guilt in regard to sin and righteousness and judgment …" (John 16:8).

What Jesus tells his disciples about this work is not easy to understand. In part, that is because the language itself is difficult (as we will lament later). What is this "convicting" work? How is it accomplished? What "sin" and "righteousness" and "judgment" is Jesus talking about?

But in part this teaching is hard because the common view of humanity is so different from the view of Jesus. We simply don't see ourselves as Jesus sees us. Our understanding of human nature—who we are, what has gone wrong with us, how we can be "fixed"—has been shaped by the Renaissance and the Enlightenment , honed by the self-improvement and psychotherapeutic culture in which we swim, and polished by an instinct for self-justification and a love of the well-crafted excuse. We are heirs to a boundless optimism regarding human potential (or, at least, of ourselves) and hold a high and happy view of our species (or, at any rate, of ourselves as representatives thereof). If you ask us, we are beloved of God, the point of the world's existence, God's gift to himself and all creation.

If we are broken, we are not *very* broken. If we need fixing, it shouldn't take much. A little teaching, a bit of moral fine-tuning, is all we require to find our way again. We are, at our core, good and wise. Given a choice (and the proper incentives), we'll do the right thing most every time.

Jesus begs to differ. In fact, he *died* to differ. In his view, humankind is broken and broken badly. Yes, we were created with great expectations.

But we fell in love with ourselves and exchanged the truth of God for a lie. Yes, we bear the image of God. But it is an image marred, sullied, and deeply traumatized.

And, according to Jesus, we are not just broken—we are *bent*. We love the darkness and hate the light. We are clever at evil, creative in the ways of sin. We are drawn to the perverse. We deny the truth. We do not think clearly or value correctly. We have lost our spiritual compass and cannot, will not, find our way home.

So badly bent are we, according to Jesus, that we must expend vast energies denying the fact, deflecting blame, constructing castles of rationalization and excuse. It is hard for us, flawed as we are, to admit any flaw at all. Our native language is self-justification. Our most urgent mission is self-protection. Our first priority is asserting our righteousness, even if the only righteousness we can claim is the sort we bestow on ourselves.

And the last thing we want is anyone telling us the truth—especially the truth about *us*.

The last thing we want, no doubt; but the one thing most needed. According to Jesus, our greatest need is the ability to see ourselves as we actually are—to see ourselves as God sees us. We need a love of truth that transcends our defensiveness. We need hearts capable of breaking over our brokenness. We need honesty about just how bent we are.

But that will require a cure far more radical than a few rituals and the occasional attitude adjustment. It will require a Spirit audacious enough to convict us of guilt and powerful enough, then, to wash our guilt away. And this is the Spirit Jesus promises in the Fourth *Paraclete* Passage: a Spirit who knows how to use killing sins to revive dead hearts.

## The Spirit's Convicting Work

16:8When he comes, he will convict the world of guilt in regard to sin and righteousness and judgment: 9in regard to sin, because men do not believe in me; 10in regard to righteousness, because I am going to the Father, where you can see me no longer; 11and in regard to judgment, because the prince of this world now stands condemned.

In this passage Jesus describes a Spirit who is hounding the world, watching for every opportunity and opening. He describes a Spirit who loves the world enough to give it what it really needs: a deep conviction of guilt regarding its sin, its righteousness, and its judgment.[6]

The language of this text is so difficult and cryptic it has resulted in more than a few scholarly white flags. I will dare to comment briefly on the details of this passage only because those details can shine light on the Spirit's work in the world.[7] But clarity about the details is not really necessary to understand the main point Jesus makes here: the Spirit is hard at work convicting the world of guilt.

According to Jesus, the Spirit's convicting work revolves around "sin and righteousness and judgment." We best understand what that means when we remember that the Spirit is Jesus, his words and works are Jesus' words and works, his mission is Jesus' mission. (See Chapter Eight.) I believe we learn a great deal about how the Spirit does his convicting work by watching how Jesus did it.[8]

Convicting the world of "sin" was an important part of Jesus' ministry.

> [15:22]If I had not come and spoken to them, they would not be guilty of sin. Now, however, they have no excuse for their sin... [24]If I had not done among them what no one else did, they would not be guilty of sin. But now they have seen these miracles, and yet they have hated both me and my Father.

Jesus took sin seriously. He believed it was killing humanity (John 8:24). He warned against it and begged people to stop doing it (John 5:14). He lamented a blindness to sin that kept people from penitence (John 9:41).

Of course, his purpose in talking about sin was not to condemn the world but to save it (John 3:17). Jesus longed to show the world its brokenness, invite the world to turn to him for healing, and then offer the world new life. In large part, his ministry foundered on that first point: brokenness. Men loved the darkness too much; they did not want to hear the truth about their sin. Jesus' attempts to convict provoked only denial and resistance. They hated him for saying their deeds were evil (John 3:19). In the end, they killed him for it.

But killing Jesus did not stop his convicting work. Jesus simply passed it along to the Spirit. The Spirit continues to speak, to persuade, to point out the world's sin. And he does that better, more effectively, than Jesus precisely because he does it without ceasing, for everyone, on every occasion, in every heart. Even so the Spirit often fails. There remain many who resist the truth and refuse any consciousness of sin no matter what the Spirit does. But *some* hear; *some* are convicted; *some* see who they are and what they need. And when they do, it is because the Spirit has been working on them.

Convicting the world of "righteousness" was also an important part of Jesus' ministry. Jesus understood there was a true righteousness (reflecting his Father and his Father's priorities) and a *shadow righteousness* that borrowed the vocabulary of righteousness but denied the idea behind it. He was the constant champion of the first sort and the constant opponent of the other. He allowed, for instance, that the Pharisees had a certain righteousness; but he warned his disciples they would have to find a *better* righteousness to enter the kingdom of heaven (Matt 5:20). Nothing was as repugnant to him as sham righteousness, false virtue, and hypocritical morality. He rebuked those "who were confident in their *own* righteousness" and cared nothing for God's (Luke 18:9ff). When the Pharisees sneered at such charges, Jesus responded with barely suppressed fury: "You are the ones who justify yourselves in the eyes of men, but God knows your hearts. What is highly valued among men is detestable in God's sight" (Luke 16:15).

Jesus spent much of his ministry trying to teach true righteousness to his contemporaries and convict them of the lesser sort. He largely failed. But he looked forward to the coming of the Spirit who would take up that very same work: confronting ways that seem holy but are not; stripping away illusions of goodness; niggling consciences with the notion that being nice is not the same as being godly.[9] At this work, the Spirit is even more effective than Jesus. Jesus, understanding that, was eager to step out of the Spirit's way with the words, "It is for your good that I am going away."

Convicting the world of judgment (the final element of the Spirit's work named by Jesus—John 16:8, 11) was also an important part of Jesus' agenda. One of the most interesting themes in John's Gospel has to do with bad judgment and twisted thinking. According to John, people in the world cannot understand the light of God (1:5), will not recognize and receive the Word of God (1:11), refuse to believe (3:32), don't properly weigh evidence (5:43; 7:21-23), will not set the right priorities

(6:26-27), make superficial judgments (7:24; 8:15), and rush to wrong conclusions (e.g., 8:22). Jesus made repeated attempts to help his listeners think clearly—to hear the truth, to see the evidence, to believe his claims. But in the end he kept bumping into a world whose judgment was fatally flawed. He could plead, "Stop judging by mere appearances, and make a right judgment" (John 7:24), but it did no good.

The Spirit continues that plea. He exposes the bad logic, the skewed perceptions, the false assumptions of the world. He holds a mirror up to the world's judgment and shows it for the foolishness it is. Only he does it better than Jesus ever could because he has advantages Jesus did not enjoy.

## In Summary

Jesus is going back to the Father. And it's a good thing. For unless Jesus goes, the *Paraclete* cannot come. Unless the *Paraclete* comes, the greatest work of God cannot be finished. Jesus does much of that work: his teaching, his life, his death, his resurrection. But only the Spirit can complete God's work: presence without limit; teaching without cease; peace without fear; testimony that cannot be stifled …

… and cultivation of the world's heart to hear heaven's truth. Jesus promises his disciples that, when the Spirit comes, he will hound the world, seeking every opportunity to convict it of sinful living, mock righteousness, and foolish thinking. If former promises about the Spirit describe the peace, joy, and comfort the Spirit brings to the lives of believers, this promise addresses something darker the Spirit has in store for the world. The Spirit, when he comes, will trouble the world, accuse the world, disturb the world. Never again will humanity be safe from God's convicting Spirit. The Spirit loves the world too much to leave it alone.

What a relief this must have been for the disciples. In a matter of hours, Jesus is going to tear them from the womb of his protective presence and thrust them into the cold, harsh realities of life in the real world. That world will be cruel to them, hateful and threatening. Still they must testify. No matter what, they must speak the truth about Jesus. As they do so, the Spirit himself will testify.

But the Spirit will do more. Like the farmer, the Spirit works to prepare the soil into which the gospel seed will fall. He harrows hearts with the plow of conviction. Not everyone responds, of course. Some hearts remain hard and shallow and choked with weeds. But a few appreciate the *Paraclete's* efforts to "stab my spirit broad awake." They are convicted. They are broken. They are penitent.

This promise of a convicting Spirit told the disciples that their work would never be in vain, their words would never come back empty. Perhaps it took the Twelve a while to tumble to this. Maybe only later, as they reflected on all Jesus said this fateful night, did they realize what this promise meant. Still, the thought of the Spirit, working before and after them to prepare the hearts of men, must have been a source of great comfort.

They knew Jesus had called them to testify. But, especially this night, they must have been profoundly aware of their inadequacies. They could speak, but they did not have the power to persuade. They could tell the story, but they were not capable of cutting the heart. If all the disciples had were their words, their witness, they were doomed to futility and failure. The world would shut them up. The world would tear out their testifying tongues to silence their unwanted truth.

But if there is a convicting Spirit at work in the world, running into dead hearts a piercing pain, a killing sin, then the testimony of disciples can touch hearts made hungry; truth will meet conviction; seed may

---

### What We Learn about the Holy Spirit in the Fourth *Paraclete* Passage

1. Unless Jesus goes away, the Paraclete cannot come.

2. It is for our good that Jesus go away—so that the Spirit *can* come.

3. When Jesus goes away, he will send the Paraclete to the disciples.

4. There is a sense, however, that the Spirit will also come to the world.

5. The Spirit's primary work in the world is convicting the world of guilt.

6. That conviction concerns the world's guilt in regard to sin, righteousness, and judgment.

find good soil. Suddenly and miraculously, feeble words become words of life. And disciples, hand-in-hand with the Spirit, become the aroma of Christ, ministers of the new covenant, jars of clay carrying around God's treasure.

## And What of Us?

Once again, we are confronted by a promise made to *them* that we hope applies to *us*. How wonderful for *them* to hear that the Spirit will be actively, aggressively preparing the world to receive the gospel. How wonderful for *them* (for instance) to see three thousand listeners "cut to the heart" (Acts 2:37) by the convicting work of the Spirit.

But is this same promise for *us*? Does this Spirit still move in the world to prepare hearts for the seed of the gospel? Is there reason to hope there might yet be partnership possible between modern-day witnesses and a still-convicting Spirit?

Let's hope so. For the convicting work of the Holy Spirit is desperately needed in these latter times. Our world still loves the darkness, still clings to the illusion of goodness, still thinks in sin-clouded ways. We believers bang our heads against these worldly walls on a daily basis. How do you convey gospel to people who are so in love with the wrong, so blind to their own brokenness, so deluded and deceived? If the task is ours alone, if it really is "up to us," there is good reason to despair.

But God has not abandoned us. We are not alone. We must testify, but God will give the increase. We plant, but God makes the seed grow. And he does that, now as then, through the convicting power of his Holy Spirit.

What the world cannot bear to hear today, he will proclaim tomorrow. When hearts are hard, he will wait for (even provoke!) a change of attitude. When the world denies sin, boasts of righteousness, uses its twisted logic to refute spiritual truths, the Spirit will burst such pretensions with the needle of conviction.

And he does so relentlessly, eternally, without limitations; troubling the world with the truth about itself; encouraging us with the idea that our testimony might yet make a difference in the hearts of men.

It is in the hope of a *convicting* Spirit that I open my heart and life to the *Paraclete*, whatever the uncertainties and risks. For if that Spirit is meant to be a reality for us today, I believe he does the essential work of winning an audience for the testimony we are commissioned to speak: convicting the world of guilt; piercing dead hearts with killing sins so that new hearts can one day grow.

## Chapter Twelve

# THE PROMISE OF REVELATION

## (JOHN 16:12-15)

No wonder they feel overwhelmed. Too much has happened. Too much has been said. Their heads are reeling. Their emotions are raw. They cannot take anymore.

It's been building for months. Anxieties about the Jerusalem leaders—hostile and angry and plotting. The stress of Lazarus' death; the shock and awe of seeing dead Lazarus walking. Weeks of hiding in the desert. Fighting fears on the road back to Jerusalem. Jesus predicting his death. Mary anointing him for burial. Triumphal entries. Voices from heaven.

The disciples were at the end of their ropes long before they climbed the stairs to the Upper Room and sat down to their evening meal. But had they been fresh as daisies, the events of this night alone would have been sufficient to push them over the edge.

Their Master, brooding and distracted. The footwashing, witnessed in a silence of shame. Peter's proud and futile resistance. Odd words about betrayal. Judas' odder exit. Talk of death and orphans. Peter, trying to make up for one folly, committing another: "I will lay down my life for you." Jesus' wistful rebuke: "You will disown me three times." More talk of leaving. Riddles and paradoxes. The hatred of the world. Someone else, some other Companion, taking Jesus' place.

Jesus sees a look on their faces that tells him he has reached their end. The blank stares. The exhausted expressions. The look of the lost and the beleaguered. They are shutting down. They have nothing left.

Though they do not know it yet, these men still have miles to go before they sleep; the worst is yet to come.

But Jesus knows it. And he decides to show them mercy. "I have much more to say to you." Perhaps he paused; perhaps he sighed. "But it is more than you can now bear." A nod of decision, the ghost of a smile.

## A Disciple's Limits

"Much more to say" but no time to say it. "Much more to say" but no disciples who can bear it. Jesus *could* say much more, *would* say much more, but he bumps again into one of those limitations that have plagued him ever since he poured himself out and took on flesh.

As we've already noted (see Chapter Eleven), Jesus had to live within certain boundaries while walking this earth. Some involved simple physics and the fact that there are limits to what flesh and blood can do. Some involved boundaries of time: twenty-four hour days, a three-year ministry. Many of the limits belonged to his listeners: hard hearts; deaf ears; dull spiritual sensibilities.

This time, though, it is a limitation of his *disciples*—not the Pharisees or the crowds, but the very men he hand-picked to be his companions— that persuades Jesus to stop. Nor is this the first time the plans of Jesus have been stymied by the men he loved most. They've never listened very well. They don't comprehend what they hear. They won't step out of boats. They won't feed crowds. They can't cast out demons. Later this very evening, they will sleep when he asks them to pray. They will flee panicked into the night.

Jesus has expressed frustration over his limited disciples before.[1] In this instance, however, he deals quite graciously with them and the fact that they can bear no more. Yes, they are tired. And yes, they can be dull. But those aren't the only limitations that give Jesus pause this night. Not really.

The truth is, the disciples *can't* understand what he is telling them because *they don't know the rest of the story.*

Perhaps the most frustrating limitation Jesus experienced during his sojourn among us involved hard realities about ministering in a pre-Easter world. Everything Jesus said and did, everything he taught, took place before the Cross and the tomb and the blaze of resurrection. How could his disciples possibly understand many of his teachings *prior* to those defining events? No wonder they missed "Destroy this temple and in three days I will raise it up"; they had not yet experienced the horrors of Calvary and the joys of the empty tomb. How could they grasp the depths of God's love for the world until Jesus (God's love offering) had been "lifted up"? How could they embrace the true meaning of dying to self, the new birth, or "I am the resurrection and the life," except in the light of the events of Easter?

The Cross and resurrection were still in their future. What could words like the following have possibly meant to them?

> Now is the Son of Man glorified. (13:31)
> Where I am going, you cannot follow now, but you will follow later. (13:36)
> I am going there to prepare a place for you. (14:2)
> I will not speak with you much longer, for the prince of this world is coming. (14:30)
> I did not tell you this at first because I was with you. (16:4)
> You will weep and mourn while the world rejoices. (16:20)
> Take heart! I have overcome the world. (16:33)

Jesus has to stop. There are lessons he cannot teach, ideas his disciples cannot grasp, until he gasps out his life on the Cross, lies in the cold tomb, and rises victorious from the grave. Until the whole story unfolds, the disciples won't "get it," no matter how long or how frankly Jesus speaks.

## Revelation

We've reached the fifth and final *Paraclete* Passage. Jesus has one thing more to say about the Holy Spirit before he ceases teaching and commences dying. The dinner is done. The hour is late. Calvary beckons.

> 16:12I have much more to say to you, more than you can now bear. 13But when he, the Spirit of truth, comes, he will guide you into all truth. He will not speak on his own; he will speak only

what he hears, and he will tell you what is yet to come. [14]He will bring glory to me by taking from what is mine and making it known to you. [15]All that belongs to the Father is mine. That is why I said the Spirit will take from what is mine and make it known to you.

Four times Jesus has spoken to his disciples about the Holy Spirit, telling them how the Spirit will help them in the future. Are the disciples worried about Jesus abandoning them? The Spirit will be the presence of Jesus, available to them forever (the First *Paraclete* Passage). Do they wonder how they can carry on the mission of Jesus in his absence? The Spirit will teach them everything they need to know and do (the Second Passage). Are they concerned about witnessing to a hostile world? The Spirit himself will testify to Jesus and give them courage to testify (the Third). Do they question whether their feeble voices can possibly make a dent in a hard-hearted and sin-deadened world? The Spirit will do a convicting work in the hearts of men, revealing their guilt and their need for a Savior (the Fourth).

The fifth time Jesus speaks of the Spirit, he tells his disciples about a *revealing* Spirit: a Guide who will disclose "all truth," "what is yet to come," "all that belongs to the Father," and all of "what is mine."[2] The context of this promise is, of course, the fact that there is so much more to say than the disciples can bear. And the central question is: what is that "much more"?

It is at this point some readers jump all exegetical fences and run wildly down the road of conjecture. *"All truth"?* Is there some secret and mysterious wisdom Jesus has left to the last but doesn't have time to talk about now? Has he forgotten some critical piece of information for being a disciple that the Spirit must supply in his absence? *"What is yet to come"?* Is Jesus talking about a prophetic gift here, the Spirit enabling disciples to know the future and see around the corners of tomorrow? Is he promising that faithful disciples can know everything about *everything* because the Spirit will reveal every mystery and disclose future events?

Hardly. This has nothing to do with predicting stock market trends or unveiling DaVinci-Codes-of-the-soul or filling fatal gaps in Jesus' teachings or creating know-it-all Christians. (We have too many of those as it is.) This promise is nothing more nor less than an assurance that, in spite of limits and time constraints and stress levels, the most fundamental work Jesus came to accomplish will continue through the on-going ministry of the Spirit.

And what is that *most fundamental work*? Revealing God to the world. Making the invisible God known. Shining the light of God into the world's darkness. Letting God walk in his world once more and be recognized. "Now this is eternal life: that they may know you, the only true God" (17:3). No theme comes closer to John's heart. From the opening words of his Gospel, and repeatedly throughout, John trumpets the truth that Jesus makes God known.

Jesus is the Word, who was with God and who was God (1:1), and now shows himself to the world. He is the Light who shines in darkness (1:5), revealing (in Paul's pithy phrase) "the light of the knowledge of the glory of God in the face of Christ." He becomes flesh so that we can see his glory, the glory of God himself (1:14).

"No one has ever seen God, but God the one and only, who is at the Father's side, has made him known" (1:18). Jesus is the Son of God (1:34), the Lamb of God (1:29), the Holy One of God (6:69), the Gift of God (4:10), and the bread of God (6:33); tied by every device in John's vocabulary to the Yahweh who sent him. He is the one who came "from heaven" (3:13) and "from above" (3:31; 8:23) in order to testify to what he has seen and heard of his Father in the heavenly realms (3:11, 32). It saddens Jesus that there are those who "have never heard [God's] voice nor seen his form" (5:37), but he does not count himself among that number. He has seen the Father (6:46) and knows the Father (8:55; 10:15) and exists in the flesh to make God known.

In fact, when the world wants to see God, Jesus simply points to himself. It is Jesus *himself* who best reveals the Father (a principle we stressed in Chapter Eight). Look at Jesus and you see God (12:45). Know Jesus and you know God (8:19; 14:7).

At the highest level Jesus did not come to earth to expound on Moses or set up an improved moral code or institute a new religion. He didn't come to preach the Sermon on the Mount or heal the lame man or walk around with Matthew. In the ultimate sense, he didn't even come to die on the Cross.

Jesus came to reveal his Father. Everything else was a facet of that overriding mission, a means to that greatest end.

There is a prayer at the end of this evening that closes out Jesus' ministry. It is known as the High Priestly Prayer (John 17). In it, Jesus gives his Father a final report on his mission to earth and makes a few last requests. The prayer begins: "This is eternal life: that they may know you" (17:3). Knowing God is a life and death matter—an eternal life matter. Jesus then assures his Father that he has made that matter a priority in his ministry: "I have completed the work you gave me to do…. I have revealed you to those whom you gave me out of the world" (17:4, 6).

As he finishes the prayer, however, Jesus says something that suggests he has more in mind than his own accomplishments: "I have made you known to them, and will *continue to make you known*" (17:26—emphasis mine). Odd. In a few hours, he will be dead. He has just spent most of this evening breaking the bad news of his imminent departure. How can he talk about "continuing" the vital work of revealing his Father when he is leaving the world behind to go home? Is he talking about the Cross and resurrection?

Perhaps. But it is more likely that he is pointing beyond himself and his earthly ministry to the Holy Spirit, the *Paraclete*, who is coming to continue his revealing work.

## The Revelation Chain

In the Fifth *Paraclete* Passage, Jesus tells his disciples about a revelational chain: a revealing work passed on from Father to Son, Son to Spirit, Spirit to disciples, and (implicitly) disciples to world. "I have much more to say to you, more than you can now bear…. All that belongs to the Father is mine…. the Spirit will take from what is mine and make it known to you" (16:12-15).

The chain begins with the Father. The Father has a great deal that "belongs to" him (16:15): who he is and what he is about; this world; his purposes and plans. God is the source of all good words and works, all wisdom and knowledge, all life and light. Everything that is high and holy belongs to him.

But the Father is not tight-fisted; he longs to share all that belongs to him. So, the Father's *belongings* have been handed over to the Son (16:15):

the Father's words, work, and will; the Father's essence. Everything has been given by the Father to the Son. "All that belongs to the Father is mine."

Like his Father before him, Jesus wants to share what has been given to him. In fact, revealing the Father is his Job One. So he turns to us. He uses words when he can. But some revelations are too big for words. They require crosses and empty tombs; they must be shown rather than spoken.

And we are bedazzled by it all. We do not understand the words. We cannot bear the Cross. We cannot even imagine resurrection power. He reveals to us what the Father has entrusted to him and we cannot handle it.

Imagine, if you will, a suitcase handed from Father to Son to us. It contains all that belongs to the Father: his character and purposes, his hopes for this world, his will for our lives. (Perhaps we should imagine a shipping container rather than a suitcase!) That suitcase has been carefully packed by the Father. Everything needed is in there.

God hands that suitcase to his Son. The Son is strong. He can do the heavy lifting of carrying that case to the world. And the Son is smart. One look inside and he understands everything packed away there. He knows it intimately, in detail.

Now Jesus hands that suitcase on to us. He intends to unpack what belongs to his Father before our very eyes. Only we're not as strong as the Son: we cannot bear the weight of God's glory. Nor are we as smart as the Son: what he grasps in a moment, we require a life-time to comprehend; what he understands intimately, we see only darkly and in part.

It is too much for us. It overwhelms us. We are thimbles trying to hold a cistern of truth. We are 98-pound-weaklings attempting to bench-press the Mystery of the Ages. What Jesus reveals is simply beyond our capacities. We are not large enough to contain it. We cannot bear it.[3]

But Jesus doesn't chide us for our limits. He doesn't exchange us for more capable disciples. He shows us mercy. "I have much more to say to you." Perhaps he pauses; perhaps he sighs. "But it is more than you can now bear." A nod of decision; the ghost of a smile.

## Another Link

In this Fifth *Paraclete* Passage, Jesus forges another link in the revelational chain. He makes room between himself and his disciples for a

Spirit who will "take from what is mine" and reveal it to limited disciples.[4] Think of the Spirit as a transformer, stepping down the current of Christ to a wattage we can bear.

> … more than you can now bear. But when he, the Spirit of truth, comes, he will … bring glory to me by taking from what is mine and making it known to you. All that belongs to the Father is mine. That is why I said the Spirit will take from what is mine and make it known to you. (John 16:13-15)

The reason the Spirit becomes involved in this chain is the disciples—what they can handle or, better put, what they cannot. Jesus wants them to know the Father. He has shown them himself, the "fullness of deity in bodily form" (Col 2:9). But it is not enough. Rather, it is too much. They need something other, something *less*. They need slow, steady, consistent infusions of the knowledge of God that will reveal what they can bear as they can bear it. They need a revelation of God that won't overwhelm or squash them. They need someone to bridge the gap between God's greatness and their own puny capabilities.

"The Spirit will take from what is mine and make it known to you" (16:14-15). Jesus says it twice, just so the disciples (in their befuddled state) get the point. He promises that the Spirit will continue to do for the disciples what Jesus has been doing: take holy things and unpack them for believers.

Only the Spirit will be able to do this without blowing the disciples' circuits. He will make the Father known when disciples are ready, as they can receive it, in doses they can handle. He will parse out the knowledge of God slowly, in small words. When disciples cannot "bear" any more, the Spirit will bide his time until they have room for another installment. When they do not understand, the Spirit will try again, in another way. When sin deadens and deafens disciples to revelation, the Spirit will do his teaching and testifying and convicting work to prepare their hearts once more for more God.

The Spirit will mature and deepen disciples, turning their thimbles into cups then buckets, then barrels, expanding their capacity to hold the glory of God.

## He Will Guide You into All Truth

In the Second *Paraclete* Passage (John 14:25-27), Jesus promised a *teaching* Spirit who would help disciples remember "everything I have said to you" and instruct them in "all things." This (I believe) was a promise that, in the particulars of mission and ministry, the disciples could expect the Spirit to provide practical and equipping guidance.

Now Jesus focuses on a *revealing* Spirit, teaching "all truth" and "what is yet to come," not to repeat what he's already promised but to suggest there is a work of the Spirit more profound than the "practical and equipping." Disciples are more than the sum of their missional parts. And their calling is far more fundamental than remembering certain words or grasping particular precepts.

The Spirit's "all things" are, in fact, the "much more" Jesus would say if the disciples could only bear it. The "what is yet to come" is all that revelation of the glory of God stuck at the point of their incapacity, dammed up behind the narrows of their comprehension. This has nothing to do with revelations involving end-times surprises or unique theological twists. It has everything to do with continuing and culminating the work Jesus began: revealing his Father; unpacking his Father's

---

### What We Learn about the Holy Spirit in the Fifth *Paraclete* Passage

1. Jesus has much more to teach the disciples.
2. It is more than the disciples can bear at the time.
3. The "Spirit of Truth" is coming soon.
3. He will finish Jesus' teaching work, guiding disciples into "all truth."
4. His teaching will not be original … it will come from Father and Son … an extension of their teaching.
5. He will tell the disciples "what is yet to come."
6. In the process, he will bring glory to Jesus.
7. The Father has given everything to Jesus. In turn, Jesus has given everything to the Spirit. In turn, the Spirit has given everything to the disciples.

belongings; making known his Father's essence and business. "That is why I said the Spirit will take from what is mine and make it known to you."

Through the Spirit, the disciples can continue to listen to Jesus as he reveals his Father and his glory and the kingdom he rules. Because the Spirit is present, when disciples ask "show us the Father," Jesus still has a way to do so. The Spirit who guides "into all truth" is the One who keeps breaking the "Bread of God" so that disciples can feast on "all that belongs to the Father."

For the Twelve, there is a cross just ahead that will rock their world. But it needs to keep rocking their world, keep revealing the hidden layers of the Father and his plans and his love. The Spirit will ensure that happens. There is an empty tomb looming that will open the door to a new reality. But there are a thousand doors the resurrection must open: about God, about the world, about the life of disciples. The Spirit will be responsible for opening those doors and then leading believers to walk through them to undiscovered countries.

The Spirit will help the disciples understand the full truth of God's love, Jesus' mission, and their calling.[5] The Spirit will disclose God so disciples can comprehend the full truth of God's plan, Jesus' obedience, and their salvation. The Spirit will "make God known"—more completely, more profoundly—by taking the life and teachings of Jesus, adding in the death and resurrection of Jesus, to help disciples "see the face of God." [6]

As he does this revealing work, the Spirit also matures the disciples, deepens the disciples, so that they can understand who *they* are and what they should do when times change and new circumstances arise and fresh challenges must be faced.

> The best Christian preparation for what is coming to pass is not an exact foreknowledge of the future but a deep understanding of what Jesus means for one's own time. [7]

## And What of Us?

One last time, you and I are confronted by a promise made to the original disciples that we hope, we pray, applies to us. It is wonderful for the Twelve to hear that God's revealing work is not finished, that God is not limited by their fatigue or their immaturity or their tiny capacity to hold heavenly truths. It is wonderful for Jesus to promise them a Spirit who will "take from what is mine and make it known to you."

But is this same promise for *us*? Is there still a revealing Spirit working to unpack the Father for us, to explain the Father in small words, to grow in us the capacity to bear the unbearable glory of God?

We must hope so. For we are still desperate for that revealing Spirit, a guide who will lead us into "all truth," someone who yet discloses God in the kind of bite-sized portions we are able to take in and chew. We need a Spirit who walks us beyond the "sacred page" to the one who is, himself, God's Word.

Without that revealing Spirit, constantly and compassionately unpacking the things of God, what we "cannot bear" will be reduced to something more attuned to our limits. We settle for a diminished God. The hunger for the Holy is appeased with church and ritual. The Cross is devalued into a religious construct or a piece of jewelry. Faith devolves into religion, devoid of true worship. Mission becomes program rather than calling.

We go through the motions. We check the boxes. We jump through the hoops.

I believe there yet remains in the world a Spirit who is committed, now as then, to guiding us into all truth, to everything that "belongs to the Father," to the "much more" Jesus has to say when (at last) we are ready to bear it. I believe there is still a Spirit who will not settle for our partial understandings and our in-the-mirror-darkly points of view and our immature approximations of truth. What if there is a Spirit who loves us too much to leave us alone, who helps us grow up so we can understand more, who guides us past the milk to the meat of life in God? What if there is still a Spirit who shows us the Father and, in doing so, consistently, persistently breaks our hearts and blows our minds and enlarges our lives?

It is in the hope of a *revealing* Spirit that I open my heart and life to the *Paraclete*, whatever the uncertainties and risks. For if that Spirit is meant to be a reality for us today, I believe he will lead us, in these best of times and worst of times, to a far, far better truth than any we have known before.

# THE SPIRIT, YOU, AND ME

If you've made it this far, congratulations!

I recognize that you've had to work hard to get to this point. But it was necessary work, foundational work. We could not get to *application* without a thorough grounding in *principles*.

The Bible attests to the presence of the Spirit whenever God encountered his people in the Old Testament. Jesus—the Messiah—unleashed the Spirit into the world in an unprecedented way. Then in the Upper Room he promised his disciples a continuing experience of the Spirit that would be forever and powerful and personal. This experience of the Spirit would be necessary for their survival. The *Paraclete* would be their life-line, their sustenance.

The focus to this point has been on the past. What did the Spirit do *then*? What did Jesus promise to the Twelve on that long-ago night?

Now the time has come to shift our focus. What about all the nights that followed? What about all the disciples to come? What do these promises mean for the rest of time and the rest of us? If this Spirit is available still, for you and me, what does that mean? What would that look like? What difference could that make?

Section Three is where theory becomes practice.

In Chapter Thirteen we finally answer the question, "Are these promises for us?" Yes! Unequivocally yes! And in this chapter, I give you some good reasons for thinking so.

Chapter Fourteen asks the "So what?" question. How does the Spirit act as our *Paraclete*, today, in modern times? What difference does he make in our lives? How does his power fuel our disciple-ship? I'll show how the promises of Jesus in the Final Discourse apply to us and, in the process, paint a portrait of a Spirit we can't live without.

Chapter Fifteen looks at how we welcome the Spirit to be a greater, more influential part of our lives; how we develop a renewed awareness of the Spirit's presence and a fresh readiness to experience his transforming power. I describe "Ten Disciplines for Seeking the Spirit" that will help you—in basic, practical ways—pursue a relationship with the Spirit that is more intimate and tangible than anything you've known before.

The Spirit is for us. But, like every gift, it must be accepted and enjoyed. I can show you that the gift is real. It's up to you to unwrap it for your own life.

Chapter Thirteen

# ARE THESE PROMISES FOR US?

A re the promises of the Final Discourse for us?
What Jesus said about the Spirit in the course of this long evening must have sounded wonderful to the Twelve. But are those promises wonderful for us? Do we have any reason to hope that the living, indwelling, powerful, comforting, transforming *Paraclete* might be available for you and me?

This is the critical question we've postponed so far in this book. But it is the key question that drives this writing. And the time has come for us to attempt an answer.

There are those who insist that the words of this Discourse apply only to Jesus' immediate audience—the Twelve—and to the immediate future of that last night. Jesus tells Judas, "What you are about to do, do quickly." But he is addressing *Judas,* not all disciples throughout history. He tells Peter, "You will disown me three times," but he doesn't expect other disciples to take those words personally.

In a similar way, these people would limit *all* the words of the Discourse to the Apostles alone. These words (and especially these promises) are only for the men Jesus called from fishing boats and tax tables, and for that brief-but-shining-moment between the death of Jesus and the deaths of his chosen few. The rest of us can listen in with some historical curiosity ("My, isn't that interesting!"), but we shouldn't go looking for words that apply to our own lives.

So are these promises reserved for Apostolic ears? Some would answer with a resounding "Yes." Could Jesus be speaking over the heads of his Apostles to a larger audience; an audience that encompasses all believers of every age; an audience that includes us? Some would answer with an emphatic "No."

I believe those people are mistaken. Let me give you three reasons why I think so:

1 John focused long and hard on the Final Discourse. The fact that he did so suggests *he* believed Jesus said something that night the rest of us need to hear.

2 All disciples are not apostles. True. But we have so much in common with the Twelve (struggles, circumstances, need), it would be cruel for Jesus to offer the *Paraclete* to them and withhold him from the rest of us.

3 Jesus promised the Spirit would "be with you *forever*" (John 14:16). I tend to think he meant what he said.

## Why the Final Discourse?

It is abundantly clear why Jesus had this conversation with the Twelve. They needed these promises, and needed them desperately, to survive the difficult days ahead.

But why should John preserve this Discourse, at such length and in such detail, for people who lived at the close of the Apostolic Era? Why would he think these promises important enough to repeat for believers who had their own struggles and circumstances to deal with?

These are difficult questions. But they are not merely academic. They go to the heart of how we read this Discourse and the sense in which these words are "for us."

The premise of this book is that Jesus made these promises because his disciples needed them, that John passed on these promises because his first readers needed them, and that the Spirit preserved these promises because every subsequent believer needs them as well.

Consider this: John tells us not a single parable of Jesus. He does not record the Sermon on the Mount. He omits any reference to Jesus' birth or the Transfiguration or the institution of the Lord's Supper. Five of the twelve Apostles (including Matthew and James) are not even named in the Gospel of John. Of all the things John included in his story, of all the things he chose to leave out, he decided to feature this one conversation. In fact, it dominates his Gospel. He gives more space to the Final Discourse (by far) than to any other event in Jesus' ministry—more space than he devotes to all the signs combined, to the temple controversies, and even to the events of the Cross and resurrection.

The gospel of John has twenty-one chapters. Of those, seven chapters (13-19) report the events of a single, twenty-four hour span. Four chapters (13-16) record the particulars of a single conversation. Nearly a *third* of all the words Jesus speaks in the entire Gospel of John are used right here.

I do the math on this point to underscore the significance John places on these words. Certainly, this Final Discourse is significant because of the situation: Jesus is about to die. It is significant because of the weighty themes Jesus addresses: "Love one another;" "I am the way, the truth, and the life;" "Remain in me." The emotional intensity of this conversation would alert us to its significance, if nothing else: themes of betrayal and abandonment, fear and separation, love and loss, persecution and hatred, grief and joy.

But with all that said, I still ask you to look at the numbers. Judging by them, John thought this Final Discourse was the most important exchange, containing the weightiest words, in all of Jesus' ministry.

The question we need to ask is, "Why?"

If current scholarship is correct, the Gospel of John was written during the closing years of the first century—after most of the other books of the New Testament were already in circulation. If the author was, in fact, the "beloved disciple" and an actual eye-witness of the events he recorded, he was nearing the end of a long life by the time he finished his story of Jesus.

According to the theory that miracles ceased with the death of the Apostles, that the Spirit's active work in Christians and the church came to an end with the completion of the canon, John was writing at the very end of the time when a living, indwelling, miraculous Spirit could be experienced. John himself was finishing the final installment on the New Testament. He was the last of his kind and soon to be dead.

Yet he devoted a significant portion of his gospel to a conversation dominated by teachings about the indwelling Holy Spirit! If the Spirit was soon to replace himself with the New Testament, why did John recount these promises of a living and intimate Spirit at such length? Why talk about such an experience of the Spirit if John knew that experience was about to change radically?

Was John simply playing the good historian here, reporting what happened that evening whatever the relevance to his readers? Was this conversation something he found personally interesting even though it had no application to those who read his gospel? Were these just the fond memories of an old man who had lost touch with the larger needs of his people?

If they are right—those who limit these promises to the Apostles—John belabored a Spirit who was already moot. He taunted an audience, soon to exchange an indwelling Spirit for a stack of scrolls, with promises of a spiritual experience that was not really for them.

No. Things were too critical at the time John wrote to permit that. The believers he addressed with his Gospel were in bad shape. They were suffering, discouraged, uncertain about the future, and wondering why Jesus had not returned. As much as that, however, they were frightened by the thought of losing John. He had been their Apostle for a long time. They depended on him, needed him, and were especially conscious of it now that he was old and failing.

In fact, when you think about it, you realize that the Johannine community faced circumstances very similar to those of the Apostles on that final night. Time was running short. Their "Master" was going away. Soon they would be left on their own in a hostile world.

That's why John spent so much time on the Final Discourse. He retold the events of that last evening because he saw profound similarities between the Apostles and his first readers. "Do not let your hearts be troubled and do not be afraid," Jesus told the Twelve. But John was thinking about his own people as he wrote those words. "I am going away," Jesus announced. But John was also going away and wanted to prepare the church he was leaving behind.

John is playing Jesus to their Twelve. The balm Jesus used to soothe his troubled disciples is the same medicine John applies to the wounds of his church: the Holy Spirit. And *that* is why John pounds home the promises of the *Paraclete* with the Final Discourse. Just as Jesus left his Apostles with words about the Spirit on his lips, so John wants to leave with those same words for his frightened people. "There is a *Paraclete*," John says through the story of the Gospel, "who will never leave you, who will teach and comfort you in my absence, who will continue the work of God in you and in this world."

John believes the promise of the Spirit is as much for believers at the close of the first century as for Apostles sixty years before. The same power that sustained the Twelve when Jesus left will sustain John's church when he leaves. Not a completed New Testament. Not inspiring worship services and pot-luck dinners. The Holy Spirit. A Spirit who accompanies and comforts and teaches and reveals. A "Final Discourse Spirit" who will do for John's readers what he did for Jesus' Apostles. A Spirit not just for the privileged few but for the rest of us.

I am convinced that God, through the work of inspiration, canonization, and preservation, has kept this Discourse available to us for exactly the same reasons. The promise of the *Paraclete* is as much for believers *today* as for those who knew John or walked with Jesus. The same power that sustained the Apostles and John's community is available to sustain us. That's why—at least in part—we have the Gospel of John with its lengthy and detailed account of Jesus talking to his Apostles about the Spirit his Father would soon send.

## Common Ground

The people who limit these promises to the Twelve and only to the Twelve place great emphasis on the *differences* between the Apostles and all other disciples. The promises about the *Paraclete* were only for the Twelve because they were set apart from the rest of us. They were specially chosen by Jesus. They walked and talked with him. They were given the keys of the kingdom and commissioned to shepherd the first-century church. All of them had miraculous powers. Many of them wrote inspired books. When Jesus spoke to these unique Apostles, it should be expected that he would say things that don't always apply to ordinary disciples like ourselves.

True enough. The differences between the Apostles and the rest of us are real. I appreciate and respect that fact.

In the matter of the Final Discourse, however, these may be differences that don't make much of a difference. It isn't the *differences* between his Apostles and regular disciples that motivates Jesus to talk about the *Paraclete*. It is, in fact, the very things *all* disciples have in common that prompts Jesus to raise this subject.

The words of the Final Discourse aren't aimed at the Twelve because of their Apostolic status, but because their hearts are troubled and they are afraid. The men Jesus addresses in these chapters aren't bold, brave Apostles, full of spiritual courage and wisdom, pregnant with inspired words and miraculous powers. Jesus isn't talking to haloed giants eager to turn the world upside down.

The men we meet at table this night strike us as lesser mortals who seem intimately familiar. They remind us of ourselves. Jesus talks to them of the Spirit because they are feeling inadequate and insecure and confused. They don't understand. They don't know what to do. They can't fathom what comes next. Their hearts are troubled. They are timid and limited and lonely. They have a mission bigger than they are. They have a calling that is larger than themselves.

Jesus doesn't promise them the *Paraclete* because of who they *are* but to help them become the men he needs them to be. He promises them the *Paraclete* because they will fail miserably as *disciples*—much less as *Apostles*—unless he leaves behind someone to help them in his absence.

We can identify with that. You and I may not have an apostolic calling or role. But we certainly share the Apostles' fears and anxieties, their insufficiency and doubt, their need for a power beyond themselves. Every disciple has felt this—not just the Twelve. If there is anything disciples of all ages have in common beyond their commitment to follow Jesus, it is the certain knowledge that none of us is equal to the task.

So when Jesus promises the Twelve someone who will *make them equal* to that task, we should not be surprised when disciples through the centuries prick up their ears and crowd closer and ponder whether that promise might be for them.

There is more. Jesus doesn't talk to them as he does on this final night because they have seen him in the flesh and witnessed his miracles and heard his voice with their own ears. Yes, the fact that the Apostles experienced Jesus during his earthly ministry makes them different from almost every other disciple who ever lived. But Jesus does not offer them the Spirit on this final evening because they've seen him up-close-and-personal. He offers them the Spirit precisely because they must remain disciples *without* his up-close-and-personal. The whole point of the Final Discourse is that Jesus is going away and they must stay behind. He is leaving and they cannot follow.

They will spend the remainder of their lives pursuing their mission in the absence of their Master. They will face a hostile world and endure its hatred without Jesus as buffer and shield. Never mind that they feel inadequate to the task. Never mind that the mission scares them to death. The real issue is that Jesus will be dead and gone and they must find a way to muddle through without him.

And this, again, is common ground. Just as we identify with the Apostles' fears, we can also identify with their circumstances. We know all about being disciples *here* while Jesus is *there.* Every disciple of every era knows the loneliness and uncertainties of stepping into a future where Jesus does not live. If there is anything disciples share in common—whenever and wherever they are—it is the need for Jesus to walk with them through changing circumstances and times.

So when Jesus promises a *Paraclete* who will show the Twelve how to be disciples in a future Jesus cannot share, we should not be surprised that disciples throughout history take notice and listen harder and wonder whether this offer might be for them.

Common fears. Common circumstances. Common limits.

When Jesus talks to the Twelve about the *Paraclete*, it's not because they were "super-sized" disciples with special capacities and supernatural aptitudes. He doesn't have this conversation with them because, as Apostles, they've got it all together and know everything they need to know and have fathomed all mysteries and all knowledge.

Just the opposite. Jesus offers them the *Paraclete* because they have reached their limit and cannot bear any more. Only through the *Paraclete* can these limited Apostles experience more communion with Jesus, more teaching, more peace, more courage, more traction with the world, more capacity for God. Jesus offers them the *Paraclete* precisely because, even as Apostles, they need to be further equipped and matured.

So do we. You and I will never write an inspired book. We may never get our hands on the keys to the kingdom. But we share this in common with the Apostles: a great need for the *Paraclete* to work within our spiritual limitations to transform us into the disciples God wants us to be.

Why then, with so much common ground between the Apostles and the rest of us, would Jesus offer the Twelve one solution and all other disciples a different one? He promises them the *Paraclete* to help them with their fears, to see them through their circumstances, and to meet their crying need.

According to some, however, the Spirit-solution is for *them*, not *us*.

For *us*, there is everything Jesus does *not* offer the Apostles. We get the writings of the Apostles. We get pep talks about what fine disciples we are and how, by staying the course and sticking to our commitments, we can survive until Jesus comes again. We get each other and sermons about hanging together lest we hang separately. We get baptism and the Lord's Supper—rituals, we are assured, that will keep us spiritually vital until the Last Day. We get the one-true-church and doctrinal correctness and The Pattern to sustain us through all the difficult days between our decision to follow Jesus and his return.

I am thankful for the church and the sacraments and the Scriptures. I prize and revel in them. I believe they are blessings from God and necessary to our walk as faithful disciples. I just don't think they are enough. They weren't enough for the Apostles. They weren't enough for the Jerusalem church or Paul's churches or John's community of believers.

Always there has been the need for "another *Paraclete*," the Holy Spirit of God, the One who is for our good, the One who guides disciples into all truth. So when Jesus says this *Paraclete* will be present "forever," it at least suggests we're not being silly for thinking this "forever" Spirit might still be around for us to enjoy.

## Forever

"I will ask the Father, and he will give you another *Paraclete* to be with you forever—the Spirit of truth ..." (John 14:16-17).

What does Jesus mean when he says "forever"?

Those who would limit these promises to the Apostles must limit this "forever" as well. They do so by pointing out that, if the promise of the *Paraclete* is only for the Apostles in any case, the promise of "forever" means the *Apostles'* forever: for as long as they live, the Apostles will have the *Paraclete*. But since Jesus never meant to extend the promise of the *Paraclete* beyond the Twelve, he never intended this "forever" to mean *everyone's* forever. They tell us to read this passage in this way: "I will ask the Father, and he will give you [only the Apostles] another *Paraclete* to be with you [only the Apostles] forever [as long as you, the Apostles, live] …."

The problem with this reasoning is, as so often, the *premise*. Just because Jesus is talking to the Apostles doesn't mean that what he says is meant *only* for them. There are lots of things Jesus says to the few he intends for the many.

Take the Great Commission, for example. Jesus is standing on a mountain in Galilee. The eleven disciples have traveled there to meet with their Master. No one else is around. No one else hears Jesus say, "Go and make disciples of all nations, baptizing them in the name of the Father and of the Son and of the Holy Spirit" (Matt 28:19). Yet every disciple of Jesus through history has felt the weight of these words and acknowledges the burden of this commission. Jesus spoke only *to* the Apostles. But what he said wasn't meant only *for* the Apostles.

In Matthew 24 Jesus is on the Mount of Olives enjoying—apparently—a quiet moment. The Apostles come to him "privately" (24:3) to ask a few questions. Jesus tells them a series of his most powerful parables about discipleship. This is the context for the Parable of the Wise and Foolish Virgins, the Parable of the Talents, and the incomparable Parable of the Sheep and Goats (see Matt 25). It is just Jesus and the Twelve. No crowds to overhear. No Mary and Martha and Lazarus to round out the audience. But no disciple since then, on the premise that these parables were addressed only to the Apostles, would excuse himself from the duty to "keep watch" or pour himself into the Master's business or care for "the least of these."

The same thing is true of the Final Discourse, Jesus is secluded with the Apostles. They are in a private Upper Room. No one else is present. Even Judas has gone away. What Jesus says here is said to them. But is it meant only for them?

Apparently not. When Jesus commands the Apostles (in the course of this Final Discourse) to "love one another" (John 13:34-35), we understand the command is for all of us. When he promises them that there are "many mansions" (14:2-3), we believe one of them has our name on it. When he says, "If you love me, you will obey what I command" (14:15), we recognize that Jesus is speaking past the Twelve to all disciples to follow. It's the same with "Remain in me" (15:4) and "Bear much fruit" (15:5) and "The world will hate you" (15:19)—words addressed to the Twelve but meant for us all. The warning about persecution (16:1-2)? The invitation, "Ask and you will receive" (16:24)? These are the bane and blessing of all disciples, not just the Apostles.

In fact, when you really look closely at the Final Discourse, *everything* Jesus says to the Twelve applies to *everyone* who follows after him. Except, apparently, what he says about the Spirit. *That's* not for us, so we've been told. *That* is only for Apostles, in the time before Scripture came.

Sounds like special pleading to me. "We don't understand this Spirit, we're not comfortable with this Spirit, so Jesus could not be talking about the Spirit *to us*. Those promises are for the Twelve alone."

But that's just plain wrong. These words are meant for all believers—for disciples of every age and place—and this "forever" means just what it seems to say. We are meant to read this passage as: "I will ask the Father, and he will give you [the Apostles, yes, but also all disciples] another *Paraclete* to be with you [the Apostles, certainly, but also all disciples] forever [from this time forward, for all eternity] ...."

This reading certainly fits better with the phrase translated "forever" in this passage. The Greek here literally reads *into the ages* (*eis ton aiona*). It is a phrase John uses a dozen times. And in every single case the meaning is clearly "forever"—as in the rest of time, all eternity, ever-and-ever-without-end-amen.

Drinking living water means never thirsting again *into the ages* (John 4:14—it will become a spring "welling up to eternal life"). Eating living bread means living *into the ages*, forever, eternally (6:51, 58). Keeping Jesus' word means never dying *into the ages*, ever, without limit (6:51, 52). When Jesus promises the presence of the Spirit *into the ages*, there are no time constraints involved, no statute of limitations, no impermanence implied. He isn't promising something for the next thirty or forty years; just until the Apostles die off; just until the New Testament is finished.

This promise is for a "forever Spirit" who will remain *into the ages*. The One who was baptized in the Spirit and baptizes with the Spirit has made the Spirit available for all and forever. That Spirit is still here, doing his vital work, empowering inadequate disciples, convicting a sinful world.

And the promises still apply. This Spirit is for us. This comfort and power is for us. Jesus has not abandoned us anymore than he abandoned them. He has gone away, yes. But someone has come: the *Paraclete* who is our constant Companion, our forever Teacher, our fellow Witness, our convicting Partner, and our patient Revealer.

John tells us about this Spirit because he wants us to experience the same Presence promised to the Twelve. Disciples then, now, and at every age between are offered this Spirit because we all so desperately need him. And Jesus uses the word "forever" because he wants us to know that the same Spirit sent to the Apostles is available for all disciples *into the ages*.

Chapter Fourteen

# THE SPIRIT IN OUR EXPERIENCE

In the last chapter, we asked *whether* the promise of the Holy Spirit is for us and answered that question with a vigorous "Yes." In this chapter, we ask *what* the Spirit does in our lives, for modern disciples, with people like you and me.

To get at that question, allow me to return to that strange statement Jesus made to the Twelve on that final night: "Because I have said these things, you are filled with grief. But … it is for your good that I'm going away. Unless I go away, the *Paraclete* will not come to you; but if I go, I will send him to you" (John 16:6-7). Or as the New Century Version translates it: "It is *better for you* that I go away."

The Apostles, no doubt, had a hard time believing that anything could be better than Jesus. Jesus telling them, "It is for your good that I'm going away," hardly seemed credible. But as we saw in Chapter Eleven, the *Paraclete* offered them more, could do more in them and in the world, than Jesus could. Jesus was (as always) telling them the truth, the whole truth, and nothing but the truth.

But since the promise of the *Paraclete* was never intended for the Apostles alone, since it was meant for every disciple who has followed Jesus after them, we need to consider that this "going away" was *for our good* as well.

We, of course, find that as unbelievable as they did. Better not to walk and talk with Jesus? Better not to see his face and hear his voice? There's not a one of us who hasn't wished we lived during the times of

Jesus, watched him with our own eyes, listened with our own ears. We are convinced that, if only we had the privilege of being with Jesus-in-the-flesh, our faith would be stronger, our lives would be straighter, and our discipleship would be sturdier.

We don't actually believe we are better off with the *Paraclete* than with a flesh-and-blood Jesus. More than a few of us would trade a lifetime with the Spirit for three years at the feet of Jesus of Nazareth. And we would make that trade absolutely convinced we were getting the better spiritual deal. We'd do the trade, even though it directly contradicts what Jesus says on the matter. We'd trade for Jesus when Jesus went to infinite trouble and pain to bring the Spirit's presence to us in place of himself![1]

He says we're better off with the Spirit, closer to himself with the Spirit, better equipped by the Spirit, more competent and confident for kingdom work because of the Spirit. Jesus was eager to leave the flesh so disciples could be blessed by the Spirit's work. Jesus packed himself up and sent himself off so that you and I could have an encounter with the Spirit. We, on the other hand, would send the Spirit packing for a few tangible encounters with Jesus.

What does that say about us? What does it say about our trust in our Master, about our willingness to take him at his word? And what, oh what, does it say about the meagerness of our present experience of the Spirit—that we would trade him away so casually for a few days on a mountainside in Galilee?

Since the promise of the *Paraclete* is for us, the assurance that "it is for your good I am going away" is for us as well. And the reason it is for our good is exactly the same reason it was for the Apostles' good: only when Jesus returned to the Father could he send the Spirit; only when Jesus removed himself could the Spirit come; and only when the Spirit came could disciples begin to experience something better than Jesus, something that truly was *for our good.*

## The Promise of Presence

In the five *Paraclete* Passages, Jesus promised that the Holy Spirit would do specific works in the lives of disciples and in the world. So what would these works look like … in us … for us?

Jesus promised, first, that the *Paraclete* would make possible a continuing experience of our Lord's presence.

Jesus has been gone for a long time now. You and I have never seen his face, nor heard his voice, nor felt his hand on our shoulder. It's hard, in the absence of such things, to sense how much he loves us, how pleased he is with us, how closely he watches over us, how attuned he is to our hurts and needs. It's hard to have meaningful relationship with the invisible man.

In fact, the easiest thing to do with this "no-longer-in-the-flesh" reality is to interpret the silence as withdrawal or lack of concern or (even) disapproval. The easiest thing is to feel the distance and wonder whether Jesus is watching or whether he cares or whether he might have given up on us.

But the Spirit makes Jesus present once more (John 14:16-23). This doesn't mean we will see his physical face or hear his actual voice. It does mean that the *Paraclete* closes the distance between a departed Jesus and his left-behind disciples so that we can feel the intimate relationship his face and voice once conveyed.

Remember that the writers of the New Testament were addressing people who, like us, had never seen the earthly Jesus. These people needed to know Jesus and experience his presence. What Paul and Luke and John offered the first Christians was the same thing Jesus offered the Twelve: the Spirit. Paul, for instance, didn't recount more stories about Jesus to fill in the gaps and help his readers feel closer to their Master. He offered them the Spirit, confident that a vivid experience of Jesus was possible through the Spirit's ministry.

And so he wrote about the Spirit pouring out "the love of Christ" into believers' hearts (Rom 5:5; 15:30; Eph 3:16-18); setting a seal upon Christians so that they could have confidence in their salvation and in the love of the Lord who made that salvation possible (Eph 1:13; 2 Cor 1:22); letting disciples know that Jesus was alive and well and continually working for their good (Rom 1:4; 8:27, 34). Paul and the other New Testament writers believed it was the Spirit who would help readers experience the person and affection and attentiveness of Jesus. It was the Spirit who would show them that Jesus was in them and that they were in Jesus (John 14:20; 1 John 3:24; 4:13). It was the Spirit who would assure them that—in fact—they were beloved sons and daughters, valued disciples (Gal 4:6). Those writers were confident that fellowship with the Spirit would help their converts feel united with Christ and comforted by his love (Phil 2:1); that the Spirit who long ago raised Jesus from the grave would keep working to resurrect Jesus, bringing the Crucified One back to life—over and over again—for each of them and (in times to come) every one of us.

The Spirit continues that work in your life and in mine. I believe it is the Spirit who breathes new life into too-familiar gospel stories and thus allows Jesus to live again for me. I believe I hear the voice of Jesus afresh in wise words from a brother or in the forgiveness of my wife. It is the Spirit who allows me to see Jesus alive in a sunset, in a wedding ceremony, in a child, and in the church.

But it's more than that—this ability of the Spirit to make Jesus present. The Spirit touches my emotions and gives me confidence in Jesus' love and approval. The Spirit touches my sense of self and convinces me of my obedience to Jesus and my secure standing before God. The Spirit reminds me that Jesus walks with me through my day, that he is beside me when others criticize (or praise!), that he is intimately aware of my motives and struggles and efforts. My fellowship with the Spirit assures me that I am one with Jesus, a true disciple, a follower he loves and values.

In the morning, when I rise, I do so with the words, "Good morning, Lord," because the Spirit prompts those words. As I brush my teeth, I ask Jesus to stay close by me this day because the Spirit puts the thought in my heart and head. I feel embarrassed that Jesus overhears my curt response when I'm cut off in traffic because the Spirit reminds me that my Lord is listening. I ask Jesus to give me words of comfort for a grieving family, words of wisdom for a broken couple, words of witness for a doubting soul—because the Spirit whispers constantly that I am not alone, that Jesus sits beside me as I sit with these people. I don't go certain places on the internet or on the hotel TV, not because I am above such fleshly temptations, but because the Spirit pierces me with thoughts of Jesus seeing through my eyes. I listen quietly to someone tear me apart with their brutal criticism because the Spirit helps me realize that Jesus hears what they're saying; he knows what is true of me and what is not; he knows what is in their heart and in mine. I step confidently into warring congregations because the Spirit assures me that Jesus goes with me. I open my much-broken heart yet again because the Spirit convicts me that Jesus strengthens and protects me. I pick myself up, I try again, I find the courage to risk once more, because I know that the gracious, patient, powerful Jesus lives within me and will never leave me and will always help me. I know it because the Spirit tells me so.

And when, at last, I lay me down in the evening, it is with the grateful prayer, "Give me Jesus. You can have all this world, but give me Jesus." Sometimes, frankly, those words are little more than a reminder to myself—of what I value, of what I hope. Sometimes they are a desperate plea for the Father to help me keep my priorities straight. But, most of the time, it is a simple prayer to the Spirit, who makes the presence of Jesus within me of greater worth than anything the world could hope to offer.

## The Promise of Teaching

He promises, next, that the *Paraclete* will "teach you all things and remind you of everything I have said to you" (John 14:26). He made this promise in the context of passing on his mission to us. We now have kingdom business squarely in our hands. Yet there is so much we don't understand, so many ways we are inadequate to that task.

How do we continue the mission of Jesus in the twenty-first-century world? What is a faithful response to the rampant materialism of our age? What about the challenges of the Internet? What should we do with a form of modern Christianity so accommodated to culture that matters such as divorce, denominational and racial divides, and lavish lifestyles are commonplace and commonly accepted? Is God pleased by a Moral Majority that seems more interested in building voting blocs and signing petitions than in finding fresh ways to win the world with cross-shaped living? What about the dilemmas raised by medical technology and bio-ethics? What is a disciple's proper response to world hunger (brought into our living rooms in hi-def horror) or the Islamic Revolution or the American Empire?

We've never had the chance to put such questions to Jesus. We've never sat on a hillside, looking first at our meager resources, then at a crowd of opportunities, and asking Jesus, "But what are they among so many?"

It's hard, in the absence of specific directions and focused teachings, to know what Jesus thinks about such contemporary challenges, what he thinks should be done about them, how he wants disciples to handle themselves in the midst of them. It's hard to discern the will of an absent Master.

The *Paraclete* equips us for our mission. The Spirit teaches us everything we need to know to do the work Jesus has given us to do. Not just about the things that never change (adultery, hatred, envy), but about those matters that pose fresh and consequential challenges to followers of Jesus.

It was the guidance of the Holy Spirit that enabled the first-century church to wade through the practical issues that constantly plagued it. What should a Jewish church do about Gentiles who wanted a piece of the gospel pie? What about the problems posed by slaves and masters together in the same local congregation? How should disciples handle matters related to idolatry and food sacrificed to idols and the central role pagan temples played in a culture like Corinth's? What was the proper stance to take about paying taxes and showing honor to a government that was determined to persecute and exterminate followers of the Way? When Jesus did not return again as quickly as the first Christians anticipated, should they keep working to support themselves and their families? Should they marry? What was the status of believers who died in the meantime?

Jesus, in his earthly ministry, said little or nothing about such matters. In fact, some of what he taught seemed contrary to the Spirit's eventual leading (e.g., "I was sent only to the lost sheep of Israel"—Matt 15:24). Yet, in all these ways and more, the *Paraclete* provided practical instruction for the early church and showed them the deeper meaning and wider implications of everything Jesus taught.

He does the same for us. Just because Jesus never addressed the subject of designer dresses or designer drugs doesn't mean he has no "will" about such matters. He still instructs his church about being faithful in a modern context that differs radically from the world of Jerusalem or Rome.

It is the Spirit who teaches me what to think and feel about Muslim extremists or economic melt-downs or the plight of our inner cities. It is the Spirit who shows me how to weight such matters and where they fit into kingdom priorities. Surprisingly, that means I don't always line up with current conservative party lines or conventional Christian thinking. Since I am such a limited student of things spiritual, it also means that positions I once held with such certainty have changed in time … become more nuanced … become (I believe) more Christ-like. I find, because of the Spirit's teaching work, that I often know more today than I did yesterday. I see things now I didn't then. I'm aware of a bigger picture, a higher priority. What once seemed so threatening to the Kingdom (say, the gay agenda) morphs into something—often concerning myself—that is even more threatening to the Kingdom (say, my tendency to engage people as abstractions rather than as individuals; or my preference to throw stones rather than love others in sacrificial, cross-shaped ways).

Churches of Christ are a movement particularly in need of a teaching Spirit. We've tended to major in minors and minor in majors. We'll tear down spiritual mountains in order to have our way with molehills. We'll destroy the unity of the body, damn brothers to hell, and otherwise make ourselves spiritually noxious over minutia of dogma. We've strained gnats and swallowed camels. Our only hope is that God will unleash his teaching Spirit upon us, a Spirit who will help us discern what has Kingdom significance and what does not. I believe we want truth. We just haven't learned to distinguish the camels from the gnats. We need the *Paraclete* to teach us the difference.

The Spirit teaches us "all things," reminds us (and *enlightens* us) about everything Jesus said, and shows us how to make our way through the quagmire of issues that continue to plague his people. And because he does that "forever" and for all disciples, we can hear a voice strong enough to pierce our stubborn deafness and convict us once again about matters that matter to God.

## The Promise of Testimony

Jesus promised, also, that the *Paraclete* would be a "forever" witness to the truth and an active partner in the witness of disciples. "When the *Paraclete* comes … he will testify about me. And you also must testify, for you have been with me from the beginning" (John 15:26-27).

Just like the first disciples, you and I have been called to testify. We understand that "Go into all the world and preach the gospel" is for every disciple who has ever followed Jesus. We cannot evade the testimonial burden even though it frightens us.

Yet evade we do. There is, perhaps, no disobedience more characteristic of the modern church than evangelistic muteness. Our chronic laryngitis when it comes to matters of faith is widely lamented and widely ignored. We are afraid of a world that does not want to hear our witness. We feel ill equipped to witness in a world that seems so much more sophisticated than in past times. And, I suspect, we feel embarrassed by compromised lives that cannot back up our testimonial words.

Since we can't say something well, we've decided it is better to say nothing at all.

But have things really worsened so much from New Testament times—worsened enough to explain and justify our testimonial silence? Yes, our world is hostile to the Christian message, but at least they're not throwing us to the lions! And it's true we're not always "prepared to give an answer for the hope that is within us," but the first Christians were "unschooled, ordinary men" (Acts 4:13) who hadn't honed their witness in seminaries or read the latest book on apologetics. And we know way too much about the Apostles—their stubbornness and pride and ambition—to believe it was the stellar quality of their lives that gave validity and power to their witness.

Yet they managed to be the light of the world, turning it upside down with the boldness and persistence of their testimony, while we hide our faith under the nearest bowl.

The difference in their witness and ours is not the different worlds we live in or a disparity in the knowledge we bring to the witnessing task or a discrepancy in the lives we live. The difference is that their testimony was Spirit-fueled while ours, too often, is not. They believed the Spirit was busy witnessing to a lost world about the truth of Jesus, recognizing his hand at work in the Ethiopian, Saul, Cornelius, and the Antioch church. And they understood that, when *they* witnessed, it would be by the Spirit's wisdom, with the Spirit's words, and through the Spirit's emboldening power.

That same Spirit is at work witnessing to our world today. He does it through the archaeologist's spade, the NFL coach's statement of faith, the latest discoveries of science, the harsh realities of struggle and sickness and death in every life, and the writings of the most unlikely authors. He does it in a thousand different ways for a million different people every day. He is the stubborn, constant, relentless voice speaking up for Jesus even in a world as broken as ours … *especially* in a world as broken as ours.

The fact that we do not hear his witnessing voice or recognize his testifying work says nothing about him and much about us. It says that, in circumstances where the first Christians would immediately identify and give credit to the Holy Spirit, we remain oblivious, unaware, and insensible of the Spirit's activity. Let's open our eyes not just to see the "fields ripe unto harvest" but to see the Spirit already hard at work in them.

But more, the Spirit is ready, willing, and eager to do for our witness what he did for theirs: make us fearless in speaking up for Christ, give us words to say and wisdom in saying them, grant us eyes to see who is ready to hear and when the time is right. He is eager to become our partner in testimony.

We are not alone—ours is not the only voice bearing witness to the light. And we are not *alone*—when the time comes for us to speak, the Spirit will be present with us, overcoming our fears and uncertainties. His voice will speak with and in and through our voices, enhancing our timid testimony with the power of the voice that called this world into being.

## The Promise of Conviction

Jesus promised, as well, that the *Paraclete* would "convict the world of guilt" (John 16:8). Being willing to tell the truth about yourself is surely one of the hardest requirements for becoming a follower of Jesus.

Yet, just as surely, it is one of the most necessary. The initial step in any Twelve Step program is to "admit we are powerless … that our lives have become unmanageable": recovery only begins with the truth about ourselves. The first step of discipleship is to "repent": we have to acknowledge the bad news about ourselves before we ever get to good news. When Jesus teaches that the first step toward God is to be "poor in spirit," he's saying that reaching the end of ourselves is an absolute necessity.

But "admitting," "repenting," and "reaching the end of ourselves" is a tricky business. It requires divine help. Let me give you an example.

I knew someone once who was the proud owner of a sad story. His adulteries were everyone else's fault. The wife was a nagging harpy. The job was stressful. No one really appreciated him. For years he'd denied and minimized and defended himself and his actions. He and his ex had not spoken for ages. His children wanted nothing to do with him. His friends tried to maintain contact, but he required their approval as the price of his company—something they could not afford to give.

He was alone, a solitary fortress bulwarked against any accusation of personal responsibility.

Occasionally through the years, he stopped by my office to talk, bearing Starbucks as his votive offering. In his first visits he tried to explain himself, hungry for my blessing. There was a long period when he used our time together to feel sorry for himself and complain about the tatters of his life. In later chats he was obsessed with healing the rift between himself and his children.

I well remember the day, though, when he knocked at my door with empty hands and brimming eyes. He sat on my couch and, for the first time, confessed his own sins rather than everyone else's. He wept out his guilt and remorse and sorrow. He saw what he'd done, how it had wounded the people he loved, how he was tasting the bitter ashes of a life he himself had burned to the ground.

It was a beautiful moment, the first step on a long road back to himself, to his kids, to God.

I have long forgotten *what* brought this man to a penitent place, the particular pig-pen that forced him to face himself. But I do know *who* led him there.

There is a turning point in people that happens only by the power of the Holy Spirit. It's the point where they "get it," where they see themselves and what they've done with sudden clarity, where their defenses and justifications are washed away by a flood of conviction. There is a point where people can finally tell the truth about themselves without evasion or excuse. And the only thing that brings people to that point is the Holy Spirit.

Time doesn't do it. Awful consequences won't provoke it. Piling up more evidence of personal fault doesn't seem to break through. I've tried prompting repentance in all manner of folk: cheating husbands, angry

wives, rebellious children, arrogant church members, bitter septuagenar-
ians, drunks, gluttons, and the greedy. I've confronted and cajoled and
pleaded. I've used brow-beating and tears. And the hard-won lesson I've
finally learned is this: people won't see the truth about themselves until
they are ready; and readiness is a condition only the Spirit of God can
produce.

It is the Spirit who brings people to the pig-pen and to that precious
moment of self-awareness. It is the Spirit who drives people to their
knees. It is the Spirit who holds up a divine mirror to broken lives and
then grants people the nerve to look long and hard.

Only the Spirit can convict people of sin. Only the Spirit can bestow
the courage required to confess and confront sin. Only the Spirit can
lead people to that turning point when they "come to themselves" and
speak those healing words: "Father, I have sinned against heaven and
against you."

Jesus promises, in this Fourth *Paraclete* Passage, that the convicting
work of the Spirit will be necessary, will continue, forever. We see the
Spirit doing that work (through the witness of the New Testament) in
Jerusalem and Corinth and Galatia. And, if only we will open our eyes
to it, we can see the Spirit doing that same work in people all around
us—harrowing hearts with the plow of conviction so the world will be
ready for the gospel seed.

## The Promise of Revelation

Finally, Jesus promised that the *Paraclete* would "take from what
is mine—all that belongs to the Father is mine—and make it known
to you" (John 16:15). Jesus came to reveal the Father but had to pass
that job on to the *Paraclete* because the disciples couldn't handle his revelation. They did not have the capacity. Time was too short, the story
wasn't finished, their containers were too small. So Jesus offered them the
*Paraclete* who would do for them what he could not: take all the time in
the world; unpack the Father in manageable portions; connect them to
the Father at a rate they could handle.

The result of the Spirit's revealing ministry in the lives of the Apostles
and the first Christians was a deepening awareness of God, a greater
transformation of character, and a growing maturity in the Lord.

Take the Cross as but one example.

It was the Spirit who revealed to the first Christians that the Cross was not what they feared. They thought the Cross meant only death and defeat. They thought the Cross was the end—for Jesus and for them. But then came resurrection and the Spirit's patient teaching that this was just what the prophets had foretold all along, that the Cross was part of God's plan, that Jesus was the atoning sacrifice for a world of sin.

There was more to the Cross than that, however. The Cross *revealed Jesus*: the depth of his love for us, the extent of his obedience to the Father, his trust in self-giving love as an antidote to the power of sin. And the Cross revealed the *Father*: his hatred of sin, his love of the world, the extent to which he would go to win us back to himself. At the Cross, we meet a selfless God of boundless mercy and infinite grace. All of this the Spirit revealed to the first Christians; slowly; as they were able to absorb it.

By the day of Pentecost (judging from the sermon delivered then), this was about as much of the Cross as Peter and the rest seemed to grasp. Death. Resurrection. God's purposes. The Crucified One as Lord and Christ (Acts 2:14-39).

But the Spirit was not finished unpacking the Cross for these believers. By the time of Paul's first letters, the Cross that once belonged to Jesus had become a cross that all believers bore. It was the symbol and epitome of the selfless, sacrificial, surrendered lifestyle that defined disciples of Jesus. Qualities like humility, service, and dying to self became dominant virtues in the life of the church—drawn from the teachings of Jesus, certainly, but rooted in the example of his death.

Even that did not exhaust what the Spirit had to reveal about the Cross. Paul's later letters took the central dynamic of Jesus' life (Cross and resurrection, death and new life) and applied it to his churches in fresh and profound ways. Now it was not just a servant lifestyle that defined Cross-shaped lives; it was an aggressive, unnatural selflessness that only truly mature people could demonstrate. Concepts like deferring to each other (Rom 14), limiting personal freedoms for a brother's benefit (1 Cor 8), exercising gifts "for the common good" (1 Cor 12), and suffering as a redemptive act (2 Corinthians, entire), became the drum Paul thumped with increasing vigor and frequency. Each of these was a further extension of the Spirit's revelation about the meaning of Christ's Cross. One more item unpacked from God's suitcase.

This same kind of revelation is desperately needed today to help us grasp the nature of God, the mind of Christ, the priorities of the kingdom, and the contours of the spiritual realm. The work of deepening disciples, maturing them, growing them up "into the image of Christ," increasing their capacity to know God and live like him—these are central challenges of the Spirit in the church and in disciples today.

We bemoan the plague of immaturity in today's church, the cancer of selfishness. But it's going to take something stronger than small groups and adult Bible classes to kill those diseases. We lament the spiritual shallowness of our people. Yet what we offer them is, "Pray more. Read more. Try harder. Make Christian friends." Our churches have become havens for people with lots of years in the Lord and little cross in them. We've given up on expecting anything better. We won't hold ourselves and others accountable to a higher standard because we're not sure there is a power capable of raising our lives to higher levels. We're stuck with people who are stuck.

But the Spirit is still present among us, doing his revealing work, creating disciples who *know* more of God, *hold* more of God, and *look* more like God. What the Spirit did in Peter and Paul, he can still do today. What the Spirit wanted to do in the Corinthians he still wants to do in us. Transformation, now as then, remains an essential work that only the Spirit can accomplish.

## Conclusion

This is the *Paraclete* Jesus made available to his disciples two thousand years ago. This is the *Paraclete* who has sustained the church through all the centuries since. And this is the *Paraclete* who has been promised to us, if only we will welcome him into our hearts and lives.

I'm all for reading the Bible and going to church and loving neighbors. I encourage you to pray and sing and take the Lord's Supper. These are wonderful, sustaining, nurturing spiritual activities. These are "means of grace" by which we share in the abundant life of God.

Just don't confuse these things with what Jesus offers us *in his stead.* Don't think for a minute these were what Jesus meant as being "for our good" when he went away. The church was never intended to be a replacement for Immanuel: God with us. Scripture was never imagined to be "better" for us than an ongoing relationship with our Lord. The commands (and obedience to them) are no substitute for the living, indwelling, empowering, constant, ministering *gift* Jesus had in mind for all disciples as he prepared to leave this world and return to his Father.

So by all means pray and study, give alms to the poor and fast, commit yourself to a church family, get involved with a ministry.

But don't imagine these are the things that will enable you to survive and thrive as disciples in this day and time. They aren't. They were never intended to be. Jesus has something greater in store for us than this. As his disciples we are more than the beliefs we hold and the church we attend and the good deeds we do. We are more than how much Bible we've memorized or how many hours we spend in prayer or the moral code we live by.

We are the ones who have the Holy Spirit living in us. We are temples containing the *Paraclete*. We are sons and daughters of the Most High God, sealed with the guarantee of the Spirit in our hearts. We are ministers of a new covenant, made competent by the Spirit who gives life. We are those who understand the deep things of God because we have God's Spirit inside us. We are the ones being transformed into the likeness of Christ—from "glory to glory"—because of the Spirit's work within us.

Define yourself (if you must) by where you go to church, or how you choose to worship, or what you believe about this-and-that, or who your Christian friends are. Jesus defines us differently. He defines us in a way that is truly "good" for us. He defines us as people in whom the Holy Spirit has made his home.

And because (for Jesus) this is the foundational fact of our lives as disciples, it is essential (for us as disciples) to make that fact foundational in our hearts and lives. We can't afford to define our discipleship by lesser things and ignore the single truth that is the essence of discipleship. The "Spirit in us" trumps all other denominational or doctrinal or life-style cards. So long as the Spirit is in your hand, even if your other cards are weak, you can't lose.

The "Spirit in you" is that important. As Paul puts it: "If anyone does not have the Spirit of Christ, he does not belong to Christ" (Rom 8:9).

It is this Spirit who is "for our good," the One who is better for us than Jesus himself. This is the parting gift Jesus offered to help us shine as disciples. This is the Helping Presence who lives in us and works through us forever.

He will be our constant Companion, our powerful Equipper, our Comforter and Encourager, our ever-present Partner, and our Guide into all truth. He will counter our loneliness with love and joy. He will offset our inadequacies with peace and confidence. He can take away our fears by encouraging us to be faithful in witness and gentle with words. He can help us believe that we can still make a difference by granting us the courage to be patient and the wisdom to be kind. He will guide us into maturity through an ever-deepening goodness and self-control.

He will keep the promises of Jesus by pouring his fruit into our lives.

It really is "for our good" that Jesus has gone away and the Spirit has come.

## Chapter Fifteen

# TEN DISCIPLINES FOR SEEKING THE SPIRIT

We've wondered together whether the promise of the Spirit is for you and me. (It is.)

We've explored together what the Holy Spirit actually does for us. (A great deal, as it happens.)

Now it's time to think together about how we welcome the Spirit into our lives so that he can do his transforming work.

Here, for your consideration, are ten suggestions for making yourself more available to the Spirit...ten "disciplines" for seeking the Spirit. For those of you with a practical bent, this is where all the hard slogging through the Spirit-theory pays off. For those who would rather stick with theory, this is where you have to face the challenge of putting theory into practice. Either way, this book won't be complete without applying the principles we've studied to our daily life.

As you read this, don't get discouraged and start thinking, "This is all too much!" Let me confess that I am outlining a *lifetime's* agenda. You don't have to accomplish any of this today. I'm not asking you to master these disciplines by next week. I'm not suggesting that we can ever wrap our minds and our lives around the whole thing.

What I am trying to do is paint a different way of looking at discipleship. I'd like you to consider the possibility that—behind all the church-going and elders' meetings and Bible-reading—there is a higher agenda, another dimension, a life-building work going on. I want you to step into the Spirit's realm and experience your life from his perspective. And then I hope to give you some practical guidance about letting the Spirit step into your life and change your perspective forever.

## 1. Ask for the Spirit

Relationship with the Holy Spirit begins with an invitation. "If you then, being evil, know how to give good gifts to your children, how much more will your heavenly Father give the Holy Spirit to those who ask him" (Luke 11:13).

Yes, there are times in Scripture when the Spirit falls, unasked and unexpected, on people like Cornelius. And, yes, the Spirit can do what he wants, when he wants, with whom he wants. But, as in so much of our interaction with God, the Spirit demonstrates a remarkable respect for and deference to our wills and our wishes. Just as Jesus does not come barging into our lives, demanding faith and obedience "or else," so the Spirit will not force himself on us, taking up residence where he has not been welcomed. He wants a partner, not a puppet.

And so the Spirit waits for us to invite him inside. We can do this through baptism (a request, not just for forgiveness of sins, but for "the gift of the Holy Spirit"—Acts 2:38). We can do it through prayer (as when Peter and John prayed for Samaritan believers that "they might receive the Holy Spirit"—Acts 8:15). I personally believe we should make this request whenever we participate in communion—inviting the Spirit into our hearts through the medium of the bread and wine.

So eager is the Spirit to collaborate with us, our invitation doesn't have to be very "correct." Don't get hung up on wording or rituals. You don't need to stand on one leg, rubbing your stomach with the left hand while patting your head with the right in order to convince the Spirit of your sincerity. Just ask, in simple, heart-felt words:

> *Father, I believe you have sent the Holy Spirit—the Paraclete—to be my Companion and Comforter. I believe your Son wants me to have a close and forever relationship with the Spirit. So I open my heart and life to him. I ask you to give me the gift you have promised. I trust your Spirit because I know you. He is everything I have come to know and love about Jesus, my Lord. Let your Spirit do his*

*transforming work in me. Make me the disciple you, your Son, and your Spirit want me to be.*

Once you ask, however, it is important that you trust God—your good Father—to give you the gift you've requested.

> If you don't know what you're doing, pray to the Father. He loves to help. You'll get his help, and won't be condescended to when you ask for it. Ask boldly, believingly, without a second thought. People who "worry their prayers" are like wind-whipped waves. Don't think you're going to get anything from the Master that way, adrift at sea, keeping all your options open. [Jas 1:5-8—The Message]

So many of God's gifts are second-guessed, I fear: salvation, forgiveness of sins, reconciliation, our status as sons and daughters ... and especially the indwelling presence of the Spirit in our lives. We may call such second-guessing "humility" or even "insecurity." The Bible calls it "lack of faith."

So when you ask God for his promised Spirit, do so with confidence that he wants to give the Spirit to you, believing that what you have asked he will accomplish, trusting that your Father will keep his promise. Ask God and then expect him to deliver, expect him to have *already* delivered.

## 2. Become a Spirit Student

"God has chosen to make known ... the glorious riches of this mystery, which is Christ in you ..." (Col 1:27).

Our education about the Spirit has been sadly lacking. We don't talk about him a great deal in our churches. We don't preach and teach about who he is and how he works and why he is important to discipleship today.

Even those of us who have walked with Jesus a long time need to go back to school when it comes to the Holy Spirit. Though asking the Father to give us his Spirit is a good start, that's all it is—a start. Now we need to devote ourselves to becoming students of the Spirit, getting to know this *Paraclete* who promises to be our Companion and Present Helper.

*Father. I have invited your Spirit into my life. Now I need to know him. I want to learn who he is and what he does and how he acts. Teach me about your Spirit. Allow your Spirit to show me what I have the capacity to see. Let me understand his names and his nature. Teach me his ways and his work. Let him be my Companion in word and deed. Allow me to walk with him intimately, as I long to walk also with you and with your Son.*

The learning process begins by going back to Scripture and meeting the Spirit in the pages of Sacred Writing all over again. Spend some time in the surveys of the Spirit in Scripture I've provided in this book. Contemplate the Spirit in the lives of Moses, David, and Paul. Memorize the Final Discourse. Immerse yourself in the eighth chapter of Romans. Think long and hard about the second chapter of 1 Corinthians ("no one knows the thoughts of God except the Spirit of God"). Learn what's really being said about the Spirit in the twelfth chapter of that book...and the loving lifestyle that (in chapter thirteen) Paul calls the Spirit's "most excellent way." List out the "fruit of the Spirit" and measure yourself by that standard (Gal 5:22-23—need any help to measure up?) Linger over Paul's prayer for the Ephesians (3:14-21) and notice both the central role played by the Spirit and how much Paul's prayer speaks to our highest hopes. There is a great deal the Bible says about the Spirit we've seldom heard. So hear it now. And learn.

What begins with personal study will be enhanced by discussion. Ask a couple of friends to meet you at Starbucks one morning a week for the next few months to talk about the Spirit in Scripture, in the plan of God, and in your lives. Pray together for God to give you wisdom as you seek to know him better.

## 3. Develop Spirit Eyes

"So we fix our eyes not on what is seen, but on what is unseen. For what is seen is temporary, but what is unseen is eternal" (2 Cor 4:18).

I am convinced most of our inability to see the Spirit at work in us and in our world is due to our Spirit-blindness rather than any inactivity on the Spirit's part. Like the poor man of Bethesda, we see nothing or—at best—we cannot make sense of what we see (Mark 8:22-26). We require repeated touches of the Master's hand before our spiritual sight can be restored…before we see more clearly.

So ask God to touch your eyes and open your heart so that you can see the Spirit's work. Ask him today and tomorrow and the day after. Cry out and do not allow anyone to shush you.

> *Father, forgive my blindness to your Spirit. Heal me so that I may see. Once, it is true, I was convinced I saw everything clearly and, so, I remained blind. But now I know I need your healing touch, opening my blind eyes and deaf ears and weak heart. Grant me the ability to see your Spirit, Father, and—in turn—I will give you my fixed attention.*

What good are healed eyes if they won't focus on heavenly things? Some of our blindness to the Spirit, frankly, isn't a matter of incapacity but inattention. We walk through life with our Spirit-eyes wide shut. We don't expect to encounter the Spirit. We don't look and so we don't see.

We need new disciplines that allow us to "fix our eyes on what is unseen," with the operative word being "fix," as in: "fasten," "glue," "habitual focus," "unwavering attention." Watch for the Spirit at work in the morning headlines, in the events of your day, in the people you meet and the opportunities you are given. Look to see how he shows up in times of worship, in moments of need or crisis. Pray that God would not only heal your spiritual blindness but treat your SADD—Spiritual Attention Deficit Disorder.

## 4. Build a Spirit Vocabulary

"This is what we speak, not in words taught us by human wisdom but in words taught by the Spirit, expressing spiritual truths in spiritual words" (1 Cor 2:13).

One of the things I admire most about my charismatic brothers and sisters is their eagerness and eloquence in witnessing to the Spirit's work in their lives. Not only do they see his fingerprints everywhere, they talk about the Spirit with great ease and joy. "The Spirit convicted me …" "I haven't felt released by the Spirit …" "I've been seeking the Spirit's wisdom on this …."

You and I lack the vocabulary to talk like that. Even if we found the courage, we wouldn't have the words. Speech about the Spirit might as well be a foreign language to us. We stammer and struggle. Spirit-phrases feel odd on our tongues. We'd much rather talk Bible or church.

> *Father, I confess that I am "slow of tongue" when it comes to matters of the Spirit. Jesus, please touch my tongue—as you did with the mute man—so that I can "speak plainly" about the Spirit's work within me. Forgive me for hardly understanding much less being able to talk about spiritual truths in spiritual words. I want my speech to honor the Spirit and to be a constant testimony to his grace, goodness, and power.*

So learn to use the Spirit's names in prayer and conversation. Hear the phrases used in Scripture (live according to the Spirit; set your mind on what the Spirit desires; the mind controlled by the Spirit is life and peace; we are led by the Spirit of God; the Spirit helps us in our weakness; the Spirit intercedes for us; the fruit of the Spirit is love, joy, peace, etc.; we are "saved" and "sanctified" and "sealed" by the Spirit) and allow these Spirit-idioms to imprint onto your own mental and verbal routines. Become comfortable talking about the Spirit, giving credit to the Spirit, acknowledging the Spirit's work in your life, in your church, and in the world.

Before our Spirit-speech can ever be heard, of course, it must be *authentic*. We have permission to talk the Spirit-talk only when we walk the Spirit-walk. I've seen people who had the lingo down but lacked the life. Such speech is hypocritical and dishonest. Better to say nothing and have everyone think you a Spirit-fool than to open your mouth insincerely and remove all doubt.

## 5. Live in the Spirit

"Since we live by the Spirit, let us keep in step with the Spirit" (Gal 5:25).

It's all very well to accept that the Holy Spirit lives in us. It's another thing to understand that *we also live in the Spirit*. There is a sense in which the Spirit "keeps in step" with us by ministering to our particular wounds, recognizing our individual limits, and knowing our specific strengths and weaknesses. But there is also a sense in which we "keep in step" with the Spirit, learning his will and adapting to his ways.

Paul gets at this idea with phrases like: "live according to the Spirit" and be "controlled by the Spirit," "keep in step with the Spirit" and be "led by the Spirit." He believes Christians inhabit a Spirit-environment in which they "speak by the Spirit," "worship by the Spirit," "pray in the Spirit," "love in the Spirit," and bear the "fruit of the Spirit."

Everywhere we turn, everything we do, every action we take—according to Paul—is done within an environment of God's Spirit. We live, breath, and have our very being within the Spirit's realm.

John, of course (in the Final Discourse), is getting at the same idea. The *Paraclete* is our Companion, Teacher, Equipper, Partner, and Guide. He is our new reality. We live our lives in constant reference to him. The Spirit lives in us. And, because of that, we must consciously, faithfully, live in him.

This is the new perspective that shapes disciples' lives. We stepped out of Adam's world and into the realm of the Spirit when we trusted in Jesus. Now we walk in the new way, according to the new realities, of the Spirit's presence.

Without this Spirit-consciousness, we pretend to set goals for our lives: marriage, career, retirement. Sorry. For disciples of Jesus, there is only one goal: to keep in step with the Spirit.

Apart from the conviction that we live by the Spirit, we act as though we were masters of our fate, captains of our personal ship. How foolish! We are, in fact, slaves of righteousness, controlled by the Spirit, doing what pleases the Spirit. The Spirit leads us; the Spirit shapes us; the Spirit owns us.

Our forgetfulness of this new reality results in a kind of tepid living that throws us back on our own power, exercising our own self-control, and boot-strapping our way through life. But Paul has an antidote to such forgetfulness and such meager living: keeping in step with the Spirit.

*Holy Father. You have promised that the Paraclete will live in me and walk with me through all the highways and byways of my life. Teach me that I also live in him and walk with him. Let me devote my life to the Spirit's control and to his leading. Help me to live in Spirit-ways, according to the Spirit's wisdom and power. Let me keep in step with the Spirit, even as he walks beside me as my Companion and Guide.*

## 6. Pray "in the Spirit"

"But you, dear friends, build yourselves up in your most holy faith and pray in the Holy Spirit" (Jude 1:20).

Prayer is a difficult subject for people who aren't sure whether miracles still happen, whether God still personally intervenes, or whether the Spirit is still living and active. Why pray if God no longer reaches into our world to do something ... well ... divine? Why ask God to act (heal, convict, transform, right wrongs, punish, strengthen, etc.) if we don't believe he does those things directly and by his own hand?

The result of such questions is that, too often, we don't pray. Not really. At mealtimes, maybe. Before we drift off to sleep at night. But prayers become rote when we're not sure God listens. Prayers become formulaic when we aren't convinced they change anything.

The alternative to tepid prayers, I suggest, is to pray "in the Spirit."

I recognize that "praying in the Spirit" may have referred to some kind of ecstatic experience for first-century Christians, a prayer practice in which disciples were "caught up to the third heaven" (2 Cor 12:2) and spoke in prayer tongues (1 Cor 14:14-15).

But it is more likely that Jude's exhortation to his readers (Jude 1:20; and Paul's similar injunction—Eph 6:18) had little to do with ecstasy and much to do with mindset. "Pray in the Spirit" most likely meant to pray *with* the Spirit, *in the context* of the Spirit, with *confidence* in the Spirit, through *the agency* of the Spirit, and *because* of the indwelling Spirit. "Pray," says Jude, "and do it with the Spirit very much in mind."

*Father, you have given me the Paraclete to stand beside me and speak up for me. Remind me that I am not alone when I pray to you, that your Spirit gives my prayers power and boldness. And help me trust that your Spirit will speak up for me, that he will groan and plead on my behalf. Teach me to pray in the Spirit and with the Spirit and through the Spirit ... to pray because the Spirit is in my heart and on my mind.*

Praying "in the Spirit" would radically change the way we pray, our dependence on prayer, and what we pray for. It would allow us to pray with the confident knowledge that the Spirit is in us and provides us access to the Father (Eph 2:18). This kind of praying would remind us constantly that the Spirit is helping us pray, interceding for us, translating our groans into groans of his own that the Father understands (Rom 8:22-27). We could pray for the Spirit to strengthen us emotionally, in our inner being, with peace, joy, hope, confidence, and love (John 14:27; Eph 3:16; Ro 8:6; 14:17; 15:13; 1Th 1:6). We could pray for the Spirit to equip us for effective ministry and for carrying out the mission Jesus has given us to do (1 Cor 12). We could pray for the Spirit to deepen and mature us, making us more like Christ (Rom 8:29; 2 Cor 3:18; Col 3:10).

## 7. Discover Your Spiritual Gifts

Do you know what your gift is?

There are (at least) two lists of spiritual gifts found in Scripture: Romans 12:6-8 and 1 Corinthians 12:8-11. Read these lists and see if you find yourself there. You may have more than one of the gifts listed—good for you. But you have *at least* one. It's part of God's plan for you. It's part of God's plan for the church.

So what is your spiritual gift?

> *Father, please give me the wisdom to know what my true gift is and the courage to use it selflessly in the service of your kingdom. Forgive me when I have hidden your gift away and kept it from the Body. You, through your Spirit, have equipped me to make a difference for your people and in the world. Convict me, by your Spirit, of the need to use my gift for your glory.*

You may not be comfortable with the gifts Paul lists for Corinth: messages of wisdom and knowledge, faith, healing, miraculous powers, prophecy, discerning spirits, speaking in tongues, interpretation of tongues (1 Cor 12:8-11). Okay. Go to Romans and find your gift there: service, teaching, encouragement, generosity, leadership, and showing mercy (Rom 12:6-8). Which gift has God given you "for the common good"?

What is critical is not which list your gift appears on. What's critical is not even which particular gift you've been given. No. What's critical is that you have *identified* the gift God has entrusted to you and are *using* your gift for his glory.

According to Paul (see 1 Corinthians 12), the church you attend will never be the beautiful, functional, powerful body God wants it to be unless you play your part. A gift given "for the common good" becomes—unused—a disability in the body of Christ. The church limps and gasps and blanches when it is missing vital pieces and functions.

And, according to Paul, you will never be the integral, valuable, mature, considerate, cooperative disciple God wants you to be until you put your gift to the use it was intended. You'll be constantly insecure ("The church doesn't need *me*"—12:15) or constantly self-important ("The church doesn't need *you*"—12:21). What you *won't* be is a connected part of the body, living out God's purpose for your life in the context of his church.

Yet, as critical as this matter is, many of us have no clue about our giftedness, no understanding of the important part we play in the body of Christ, and no active involvement in the life and ministries of our churches. The Spirit has given us a gift—just the gift he wanted us to have, just the gift our church needs—and (as often as not) we've buried that gift in the ground.

Inviting the Spirit into your life, becoming a student of the Spirit, learning to see with new eyes, learning to talk in new ways, living and praying in the Spirit mean you no longer have the luxury of ignoring spiritual gifts. Your growth depends on finding your gift. The people around you depend on your finding it. The church you attend needs you to find it.

## 8. Discern the Spirit in Others

It really does take one to know one.

Who has God's Spirit in them? In whom has that Spirit grown large? Who demonstrates the Spirit's fruit in such a way that, clearly, he or she has walked "a long obedience in the same direction" with the Spirit? Who has experienced an authentic, transforming, character-building encounter with the Spirit that you can rely on?

Questions like these sound nebulous until you consider how much of our interaction with other Christians is built on assumptions about good motive, spiritual maturity and wisdom, common commitments, and shared values and priorities. Seeing the Spirit in others, knowing he is present and active in someone else's life, helps us develop trust and confidence in each other. Failing to see that Spirit in some, or seeing him only dimly, helps us identify people we can't—for now—put much spiritual weight on.

Discerning the Spirit in others does sound vague—even judgmental!—until you recognize how much our discipleship hinges on decisions we make about who we consider wise, whose advice and teaching we seek, who we give permission to shape our thinking, who we turn to at moments of crisis, who we choose as Christian leaders, mentors, and friends. Ever chosen poorly? Ever been deeply disappointed in, deeply wounded by, someone you looked up to spiritually?

We're going to base such relational decisions on *something*. Personality. Persuasiveness. Chemistry. Common history. Demeanor. Public actions. Stated beliefs. Financial success. The Bible suggests there may be another way to make such choices and exercise discretion about other people. It involves asking the Spirit to help you discern his presence in others. It involves looking at others with spiritual eyes rather than fleshly eyes, and making decisions based on spiritual discernment rather than more surface considerations.

> Dear friends, do not believe every spirit, but test the spirits to see whether they are from God, because many false prophets have gone out into the world. This is how you can recognize the Spirit of God: Every spirit that acknowledges that Jesus Christ has come in the flesh is from God, but every spirit that does not acknowledge Jesus is not from God. (1 John 4:1-3)

Such an interesting way for John to put this: "Test the spirits." Why not just give his readers a doctrinal check list and tell them to "test the positions."[1] Why not give them an ethical check list and tell them to "test the life"?[2] Instead, John says "Test the spirits"—as though more is involved with this discernment than particular beliefs or specific lifestyles. He's not so much interested in learning about positions or morality as he is in knowing whether someone has the Spirit of God or not.

In fact, the first Christians did this "testing" all the time. The Apostles, for instance, asked the Jerusalem church to "choose seven men from among you who are *known to be full of the Spirit* and wisdom" (Acts 6:3ff) to be given special responsibilities within the church family. And the church responded, not with questions about what in the world "full of the Spirit" meant, but with specific nominations. When the Apostles needed to send a representative to Antioch to check out news of the first Gentile church, they chose Barnabas—the right man for the job because "he was a good man, *full of the Holy Spirit* and faith" (Acts 11:24).

The early church did not give responsibilities or leadership roles to people in whom they could not see the Spirit at work. It's easy to see why. Only people "full of the Spirit" were equipped to understand the essential business of God's kingdom. Someone who lacked this Spirit would not be able to "accept the things that come from the Spirit of God, for they are foolishness to him, and he cannot understand them, because they are spiritually discerned" (1 Cor 2:14).

> *Father, give me Spirit eyes. Help me see the world, other people, and myself as you do. Teach me to recognize your Spirit in my brothers and sisters, to discern whether the Spirit is burning bright or dim in them. Give me compassion and patience with those who do not know your Spirit as well as I do. Give me humility and respect for those who know your Spirit better. Grant me the gift of discernment so I can know whom to lead and whom to follow.*

## 9. Think Trinitarian

Whenever I use the word "Trinity" in public, someone is sure to sit back, fold his arms, and inform me that "Trinity" is not a word found in Scripture.

(Sigh.)

I find it interesting that we are quick to use other words that don't occur in Scripture to talk about the concepts and practice of our faith: necessary inference, acapella music, pulpits and pews, for instance. But some people have a special aversion to the word "Trinity."

Of course, these people are right in saying "Trinity" is not found on the lips of Jesus or his Apostles. That doesn't mean, however, that the Bible doesn't "think Trinitarian." Indeed, in the pages of Scripture, Father/Son/Spirit are constantly linked. While this is not the place to document this statement (it has been done exhaustively by others), I do suggest that the idea of "Trinity" is foundational to Scripture, even if the word is never used. We cannot understand Jesus or the Spirit or (for that matter) the Father without resort to the notion that God is one-in-three.

So don't use the word "Trinity" if it makes you uncomfortable. But please don't throw out the biblical baby with the extra-biblical bath!

God is one. Father, Son, and Spirit are one. The Father is God. The Son is God. The Spirit is God. Jesus was God incarnate. The Spirit is God in us. One God in three persons. One God in three expressions. Blessed Trinity.

I realize, of course, that some find this concept incomprehensible. It is more than "mystery"; it is babble, nonsense. Others are simply impatient with the idea. It's not incomprehensible so much as inconsequential. Who cares? The whole discussion is theological hair-splitting. The whole debate is "much ado about nothing."

But at the heart of the trinitarian idea is a notion that goes to the heart of our faith. Jesus was not just a good and wise man, a man uniquely equipped to talk to us about God. Jesus was God himself, God in the flesh, God with us (Immanuel!). Jesus is not simply someone we admire; he is someone we *worship*—the "fullness of God in bodily form" (Col 2:9); the One who reveals God to the world because he *was* God (John 1:1, 18).

The list of people who have attempted to drive a wedge between the essence of God and the essence of Jesus is long and lamentable. Strip Jesus of his deity and you've just stripped Christianity of its central tenet. Demote Jesus to any status other than God and our whole structure of belief—revelation, salvation, sanctification—falls apart.

For our purposes, however, what's vital to notice is what this trinitarian idea says about the Holy Spirit. The Holy Spirit is not just an agent of God, a tool God used to enthuse the early disciples and inspire the New Testament writings. He isn't merely a good influence and a helpful presence. He is God himself, God in other form, God *in* us. The Spirit is not simply someone we admire (or, worse, some*thing* we admire); he is someone we *worship*—the fullness of God in indwelling form; the One who continues to reveal God to the world because he *is* God (John 16:12-15).

The list of people who have attempted to drive a wedge between the essence of God and the essence of the Spirit is also long and just as lamentable. Strip the Spirit of deity and you've just stripped Christianity of its central power. Demote the Spirit to any status other than God and ideas like indwelling, transformation, revelation, and eternal-life-here-and-now lose their meaning.

It is grappling with the idea of "Trinity" that helps us understand that the Spirit in you is Christ living in you—the presence of Christ, the teachings of Christ, the fullness of Christ, and the mind of Christ. The Spirit in you is God dwelling in you—bestowing the words of God, the power of God, the will of God, and the presence of God. The Spirit in you is eternal life: not heaven as yet, but what makes heaven "Heaven"— the presence of God, the life of God, a life *with* God.

> *Father, I know that everything that belongs to you has been given to your Son. And I know that everything Jesus had, he gave to the Holy Spirit. And now, I know, everything you have entrusted to the Spirit is being poured into me. I am too small to contain it all. I am weak and blind and so limited. Let your Spirit show me the fullness of your Son and the glory of yourself. I praise you and worship you and gratefully give my life to you. I pray this in the name of the Father, the Son, and the Holy Spirit.*

## 10. Spread the Word

Jesus changed the world with eleven men because he was able to convince them, not just to believe, but to witness. I'm thankful you have read this book. I hope it will make a difference in your life. But for this message about the Spirit to take root and grow, you must do more than nod assent and find personal benefit. You should testify.

It's good to "hear and believe." It's better to "hear, believe, and apply." Best of all, though, is to "hear, believe, apply, and tell."

> *Father, thank you for revealing yourself and your will and your Spirit to me. I'm eager for more. Give me the courage to share this good news with others. Give me the wisdom to share it well. And give me the compassion to love people whatever their response, however ready or not they may be. Prepare the hearts of those I love to hear my testimony to the indwelling Spirit. I trust you to open ears,*

*to determine the time, and to anoint my conversations. May my every effort be for your glory and the good of your people.*

"Telling" will help you understand the Spirit better yourself. "Telling" will encourage you to walk in the Spirit more fully, more deeply. But "telling" will also invite the people you love to a richer spiritual experience than they have known. If the ideas expressed in these pages have impacted you, please share them with others.

# THE SPIRIT AND THE AMERICAN RESTORATION MOVEMENT

I've left this discussion to the end of the book because an overview of notions of the Spirit within the Stone-Campbell heritage/ Churches of Christ would bewilder those who do not share this heritage and perplex many of us.

Our traditional take on the Holy Spirit is unique. At the heart of our movement is a deep, rationalistic streak that tends to make the subject of an indwelling Spirit—communing with us in ways that transcend the ordinary senses, mysteriously touching and transforming our characters—disturbing.

Chapter Sixteen traces the manner in which we "reasoned" our way out of any need for an encounter with or a theology of the Holy Spirit. We used three arguments to distance ourselves from a living Spirit.

Chapter Seventeen looks at some of the fears that drove us away from the Spirit and what those fears did to our reading of Scripture. Not only did we do bad exegesis in our flight from the Spirit, we were also required to live with a series of theological losses that worked against a vital faith.

The final chapter, Eighteen, is an unscientific postscript: a parable for your consideration.

Chapter Sixteen

# A Trickle of Spirit

The subject of the Holy Spirit is a difficult one—particularly for those of us who stand in the stream of the American Restoration Movement at this particular time. Admit it: our relationship with the Spirit has long been a troubled one.

It's not *just* that, in this multi-channeled stream that makes up the wider church's varied experience of the Spirit, our stream happens to be of the "minimalist" sort. If that explained our Spirit-impairment— our particular channel runs a little shallower than most—there might be no need for a serious discussion of the Spirit or for the writing of this book.

But it's more than that. Much more.

We've gone far past merely accepting that our Spirit-experience is of the "trickle" variety. Our movement has attempted to dam up even the dribble, re-channel it into Scripture, and reduce the Spirit to an influence that touches us only through the pages of inspired writings. We have tended to deny any need for an indwelling and living Spirit. We have relied solely on the Bible and the Pattern, and insisted to all who would listen that *that* should be sufficient. Some have even gone so far as to claim that a continuing role for the Holy Spirit today would be counterproductive; it muddies the clarity of a faith built on command, example, and necessary inference and opens the door to all sorts of subjective troubles.

We have moved dangerously close to the point of resisting the Spirit, grieving the Spirit, and quenching the Holy Spirit's fire: a position that

Scripture repeatedly—and sternly—warns us against (Matt 12:31; Acts 7:51; 1 Thess 5:19; Eph 4:30; Heb 10:29).

## Reasoning Ourselves Out of Spirit

What follows is an attempt to summarize the teachings characteristic of the Stone-Campbell Movement and, particularly, of Churches of Christ on the subject of the Holy Spirit. Such a summary poses numerous difficulties, among them the problem of drawing together a coherent picture from such an autonomous and idiosyncratic collection of people. I don't mean to imply that everyone everywhere in this heritage learned the same things (regarding the positions I'm about to describe) in exactly the same way. I plead guilty to a certain amount of generalization and oversimplification.

What I am reaching for, however, is a truth to be found in the big picture. I thought about peppering this analysis with footnotes and references and quotations—only to realize that if my description of the whole does not resonate with your own experience of what we've taught on this subject, footnotes won't help. Instead, I'm going to put on the table what I believe to be characteristic of our teaching on the Holy Spirit. And I'm going to ask you to remember the sermons you've heard and the classes you've attended, to see whether—in the main—my summary captures the positions we have taken.

Our understanding of the Holy Spirit begins where you would expect a biblicist people to start: with a strong affirmation that the witness of the New Testament to the person and work of the Holy Spirit in the lives of the first Christians is accurate. We accept everything the Bible says about the Spirit and believers as a reliable depiction of what our original brothers and sisters experienced. The Spirit was alive and present in those first disciples. The Spirit empowered them to heal and prophesy and speak in tongues (though we still argue over whether those "tongues" involved foreign languages or a heavenly jargon). The Spirit was actively and directly engaged in a transformative work in their lives that conferred love, wisdom, knowledge, and unity. We believe that—by the power of the Spirit—Peter healed a lame man (Acts 3:1-10), Paul cast out demons (Acts 16:16-18), the Corinthians received revelations (1 Cor 2:10), and the Thessalonians were sanctified (2 Thess 2:13).

What we do *not* believe is that this Spirit—this active, indwelling, gift-giving, life-transforming Spirit—is available to believers today. That sort of Spirit may have been necessary for the birthing of Christianity, when doctrine was being revealed and the church established and disciples moved miraculously from spiritual infants to giants of the faith. But conditions have changed. We no longer have the benefit of miraculous gifts (so we've been taught) because we no longer need what those gifts conveyed. The church is at a different stage of her development. The gifts are gone and with them (and here's the rub) the Gift-Giver—the active, present, indwelling Spirit working directly on the hearts and minds of believers.

Thus we drew a line in time and created two distinct experiences of the Spirit in the church: a full, rich, miraculous, transforming experience of the Spirit for the first generation of Christians; and something radically different for generations that followed.

To chisel that line in stone, we advanced three arguments.

The first made a careful distinction between the "ordinary" gift of the Spirit (granted in water baptism—Acts 2:38) and the "extraordinary" gifts of the Spirit (granted in Spirit baptism—Acts 2:1-4). The Spirit received in water baptism was (we taught) the indwelling Spirit enjoyed by the first believers. His power and presence were limited in scope, however. He could bestow peace and wisdom and words on disciples, but this measure of the Spirit did not include the miraculous, supernatural powers of the Spirit's full gifts. The full gifts required a second touch, granted directly by God or through the agency of the Apostles. This second touch (frequently referred to in Scripture as "baptism of the Spirit" or by code phrases such as the Spirit being "poured out" or "coming on" the disciples or the disciples being "filled with" the Spirit—Acts 2:4, 17, 18, 33; 4:8; 9:17; 10:44-45; 19:6; Eph 5:18) included all the miraculous gifts and powers evidenced in the first-century church.

The second line of argument linked the "full measure" of the Spirit to the Apostles. The reason the earliest church experienced the Spirit in such a remarkable way was because the Apostles were present. The Twelve had the Spirit in full measure because Jesus had breathed on them and given them the Spirit (John 20:21-23). They were not the only ones to receive this direct gifting of the full measure of the Spirit (e.g.,

Cornelius and his household—Acts 11:15-17). But the Apostles' gifting was unique in one important respect: not only did they experience the Spirit in full, they could—through the laying on of hands—grant this experience of the Spirit to others (Acts 8:14-17; 19:1-7).

We took Acts 8:14-17 as one of our proof texts:

> When the apostles in Jerusalem heard that Samaria had accepted the word of God, they sent Peter and John to them. When they arrived, they prayed for them that they might receive the Holy Spirit, because the Holy Spirit had not yet come upon any of them; they had simply been baptized into the name of the Lord Jesus. Then Peter and John placed their hands on them, and they received the Holy Spirit.

From this passage we drew several key ideas. One must distinguish between the Spirit received in baptism and the Spirit "coming upon" believers because these disciples (who had been baptized) still needed to "receive the Holy Spirit." Had they *not* received the gift of the Holy Spirit when they were baptized? Of course they had. That was part of the promise made of water baptism—forgiveness of sins *and* the gift of the Spirit (Acts 2:38). But now Peter and John wanted something *more* for the Samaritan disciples, an experience of the Spirit transcending anything conveyed by baptism.[1] Which led us to a second insight: For these believers to experience *more*, they needed apostolic hands laid on them. Peter and John must have been sent for this very purpose. Apostles—by prayer and touch—could pass on the full gift of the Spirit to others.

There is much to be said for this reasoning. There does seem to be biblical warrant for this "second touch" and for the Apostles having the ability to provide it. But at this juncture, we took another and critical step. We taught that *only* the hands of the Apostles could convey the full measure of the Spirit and his gifts. No one else (in our reading)—even those who themselves experienced the Spirit's miraculous working—could pass on this gifting to others. Just the Apostles. Once the Twelve died off, God no longer had any agency for imparting the miraculous gifts of the Spirit to his church. This explained why, in our view, the gifts eventually ceased.[2]

Never mind that the New Testament bears witness to the ability of others besides the Apostles to lay on hands and convey this fuller measure of the Spirit. Ananias did it with Saul (Acts 9:17).[3] Elders of the church did it with Timothy (1 Tim 4:14).[4] Timothy himself appears to have this ability to pass on gifts to his churches (1 Tim 5:22).[5] If we could just ignore these inconvenient passages, however, we could justify a cessationist view of the miraculous spiritual gifts: they stopped when the Apostles were no longer around to pass them on to God's people.

Argument #1 made a distinction between the "ordinary" Spirit enjoyed by believers through water baptism and the "extra-ordinary" Spirit enjoyed by the few (especially the Apostles). Argument #2 linked the "extra-ordinary" measure of the Spirit to the hands of the Apostles and those hands alone. No Apostles, no laying on of apostolic hands, and no passing on the miraculous gifts.

The third line of argument concerned the role of Scripture in the history of the church and the lives of individual believers. When the Apostles died, the last link to a sustainable and miraculous experience of the Spirit also died—apostolic "hands" were gone. But thankfully, Christians no longer needed this Spirit-experience because, by the time the Apostles exited, believers possessed the New Testament.

The New Testament became for us (and—in this view—for all believers living after the Apostolic Age) what the miraculous gifts had been in the first century. Did signs and wonders prompt faith then? The stories of Jesus and the Apostles' preaching (as recorded in the Bible) did so now. Did the Spirit remind disciples of "everything I have said to you?" The New Testament does that for us. Did the Spirit teach and mature and reveal God to the early church? The Bible functions to accomplish that today.

We appealed to 1 Corinthians 13:8-12 to demonstrate the inadequacy of the Spirit's gifts and the sufficiency of the New Testament canon.

> Love never fails. But where there are prophecies, they will cease; where there are tongues, they will be stilled; where there is knowledge, it will pass away. For we know in part and we prophesy in part, but when perfection comes, the imperfect disappears. When I was a child, I talked like a child, I thought like a child, I reasoned like a child. When I became a man, I put

childish ways behind me. Now we see but a poor reflection as in a mirror; then we shall see face to face. Now I know in part; then I shall know fully, even as I am fully known.

We used this passage to teach that the miraculous work of the Spirit belonged to another time, a "childish time," a time of immaturity and special measures. Now, however, the "perfect" has come and the imperfect can disappear, go away, cease.

And what is the "perfect"? The "perfect" must be the full and complete revelation of God and his will contained in the canonical books of the New Testament. With the closing "Amen" of Revelation, with the gathering of the Apostles' writings into a single collection, with the distribution of that collection for the church of the second century, the Spirit managed to exchange the fading miraculous gifts for that "living, active word" that perfectly fit our maturing needs. Thankfully and at last we were able to "put childish ways behind" us, to think like adults, and to "know fully even as [we were] fully known."

Out with the spiritual gifts, in with James and Titus and Acts.

It didn't matter that the only thing holding up this conclusion was weak exegesis. It didn't matter that Paul wasn't talking about inspired Scripture anywhere in the context of these verses or that the word "perfect" is almost always used to describe an attribute of *persons*: maturity, completion, wisdom.[6] It didn't matter that the most likely meaning of this passage is that, when we grow up enough to love each other (as Paul describes in the first half of 1 Corinthians 13), we will no longer need miracles to demonstrate that God is alive in us (which is the actual point of the second half of 1 Corinthians 13). Our selfless and miraculous love (that which is mature and "the more perfect way") will provide all the proof required that God is present in us and his Spirit is active. Who needs tongues when you've got perfect love?

We brushed right past these cautionary quibbles to put miraculous spiritual gifts out of our misery. The Apostles were gone. The New Testament had come. The time for healings and prophecies was over.

Frankly, if we had stopped there, I wouldn't have much heartburn. I feel no pressing need to resurrect miraculous gifts in the church today. My interest in the Spirit has little to do with signs and wonders. But that's not where we left it. Once again, we went a step further. It wasn't enough for us to use Scripture to put an end to the supernatural gifts of the Spirit. We used Scripture to put an end to a Spirit active in the world. Having Scripture, we actually believed (and taught) that we had no need of an indwelling Spirit. The Spirit works through the words of Scripture and only through the words of Scripture. The Spirit no longer acts directly on our hearts and minds. There is a middle-man now, operating between the Spirit and believers, who has leather covers and gilded pages.

In the Spirit's gift of Scripture we saw something comparable to Jesus' gift of the Spirit—a final, parting blessing bestowed before leaving the world and returning to the Father. A gift left behind in place of himself. Jesus did this with the Spirit. The Spirit did this with Scripture. Now, neither Jesus nor the Spirit remain with us. Each has offered (instead) a substitute for actual presence so that, in the end, we are left with a book.

That book (according to the accepted thinking) provided for modern disciples just as well as the Spirit provided for the first disciples. Did the Spirit indwell the first Christians? Now the words of the New Testament dwell in us. Did the Spirit teach "all things" to Christians back then? The Bible teaches us everything we need to know now. Did the Spirit convict and transform first-century believers? The writings of Paul and Peter and John do the convicting and transforming for us today.

Thus, we convinced ourselves that we didn't really need the Spirit; all we needed was the Word. So "high" was our view of Scripture that we saw it as an adequate and even preferable substitute for a living and active Spirit. Read the Bible. In the pages of Scripture Christians find all the guidance and help they need. To use Alexander Campbell's famous dictum: the more Bible in us, the more Spirit; the less Bible, the less Spirit. "Spirit" became for many members of our heritage little more than a synonym for reading, interpreting, and internalizing the written Word. If the death of the apostles resulted in a cessation of miraculous works, the birth of the New Testament made an indwelling Spirit moot. Baptism—which originally conveyed both forgiveness and indwelling— was reduced to an obedience which brought pardon but not *presence*. Membership in the one true church, belief in our central tenets, became the "seal and guarantee" of our status before God, not some nebulous indwelling Spirit.

The idea that there was more to the Spirit's role than could be mediated through a book has never found much traction in our movement. The notion of a living, active Spirit today—a person and presence who indwells believers—has not been a theological principle of great importance. In fact, this kind of Spirit—distinct from the Word, independent and sovereign, acting upon the church and not under the control of the church—was felt to be a dangerous thing.

Once upon a time, in the days of the Apostles, we allowed that the Spirit had a far more vital role to play in the church and in the lives of believers. But not in our day. Not in us.

This "word only" position characterized our movement for decades.[7] It hardened from "position" to "unquestionable orthodoxy" during the first half of the twentieth century. It was the standard line preached from our pulpits (if not always accepted in our pews). Dissenting voices and practices have emerged over the years, but that dissent has been muted by the high cost of speaking out. Preaching careers have been ruined by the mere suggestion that the Holy Spirit might indwell and empower the life of a believer. Churches have split over the question. Elders have been asked to resign. People have been told to leave.

## Learning to Live without the Spirit

To review: We believe everything the Bible says about the church and the Spirit *back then*. What we don't believe is that the Spirit we meet in the pages of the New Testament is a Spirit we experience today. We've drawn a firm line between the first-century church and every iteration of it since, creating two distinct experiences of the Spirit in the church— a full, miraculous, indwelling, transforming experience of the Spirit for the first generation of Christians; and something radically different (and radically reduced) for generations that followed.

Indeed, we've actually argued that we are better off *without* a living Spirit, that a continuing role for an active Spirit is counterproductive and undesirable. To take seriously a Spirit who guides and teaches and comforts and convicts, who operates on us directly and in some manner "beyond the sacred page," opens the church to a messy and individualized subjectivism. If we let *that* genie out of the bottle, surely charismatic chaos is just around the corner!

Instead, we've argued for a more reasonable approach. The Spirit is subjective; better an objective measure of beliefs and practices like the Bible. The Spirit is experiential (utilizing urges and discernment and spiritual hungers); better a rational, tangible, empirical foundation for our lives like the commands, examples, and necessary inferences of our Bibles. The Spirit is private, individualized; better a public standard, one less prone to distortion and misunderstanding—like the Bible. The Spirit is unpredictable and uncontrollable; better a clearer and orderly pattern for our lives like that contained in the Bible.

This, in my view, is how we sidestepped the subject of the Holy Spirit and constructed a church in which the Spirit has little place. In essence, our movement has said, "We can get along without you, Holy Spirit. Thanks for what you have done in the past. We appreciate the gift of Scripture. But we and our New Testaments and our restored churches will take it from here."

I can no longer say that. In fact, I believe that saying that is essentially an abandonment of historical Christian faith and a guarantee of a powerless future.

## Chapter Seventeen

# HOW DID WE GET HERE?

How did we ever come to such a pass?

Even a casual review of biblical texts must convince us our view of the Spirit has less to do with careful exposition than with other factors. It is difficult to see how any objective look at the texts that touch on the Spirit in the New Testament could have resulted in a theology and practice so devoid of a living Spirit today. Our position on the Spirit has required textual bending and twisting to an exegetical breaking point. Whole sections of the Bible have been consigned to a dusty past, describing an active Spirit *back then* who has little relevance or application to Christian living today. We have scrubbed our vocabulary clean of the very terms (transformation, spiritual power, sanctification by the Spirit, life in the Spirit, etc.) that should constitute our most precious spiritual bequest, and advocated notions (such as obedience, self-control, doctrinal correctness, discipline) that—in a vacuum of Spirit—are anemic at best and offer little beyond moral bootstrapping.

There is more going on with our attitudes about the Spirit than simply what the Bible has to say on the matter. But for a movement that has prided itself on its strict biblicism, the "more going on" is particularly painful to face, involving (as it does) reasons that have more to do with sociology, philosophy, and history-of-religion than with careful examination of biblical texts.

## An Off-the-Leash Spirit

The "more" begins with an embarrassment at our founding. Born from an emotional womb, revivalistic in our first breaths, bawling with all the hungers of the Second Great Awakening, the children of the American Restoration Movement tottered briefly on the brink of a charismatic cliff. The Cane Ridge Revival (as just one example) was marked by ecstatic seizures, jerking dances, and incoherent barking. Barton W. Stone and his disciples—always open to and, indeed, insistent on a personal and indwelling Spirit—were allowing the nascent alliance to move in dangerously subjective directions. How could a movement coalesce around the standard of God's Word and the practices of the early church, how could leadership arise to shape and mold and guide that movement, when any and every adherent could claim an intimate communion with and direct guidance by the Holy Spirit of God?

Into the breach stepped Alexander Campbell. Disturbed by what he heard and saw in the revivalism of his day, he determined to provide his followers with a viable alternative—rigorous rationalism. The key to life with God, the key to a unified and orderly restoration, was the strict application of logic and reason to the words of Scripture and the exacting implementation of those words to church and life. Only a commitment to a *reasonable* faith could unite us around a single standard (the Bible) and a shared understanding of what that Bible said. There was no room in Campbell's theology for mysterious urges, inner influences, and supernatural transforming powers. Such things threatened the preeminent role of Scripture in the church. They threatened the rational base which Campbell thought was necessary.

Campbell reached out and pulled us back from the brink. In doing so, he taught us to repent of our subjective leanings, distrust any belief nursed on feelings, embrace the purer path of propositions and precedents, and wed ourselves to a form of religion that, if uninspired,[1] was at least logical.

This deep suspicion of emotionalism and an off-the-leash Spirit was later reinforced for Campbell's followers by acquaintance with the Pentecostal/Charismatic movement in the early twentieth century. Baptism of the Holy Spirit. The "second blessing." Tongues as a sign and proof of salvation. Modern day prophecy and revelation. Healings.

Everything we saw in our Pentecostal neighbors smacked of the uncontrolled, ripe-for-abuse, sensational, spiritual free-for-all we knew would break out if Spirit were ever unchained from Word. We took one look at them and were not only deeply alarmed—we were repulsed. If *that* was what "Spirit-led" meant, we determined to run as quickly as possible in the opposite direction.

## A Textual Tension

Given these "more" factors (our commitment to a rational faith and the perceived lack thereof in others), we were then forced to face a troubling tension at the very foundation of our restoration efforts. The goal of our movement was to "restore" the New Testament church. We believed the key to pleasing God and changing the world and ushering in the millennium was to recreate first-century Christianity with all its pristine beauty in our own time. So we focused on the practices, habits, worship, governance, and teachings of the church we found in the pages of the New Testament.

But, frankly, the early church *itself* had an "irrational" component that reminded us uncomfortably of our Pentecostal neighbors. It's hard to imagine the church of Acts without the sovereign and active Spirit blowing around in mysterious and unpredictable ways. It's difficult to think about the church in Jerusalem or Corinth without the Spirit speaking and healing and gifting and (even) striking people dead. Could we restore the first-century *church* without restoring the first-century *Spirit?*

This tension and the questions it raised became especially evident when we turned in our Bibles to the writings of Luke and Paul. We loved these inspired writers, embracing them as our true mentors in the faith. We took their writings as our primary Scriptural authority. Acts and Paul's epistles became our canon-within-a-canon. Luke and Paul set the foundations and laid the parameters for our understanding of church, baptism, the Lord's Supper, polity, worship, lifestyle, and witness.

We depended on their writings to show us the way. The Gospels were good, but sadly lacking in the pragmatics of ecclesiastical conduct. John's Revelation? Well .... But Acts! Paul's letters! Now there were ideas you could wrap your *Millennial Harbinger* around!

These two writers' depiction of the first-century church seemed so elegant to us, so perspicuous. A single pattern. A clear description of acceptable worship. An unambiguous guide to organization and collective action.

Until it came to their teaching about the Holy Spirit! Suddenly, things weren't simple at all. Anointings of fire. Prophecy. Tongues and wonders. The Spirit pouring out and falling on and filling up. Visions. Healings. Paul set apart by the Spirit (Acts 13:2), prevented by the Spirit (Acts 16:7), warned by the Spirit (Acts 20:23), compelled by the Spirit (Acts 20:22). Churches saved by the Spirit (Titus 3:5), led by the Spirit (Rom 8:14), empowered by the Spirit (Rom 15:13), taught by the Spirit (1 Cor 2:13), indwelt by the Spirit (1 Cor 6:19), gifted by the Spirit (1 Cor 12:11), united by the Spirit (Eph 4:3), praying in the Spirit (Eph 6:18), worshiping by the Spirit (Phil 3:3), enjoying the fruit of the Spirit (Gal 5:22).

The Spirit described by Luke and Paul posed a significant challenge to our Lockean faith. He disrupted orderly assemblies (with tongues, prophecies, and other inconvenient interruptions—1Cor 14). He challenged our understandings of the nature of worship. (Does "worship" consist of acts we perform or spiritual and emotional responses to God that only the Spirit can prompt? See Php Phil 3:3 and John 4:24.) There was a vocabulary we were not comfortable with—groaning and grieving, filling up and pouring out, anointing, discerning, prophecy and tongues, power from on high. There was the Spirit disciplining members and granting gifts and giving fruit—all in sovereign and sometime unpredictable ways.

All of this made us nervous. How could we restore the New Testament church when it contained such a large dose of this unpredictable Spirit? Was it even possible to re-create New Testament Christianity without becoming a little Pentecostal ourselves?

Somewhere beneath the layers of logic and syllogism, questions like these lurked, monsters threatening to rise up and swallow us whole. Wasn't there something illegitimate about restoring first-century ecclesiology without restoring first-century pneumatology? Wasn't something missing in our passion for biblical forms divorced from interest in the source of spiritual power? Wasn't there a fundamental fracture in a logic that clarified church names or organizational structures but spoke hardly at all to the essential spiritual dynamic that accounted for early Christians turning the world upside down?

## A Subject Too Hot to Handle

Addressing such questions was, in the end, more frightening to us than the thought of living without the Spirit. To take seriously the possibility that the Spirit might still be at work (in believers, the church, and the world) meant stepping onto a slippery slope. It meant there was more going on between us and God than could be squeezed out of the King James Bible. It meant Scripture knowledge and correct hermeneutic were not enough. It meant God had other ways and means available for pursuing his purposes than a leather-bound book and our careful attention to textual details.

And if *that* were so, where might it lead us?

It would lead, we were told, to charismatic chaos. Slide down the slope of the Spirit and we would wind up handling snakes and lying in aisles. We'd have to deal with tongues-speaking and utterances claiming to be prophetic. We'd be faced with modern revelations that contradicted or "added to" Scripture. Our people would become more interested in wonders than in Word. Open the Spirit box, we were warned, and every ill imaginable would be unleashed in our churches.

These dire consequences were sufficient to frighten most of us away from the subject entirely. Better no Spirit than *that* Spirit. Better a Spirit confined to a book than a Spirit running wild in the church.

But veering away from one ditch, we drove hard and fast into another. And the result has been spiritual devastation. No, we're not having church wars over how to interpret tongues or discern prophecies. No, we're not arguing over healing gifts or what constitutes a "message of wisdom." But the deal we made for avoiding such controversies is a Faustian bargain, a Pyrrhic victory.

For our take on the Spirit did not simply settle the troublesome issue of modern miracles; it effectively amputated from our faith and practice the whole sphere of the mystical. By insisting that it was only through the Bible that we experienced the Spirit's influence, by eschewing any communion with the Spirit that did not come by means of the five senses and through the interpretive medium of the mind, we exchanged the supernaturalism of the first-century church for a form of empiricism more attuned to our Enlightenment era. We explained the work of God—in Christians, the church, and the world—in rational, non-mystical terms. And we cut ourselves off from some of the most important teachings and encouraging promises that God has made to those who love him.

## Skewed Reading

In order to support our single-minded resort to rationality, our distrust of the subjective, and our discomfort with the miraculous and the mysterious, we had to learn to read Scripture in a particular way. We—who claimed to read the Bible without any lenses, who taught that the plain meaning of Scripture could be plainly understood by those who came to Scripture without agenda or bias—exempted ourselves from this general rule when it came to the Holy Spirit. The New Testament witness had to be "corrected" on this subject. We needed a remedial overlay whenever the Bible talked about the Spirit.

The first of these lenses (as we've noted in Chapter 16) involved an *historical* overlay that permitted us to filter out any reference to the miraculous. Because miracles ceased after the Apostolic Age (an assumption we imported into our reading of Scripture), any reference to the miraculous must have only historical significance. It could not apply to later believers.

The second lens we brought to the reading of Scripture was a *philosophical* overlay that filtered out any suggestion that the non-rational and mysterious played a substantive role in modern faith. Nursed on Lockean epistemology as true children of Enlightenment thinking, our forefathers brought to faith a significant bias against things which could not be quantified, measured, and strictly defined. According to them, we gain knowledge through the five senses and in no other way. Communication is possible only through words, not through feelings or urges or nebulous promptings. God works on our lives using natural and rational means: he reveals his will to us (through the Bible); we read his Word; we obey his Word; we experience certain consequences that reinforce our confidence in the truth of his Word; our habits and attitudes and emotions are changed slowly, incrementally, and through natural means as a result.

The suggestion that the Spirit might work in other ways simply did not fit into our philosophical framework. Which posed a problem since the Bible gave ample testimony of the Spirit doing just that! Scripture everywhere testified to an indwelling Spirit, actively and directly engaged in the lives of disciples, using ways and means that were mysterious and defied explanation.

The third lens we brought to the reading of Scripture was an *experiential* overlay that used our current experience of God to filter out any possibility of an alternative experience of God. If *we* heard no inner voice, saw no visions, felt no urges or convictions, experienced no supernatural encouragement or wisdom or transformative power, then such things must not exist for Christians today. Our experience of God became the rule by which authentic Christian experience would be measured.

Pragmatically (and oh so ironically), this meant that our present spiritual experience was permitted to define what Scripture meant rather than allowing Scripture to define our spiritual experience. Did Scripture promise the Spirit would indwell us? We had no evidence of such a presence, alive and bubbling within us, so the promise could only refer to the words of Scripture, the sword of the Spirit, dwelling in us. Did Scripture promise encouragement, control, and leading from this Spirit? We heard no voice, felt no guiding hand or disciplining presence, so the promise could refer only to the guiding and encouraging words of Scripture. Was the promise made that the Spirit would testify to the world about Jesus, convict the world of its sin, and draw lost people back to God? We didn't see the Spirit still doing that, so we concluded the promise must now be fulfilled only through proclaiming the Bible. These promises, to the degree they were meant for us, could only be fulfilled through the words of Scripture.

The alternative, of course, was to use the plain language of Scripture to measure our experience of God. If an indwelling Spirit was promised, we could have launched ourselves on a determined campaign, an impassioned quest, to claim that indwelling. If the Spirit's encouragement, control, and leading were proffered, we could have reached for fresh ways to invite his powerful presence into our lives. If Jesus insisted the Spirit would continue to be active in the world, pursuing God's purposes in ways that would remain largely mysterious and inexplicable to us, we could have developed eyes that permitted us to see evidence of the Spirit at work in the world.

The historical lens gave us a way to read the Bible's promises of supernatural power without flinching or embarrassment. The philosophical lens demanded that we explain away any Bible teaching that bordered on the subjective or mysterious. The experiential lens gave us a powerful tool for measuring the Bible by ourselves rather than ourselves by the Bible. Armed with these three lenses, we managed to read the Spirit out of the Bible.

## Theological Losses

In this odd way (and largely, I think, unintentionally), we evolved into a sub-species of Deist.[2] God wound up the church—having gifted it with his Son and the Cross—but then left it to find its own way, using its own reasoning, and limited to its own power. Jesus ascended to his Father—after gifting his disciples with his teachings and example—but left nothing else behind for his followers except a temporary experience of the Spirit to jump-start the church. The Spirit lived in the earliest disciples—miraculously, mysteriously—but then withdrew from any direct contact with believers after gifting them with the pattern for life and faith exemplified in the first-century church and the witness of the New Testament.

What, then, is left for followers of Jesus today? We have the teachings of Jesus and his Apostles. We have the example of the early church. We have Scripture. What we do *not* have is a God who intervenes in the world to accomplish his purposes by any means other than the Bible and believers. What we do *not* have is the presence of Jesus—actual, tangible—accompanying us on our journey and assisting us in our mission. What we do *not* have is an indwelling Spirit, moving mysteriously in the church and in disciples, working directly on our hearts and minds.

These conclusions about the Spirit have led to a series of profound theological losses. It is not simply that we have forgotten how to talk about the Holy Spirit. There are implications of our Spirit-less worldview that go far beyond our peculiar positions on the Spirit himself.

For example, our deafness to the Spirit has infected our views on *transformation*—we are changed not by a surgical Spirit but by learning, obedience, and self-improvement. It has misshaped our understanding of *sanctification*—not a progressive work of a powerful Spirit but the result of discipline and moral fine-tuning. It has undermined our *security* as believers—rather than being "sealed" with the Spirit, we are left dangling in the uncertainties of our fitful obedience and incomplete understanding. It has caused us to question the efficacy of *prayer*—if God works only through Scripture, and never through the miraculous or the mysterious, why ask him to intervene in our lives?

This diminishing of the Spirit has impacted our experience of church. People who do not appreciate that they have been "baptized by one Spirit into one body" and were "all given the one Spirit to drink" (1 Cor 12:13) must necessarily have a reduced view of what membership and unity really mean. Harmony in the church gets founded on shared beliefs and practices, not in the ongoing work of the Spirit (yet see Eph 4:3-6). (In this way, dissension and division have become unpleasant by-products of the quest for faithfulness, not offenses against God's Spirit.) Worship is reduced to proper practice rather than a transcendent experience fueled by a living Spirit. The notion that the church *incarnates* God makes sense only if the Spirit is living in the church;[3] without a sense of the Spirit indwelling the church, the notion of incarnation becomes foolishness at best and blasphemy at worst, resulting in a greatly depreciated view of the body of Christ.[4] Leadership devolves to good character and judgment (and successful business practices) rather than the calling of God and the gifting of God's Spirit.[5]

Most of all, our conclusions on the Spirit have led to an effective loss of some of the most powerful passages in Scripture. Because we are no longer gifted by the Spirit, Paul's teachings in 1 Corinthians 12 (with its majestic themes of gifts for "the common good" and the unity of the body and the need for mutual respect and deference) are muted. Romans 8 (which trumpets the Spirit's help and leading and intercession; life in the Spirit; a mind controlled by the Spirit) is either overlooked entirely, demoted to an affirmation of negatives ("Don't be controlled by the sinful nature"; "Don't give up hope"), or reread with "Scripture" replacing every reference to "the Spirit." 2 Corinthians 3 celebrates the work of the Spirit in writing on human hearts, making ministers competent, and granting life, freedom, transformation, and glory—when was the last time you heard a sermon on this great chapter? It's hard to teach from Galatians 5 without considering the Spirit's equipping, leading, and fruit; so we teach around the Spirit's active work and demote the fruit of the Spirit to a list of characteristics that conscientious Christians should work on. John's admonitions (in 1 John 4) about testing the spirits and recognizing God's Spirit and being assured by the presence of the Spirit; his confidence that "the one who is in you is greater than the one who is in the world"; his conviction that the Spirit empowers our confession of Christ and our love of one another—these are themes that for a long time were rarely sounded.

Yet it is precisely at these points of loss that we feel the greatest yearning. We are thankful for God's Son and God's Word and the example of the first church. But increasingly we feel the need for a God who actively intervenes in our world and in our lives. We are hungry to experience the presence of Jesus in tangible, comforting ways. The mysterious, even the miraculous, does not frighten us as it once did. We *want* dramatic transformation and radical sanctification and lasting security. We crave communion with God in prayer, a conversation that lets us speak to and hear from our Father. We are eager for a recovery of "church" that allows the Spirit to unify, direct, and empower our feeble communities. And we are weary of the "gaps" that have developed in our reading of Scripture—the loss of all those teachings that appear in too close proximity to the Spirit and, thus, have been ruled out of bounds.

## Conclusion

There is a Spirit for the rest of us.

We aren't stuck with an absence of Spirit. Neither are we forced to become Pentecostals. We can pursue a Spirit who is authorized by Scripture, promised by Jesus, experienced by the earliest disciples, and fitted to the needs of disciples in every place and every time. We can pursue a Spirit whose prime work is to walk with us and equip us and transform us into the image of Christ. We can pursue the *Paraclete*.

The result of that pursuit will be a relationship with the Spirit in the lives of individuals and the culture of the church. The proof of that relationship will be maturing, Christ-like disciples and loving, unified communities. The measure of that maturity will be a renewed openness to the message of Scripture, to the work and priorities of the Kingdom, and to the power available through God's Spirit for God's people.

This "Spirit for the rest of us" will allow us to love God with heart and soul, as well as mind and strength. He will correct our overreliance on reason by making room for mystery and a work of God that transcends natural processes. He will grant visions—perhaps not the type that foresees the future, but surely the type that recognizes the Spirit alive and well in our lives and churches and world. He will help us recover an awareness of, an appreciation of, the centrality of his work in conversion, sanctification, and transformation; in our congregations and leaders; in navigating our way through changing circumstances and challenging situations. He will teach us the difference between theological mountains and molehills and empower us to pursue matters that matter.

When at last we meet this Spirit, his name will be *Paraclete* and his face will remind us of Jesus and his character will reflect the glory of God. He will not be a stranger to us. He will not settle for the sensational when his God-given business is to raise up the image of Christ in us.

When at last we meet this Spirit, he will change our lives. He will change our churches. And he will change our world.

## Chapter Eighteen

# A Parable

You and I, and our fathers and forefathers before us, have been hard at work constructing our religious house.

It is a magnificent thing, straight-lined and right-angled. It has all the necessary rooms any self-respecting religious house should include: a living room (for fellowship) and a library (for study); a large, public space (for assemblies) and closets (for prayer and meditation); rooms where doors can be closed (so elders can meet) and rooms where the lights can be dimmed (the Youth area). And it's a house made to last: true to the Architect's pattern; built on firm foundations.

Though still in need of some fit and finish, and being old enough now to require a bit of repair, our home is essentially completed. Some time ago, we determined to move in.

It wasn't long, however, before some of us began to suspect our house was missing something. The roof worked, the locks worked, the plumbing worked. We had all the furnishings of faith arranged in just the right way. Still, our house got cold in winter and hot in summer. It was dark inside at night. The TV wouldn't work. Food kept spoiling in the refrigerator.

The possibility began to dawn that we had constructed a religious house with every amenity except power. All the rooms we needed but no energy to heat and cool them. Every appliance of faith but not the essential dynamic that makes faith bubble and boil. Floor lamps and wall sconces and chandeliers in every room but never enough light.

In spite of all that, we did our best to make our house a home. We fanned ourselves in summer and sang against winter's frost. We ate by cooking over the open flame of our Bibles and our preachers' fiery rhetoric. We lit candles from room to room rather than curse the darkness.

The longer we lived in that fine house, however, the more we suffered the consequences. It got lonely in there, no matter how many people crowded inside. Not that we didn't have good friends or enjoy fine fellowship. But we missed the Master of the house. He'd gone away. He'd been gone a long time. We wondered what was taking him so long. To tell the truth, we felt abandoned.

In his absence, we were forced to face our own inadequacy. There were things that needed doing in the house and on the grounds and in the neighborhood—important things. "*He* would know what to do," we kept telling ourselves. But *we* didn't know. The burden of maintaining that house hung on us like an albatross, unwanted but unavoidable. We didn't have the tools. We didn't have the skills. We felt unworthy, ineffective, incompetent. It was almost enough to make us bury our talents in the ground. Some of us did.

And at night, when it was dark and cold, the fear crept in. We could hear the world howling outside our walls. We knew what the world could do. And so we huddled close together, bolting the door and shushing each other and never going outside. It was dangerous out there. Safer in here. And safest of all not to call attention to ourselves with risky attempts at timid testimony and weak witness.

The world wouldn't listen anyway. Not to us. It had its own power-grid, its own priorities, its own pursuits. What we preached about truth or crosses or sin didn't interest people outside our house. There once was a time when—like frantic Dutch boys, our finger in every dike—we tried to hold back the flood. We ventured into the world with the sense that there might be other fingers in the dike besides our own: divine fingers, cloud-of-witnesses fingers. But that sense passed and with it passed the conviction that we could still make a difference. We grew frustrated. We felt insignificant. Our every interaction with Outsiders became more strident, less graceful. Hard-hearted world! Sin-deaf world!

Maybe it was the never going outside. Perhaps it was the lack of muscle-flexing that real interaction with the world would have required. But in time, stuck in our house, we grew flabby. We stopped growing. No one new added to the family. No one old became new again. We learned it was easier to put up with each other's quirks and immaturities than expect anyone to change. The picture of the Master, hung in our hallway, became obscured with the dust of passing years. No one looked at him much anymore. No one looked *like* him much, truth be told.

## The House Down the Road

The fact that we built such a fine house with no power is all the more ironic because we patterned our plans so closely after a particular house down the road. It sat on our street some twenty blocks away (its address was 33; ours 2009). We discovered that house, fell in love with it, more than two hundred years ago. Elegant, clean, neat—it seemed to us some divine hand must have designed and built it.

So we set about measuring every wall, pacing off every room, poking around in basement and attic and kitchen. We set up our own house on exactly the same dimensions. We included the same rooms, in the same layout, using the same furniture arrangements. By the time we'd finished construction, we couldn't tell any difference between the two. To us, our house looked just like the original.

We were beside ourselves with joy. We felt faithful at last, after years wasted in homeless wanderings. We were full of confidence, hope, and not a little self-congratulation.

After the initial flush of excitement, however, we discovered to our dismay that light switches didn't work, the oven wouldn't warm, the air conditioning didn't cool. All that effort invested! All the time and sacrifice! The house was finished. The work was done. But …

No power. No *real* power. Okay, a *little* power. Candles flickering. Fans waved. Blankets spread. But nothing like the megawatt power that coursed through the walls of that first house.

Apparently, when studying the original, none of us thought to tear down to the studs and take a close look at the wiring beneath. No one poked around in the fuse box or wondered about circuit breakers. No one traced the line that ran from the side of the house, to the power pole out front, to some invisible generator beyond.

But every bit of that was an integral part of the original house: all those wires and fuses and power poles. That first house wasn't just a collection of rooms and cabinets; there were sockets on the walls and cable running to every socket. Somewhere beyond the house was a real power source. Somewhere between was a conduit streaming outside power in. Somewhere within, power flowed and diverted and became available to all. The original was more than the sum of its walls and materials and design. There was power built into its very bones; power to spare.

In fact, when we really thought about it, it was this abundance of power, this access to power, that made the first house so attractive to begin with: the Master present and alive with power; the people inside, plugged into and strengthened with power; their voices speaking out with such boldness and power; their work in the world so confident, so saturated with power; their lives full of glory and transforming power. It was the power that made the house work. It was the power that made the people within work. It was the power that gave the house and all who sailed within her an aura of beauty and grace and purpose.

But that was their house, not ours. Slowly, sadly, we realized we had meticulously copied the form of their house and left out the power that made it worth copying.

## Bad News and Good News

The bad news is that our house doesn't work like it should. Not like that first house did. But there is good news to go along with the bad—really good news. Here it is: *There is nothing broken about our house that a little power won't fix.*

Our house has good bones. The foundations are strong. The walls are plumb. The rooms are functional. We don't have to tear down our house in order to pipe in a power source. We can retrofit. We can renovate. It's what we're good at. It's what we've been doing all along. Restoration. Renovation. Replication.

Yes, we'll have to pull wire through the house we've built with such care. That will mean mess: holes in walls and dangling fuse boxes. It will require us to think carefully about where our power comes from and how we can connect to it. It will oblige us to grapple with forces we don't understand and mysteries we fear. We'll have to remove the self-generated solutions—the candles and hand-fans—we've come to know and love. It will mean construction dust again in our well-ordered house. It will mean acquiring new habits and fresh ways of living.

But think of the blessings plugging into power can bring!

Jesus piped into our house and lives without limit and without interruption. His presence available to us in every room. The warmth of affection and affirmation; the sound of an occasional, "Well done, good and faithful servant." Power tools for doing a world-changing job. The possibility of recharged batteries. Constant access to a Master Craftsman who brings centuries of experience to bear on our task. A building Companion who works independently of us (when necessary) and cooperatively with us (whenever possible). A partner who accompanies us on forays into a dangerous world.

No more loneliness. No more inadequacy. No more fear of hostility or fear of failure. No more frozen immaturity.

Presence. Competence. Courage. Confidence. Wisdom.

There are those living in our house who will insist that the old ways are good enough. They'll resist the diagnosis of powerlessness and the prescription of Spirit. They will see such measures as extreme—even unfaithful. They will feel them to be an attack on the adequacy of the house we have built and on themselves as builders.

Others, however, will agree that something is missing. They will see the blessings of power and the need for the Spirit. They will love our house enough, and the people who live within her, to do whatever is necessary to make her pulse with world-changing power once more. They will love the Master of the house enough to let him have his way with the house that belongs to him.

## The Rest of the Story

Someday, in the not-too-distant future, a stranger will come knocking at our door. "Is this the Master's house?" he will ask, provoking no small discussion among those of us huddled inside.

"Yes," we will respond suspiciously. "Who wants to know?"

The stranger will shrug. "Why aren't there any lights on? Where's the welcome mat?"

We will stare at him in silence.

"And why aren't you out in the fields, reaping the harvest?" the stranger will want to know. "Why are you hiding in here rather than working out there?"

Our silence will become a low rumble.

The stranger will look around the door frame and search the interior of the house. "Where are your young ones? Where's the next generation of faith? Where are your giants, the ones with victorious lives and vivid testimonies? Where are your wise ones, those who have grown deep and bear the blazing image?" He won't know any better than to ask such questions. He won't mean to be offensive.

But the rumble will become a swelling roar. We will rush out onto the porch to confront this stranger with his embarrassing questions.

"Who do you think you are, talking to us like this?" one of us will demand. "Don't you see this fine house we live in? Don't you see how straight and plumb everything is? Let me show you our foundations!"

The stranger will look around with great calm and dawning awareness. "This is not your house," he will say to us softly. "It belongs to another. You live here by his pleasure. You're supposed to live here by his power." He will look around again and shake his head sadly. "I'm here to inspect his house and collect what the Master is owed."

We will look at each other in stunned silence for a moment. We will try to remember that this house, indeed, does not belong to us. It is *his*. And he has an agenda for the house, purposes for the house, that take precedence over our own. It's easy to forget that. It's easy to neglect the rent. It's easy to withhold the Master's due. What's hard is remembering. We will stare and blink with the effort remembering requires.

It is at this point we will make one of the most crucial decisions of our spiritual lives.

There have been other houses, visited by other strangers, where the occupants of the house decided to rush the interloper, throw him into the front yard, and beat him for his presumption. In fact, truth be told, there have been other times, right here in our own house, when we've done the same to other messengers.

This is not the first stranger to come knocking at our door. He won't be the last.

But the story doesn't have to end that way—in anger and rejection. It could end with conviction and repentance. It could end with a huge sigh of relief. It could end with an invitation to the stranger: "We're glad you're here. It's been too long. Come in and help us."

It could end with the stranger smiling broadly and stretching out his hand. "Thank you for the welcome. I was hoping for that response." He might lift an eyebrow in faint amusement. "Sure is better than the last few times I knocked at this door."

"Come in," we'll say again, eager to chart a different course from now on.

"Don't mind if I do," the stranger will respond with great relish. He'll shake hands all around as he moves with us into the house.

Suddenly, lights will begin to flicker and burn. A low thrumming will fill the house and warm air will start to blow from dusty registers. In a back room, a radio will play soft music. The smell of coffee will fill the house.

We will stand stock-still, astounded by what is taking place in our house. We'll hear things we've never heard before, smell aromas, experience sensations of taste and touch that we never imagined. We'll stare at the stranger as he smiles back at us. He'll seem to radiate power. We'll sense it rippling from him in waves.

And then we'll recognize him. In an instant, all at once, like he stripped off a mask and revealed a face we know. We'll rush to the portrait hanging in our hallway and rub away the grime with a shirtsleeve. It's him! He's come back! We'll jump and shout and dance. We'll revel in his presence. We'll bask in all that light and warmth and the mouth-watering feast we smell cooking. We'll exult in acts, once so hard and laborious, that become simple when power is available.

We'll pause long enough to recognize that something is changing in *us*. We feel at home, secure, loved, hopeful. We feel stronger, wiser, better. We are confident that we know how to act in this house and what to do for those outside of it. We'll look around at this house filled with *him* and, for the first time in a long time, we'll feel graced and graceful and gracious.

The stranger will take everything in, smiling the entire time. He will catch our eye and wink. He will know exactly what we're thinking, precisely how we feel. And we know he knows, know it to our bones. And it doesn't scare us a bit.

We move to him and choke out our thanks.

He wraps us in an embrace and says, "This is the way our house was always meant to be. This is how the Master's house is supposed to work. Do you like it?"

We will nod in mute assent.

He will put a hand on our shoulder. "I'm glad you're here," he will say. "My name is *Paraclete*, by the way."

We'll start to give our name in reply.

But he will just shake his head and hold up a hand. "It's alright. I know who you are."

# Appendix One

## "Spirit" References in the Synoptic Gospels

| | |
|---|---|
| Matt 1:18 | This is how the birth of Jesus Christ came about: His mother Mary was pledged to be married to Joseph, but before they came together, she was found to be with child through the Holy Spirit. |
| Matt 1:20 | But after he had considered this, an angel of the Lord appeared to him in a dream and said, "Joseph son of David, do not be afraid to take Mary home as your wife, because what is conceived in her is from the Holy Spirit. |
| Matt 3:11 | "I baptize you with water for repentance. But after me will come one who is more powerful than I, whose sandals I am not fit to carry. He will baptize you with the Holy Spirit and with fire. |
| Matt 3:16 | As soon as Jesus was baptized, he went up out of the water. At that moment heaven was opened, and he saw the Spirit of God descending like a dove and lighting on him. |
| Matt 4:1 | Then Jesus was led by the Spirit into the desert to be tempted by the devil. |
| Matt 10:1 | He called his twelve disciples to him and gave them authority to drive out evil spirits and to heal every disease and sickness. |
| Matt 10:20 | for it will not be you speaking, but the Spirit of your Father speaking through you. |
| Matt 12:18 | "Here is my servant whom I have chosen, the one I love, in whom I delight; I will put my Spirit on him, and he will proclaim justice to the nations. |
| Matt 12:28 | But if I drive out demons by the Spirit of God, then the kingdom of God has come upon you. |
| Matt 12:31 | And so I tell you, every sin and blasphemy will be forgiven men, but the blasphemy against the Spirit will not be forgiven. |
| Matt 12:32 | Anyone who speaks a word against the Son of Man will be forgiven, but anyone who speaks against the Holy Spirit will not be forgiven, either in this age or in the age to come. |
| Matt 22:43 | He said to them, "How is it then that David, speaking by the Spirit, calls him 'Lord'? For he says, |
| Matt 28:19 | Therefore go and make disciples of all nations, baptizing them in the name of the Father and of the Son and of the Holy Spirit, |
| Mark 1:8 | I baptize you with water, but he will baptize you with the Holy Spirit." |
| Mark 1:10 | As Jesus was coming up out of the water, he saw heaven being torn open and the Spirit descending on him like a dove. |
| Mark 1:12 | At once the Spirit sent him out into the desert, |
| Mark 3:29 | But whoever blasphemes against the Holy Spirit will never be forgiven; he is guilty of an eternal sin." |

Mark 12:36     David himself, speaking by the Holy Spirit, declared: " 'The Lord said to my Lord: "Sit at my right hand until I put your enemies under your feet." '

Mark 13:11     Whenever you are arrested and brought to trial, do not worry beforehand about what to say. Just say whatever is given you at the time, for it is not you speaking, but the Holy Spirit.

Luke 1:15      for he will be great in the sight of the Lord. He is never to take wine or other fermented drink, and he will be filled with the Holy Spirit even from birth.

Luke 1:35      The angel answered, "The Holy Spirit will come upon you, and the power of the Most High will overshadow you. So the holy one to be born will be called the Son of God.

Luke 1:41      When Elizabeth heard Mary's greeting, the baby leaped in her womb, and Elizabeth was filled with the Holy Spirit.

Luke 1:67      His father Zechariah was filled with the Holy Spirit and prophesied:

Luke 2:25      Now there was a man in Jerusalem called Simeon, who was righteous and devout. He was waiting for the consolation of Israel, and the Holy Spirit was upon him.

Luke 2:26      It had been revealed to him by the Holy Spirit that he would not die before he had seen the Lord's Christ.

Luke 2:27      Moved by the Spirit, he went into the temple courts. When the parents brought in the child Jesus to do for him what the custom of the Law required,

Luke 3:16      John answered them all, "I baptize you with water. But one more powerful than I will come, the thongs of whose sandals I am not worthy to untie. He will baptize you with the Holy Spirit and with fire.

Luke 3:22      and the Holy Spirit descended on him in bodily form like a dove. And a voice came from heaven: "You are my Son, whom I love; with you I am well pleased."

Luke 4:1       Jesus, full of the Holy Spirit, returned from the Jordan and was led by the Spirit in the desert,

Luke 4:14      Jesus returned to Galilee in the power of the Spirit, and news about him spread through the whole countryside.

Luke 4:18      "The Spirit of the Lord is on me, because he has anointed me to preach good news to the poor. He has sent me to proclaim freedom for the prisoners and recovery of sight for the blind, to release the oppressed,

Luke 10:21     At that time Jesus, full of joy through the Holy Spirit, said, "I praise you, Father, Lord of heaven and earth, because you have hidden these things from the wise and learned, and revealed them to little children. Yes, Father, for this was your good pleasure.

Luke 11:13     If you then, though you are evil, know how to give good gifts to your children, how much more will your Father in heaven give the Holy Spirit to those who ask him!"

| | |
|---|---|
| Luke 12:10 | And everyone who speaks a word against the Son of Man will be forgiven, but anyone who blasphemes against the Holy Spirit will not be forgiven. |
| Luke 12:12 | for the Holy Spirit will teach you at that time what you should say." |

## Appendix Two

### "Spirit" References in Acts

| | |
|---|---|
| Acts 1:2 | … until the day he was taken up to heaven, after giving instructions through the Holy Spirit to the apostles he had chosen. |
| Acts 1:5 | For John baptized with water, but in a few days you will be baptized with the Holy Spirit. |
| Acts 1:8 | But you will receive power when the Holy Spirit comes on you; and you will be my witnesses in Jerusalem, and in all Judea and Samaria, and to the ends of the earth. |
| Acts 1:16 | "Brothers, the Scripture had to be fulfilled which the Holy Spirit spoke long ago through the mouth of David concerning Judas, who served as guide for those who arrested Jesus … |
| Acts 2:4 | All of them were filled with the Holy Spirit and began to speak in other tongues as the Spirit enabled them. |
| Acts 2:17 | In the last days, God says, I will pour out my Spirit on all people. Your sons and daughters will prophesy, your young men will see visions, your old men will dream dreams. |
| Acts 2:18 | Even on my servants, both men and women, I will pour out my Spirit in those days, and they will prophesy. |
| Acts 2:33 | Exalted to the right hand of God, he has received from the Father the promised Holy Spirit and has poured out what you now see and hear. |
| Acts 2:38 | Peter replied, "Repent and be baptized, every one of you, in the name of Jesus Christ for the forgiveness of your sins. And you will receive the gift of the Holy Spirit." |
| Acts 4:8 | Then Peter, filled with the Holy Spirit, said to them: "Rulers and elders of the people …" |
| Acts 4:25 | You spoke by the Holy Spirit through the mouth of your servant, our father David: " 'Why do the nations rage and the peoples plot in vain? …" |
| Acts 4:31 | After they prayed, the place where they were meeting was shaken. And they were all filled with the Holy Spirit and spoke the word of God boldly. |
| Acts 5:3 | Then Peter said, "Ananias, how is it that Satan has so filled your heart that you have lied to the Holy Spirit and have kept for yourself some of the money you received for the land?. . ." |
| Acts 5:9 | Peter said to her, "How could you agree to test the Spirit of the Lord? Look! The feet of the men who buried your husband are at the door, and they will carry you out also." |

| | |
|---|---|
| Acts 5:32 | "We are witnesses of these things, and so is the Holy Spirit, whom God has given to those who obey him." |
| Acts 6:3 | Brothers, choose seven men from among you who are known to be full of the Spirit and wisdom. We will turn this responsibility over to them |
| Acts 6:5 | This proposal pleased the whole group. They chose Stephen, a man full of faith and of the Holy Spirit; also Philip, Procorus, Nicanor, Timon, Parmenas, and Nicolas from Antioch, a convert to Judaism. |
| Acts 6:10 | … but they could not stand up against his wisdom or the Spirit by whom he spoke. |
| Acts 7:51 | "You stiff-necked people, with uncircumcised hearts and ears! You are just like your fathers: You always resist the Holy Spirit!" |
| Acts 7:55 | But Stephen, full of the Holy Spirit, looked up to heaven and saw the glory of God, and Jesus standing at the right hand of God. |
| Acts 8:15 | When they arrived, they prayed for them that they might receive the Holy Spirit, |
| Acts 8:16 | … because the Holy Spirit had not yet come upon any of them; they had simply been baptized into the name of the Lord Jesus. |
| Acts 8:17 | Then Peter and John placed their hands on them, and they received the Holy Spirit. |
| Acts 8:18 | When Simon saw that the Spirit was given at the laying on of the apostles' hands, he offered them money |
| Acts 8:19 | and said, "Give me also this ability so that everyone on whom I lay my hands may receive the Holy Spirit." |
| Acts 8:29 | The Spirit told Philip, "Go to that chariot and stay near it." |
| Acts 8:39 | When they came up out of the water, the Spirit of the Lord suddenly took Philip away, and the eunuch did not see him again, but went on his way rejoicing. |
| Acts 9:17 | Then Ananias went to the house and entered it. Placing his hands on Saul, he said, "Brother Saul, the Lord—Jesus, who appeared to you on the road as you were coming here—has sent me so that you may see again and be filled with the Holy Spirit." |
| Acts 9:31 | Then the church throughout Judea, Galilee and Samaria enjoyed a time of peace. It was strengthened; and encouraged by the Holy Spirit, it grew in numbers, living in the fear of the Lord. |
| Acts 10:19 | While Peter was still thinking about the vision, the Spirit said to him, "Simon, three men are looking for you…." |
| Acts 10:38 | … how God anointed Jesus of Nazareth with the Holy Spirit and power, and how he went around doing good and healing all who were under the power of the devil, because God was with him. |
| Acts 10:44 | While Peter was still speaking these words, the Holy Spirit came on all who heard the message. |
| Acts 10:45 | The circumcised believers who had come with Peter were astonished that the gift of the Holy Spirit had been poured out even on the Gentiles. |

| | |
|---|---|
| Acts 10:47 | Then Peter said, "Can anyone keep these people from being baptized with water? They have received the Holy Spirit just as we have." |
| Acts 11:12 | The Spirit told me to have no hesitation about going with them. These six brothers also went with me, and we entered the man's house. |
| Acts 11:15 | As I began to speak, the Holy Spirit came on them as he had come on us at the beginning. |
| Acts 11:16 | Then I remembered what the Lord had said: 'John baptized with water, but you will be baptized with the Holy Spirit.' |
| Acts 11:24 | He was a good man, full of the Holy Spirit and faith, and a great number of people were brought to the Lord. |
| Acts 11:28 | One of them, named Agabus, stood up and through the Spirit predicted that a severe famine would spread over the entire Roman world. (This happened during the reign of Claudius.) |
| Acts 13:2 | While they were worshiping the Lord and fasting, the Holy Spirit said, "Set apart for me Barnabas and Saul for the work to which I have called them." |
| Acts 13:4 | The two of them, sent on their way by the Holy Spirit, went down to Seleucia and sailed from there to Cyprus. |
| Acts 13:9 | Then Saul, who was also called Paul, filled with the Holy Spirit, looked straight at Elymas and said … |
| Acts 13:52 | And the disciples were filled with joy and with the Holy Spirit. |
| Acts 15:8 | God, who knows the heart, showed that he accepted them by giving the Holy Spirit to them, just as he did to us. |
| Acts 15:28 | It seemed good to the Holy Spirit and to us not to burden you with anything beyond the following requirements … |
| Acts 16:6 | Paul and his companions traveled throughout the region of Phrygia and Galatia, having been kept by the Holy Spirit from preaching the word in the province of Asia. |
| Acts 16:7 | When they came to the border of Mysia, they tried to enter Bithynia, but the Spirit of Jesus would not allow them to. |
| Acts 19:2 | … and asked them, "Did you receive the Holy Spirit when you believed?" They answered, "No, we have not even heard that there is a Holy Spirit." |
| Acts 19:6 | When Paul placed his hands on them, the Holy Spirit came on them, and they spoke in tongues and prophesied. |
| Acts 20:22 | "And now, compelled by the Spirit, I am going to Jerusalem, not knowing what will happen to me there. |
| Acts 20:23 | I only know that in every city the Holy Spirit warns me that prison and hardships are facing me…." |
| Acts 20:28 | Keep watch over yourselves and all the flock of which the Holy Spirit has made you overseers. Be shepherds of the church of God, which he bought with his own blood. |
| Acts 21:4 | Finding the disciples there, we stayed with them seven days. Through the Spirit they urged Paul not to go on to Jerusalem. |

| | |
|---|---|
| Acts 21:11 | Coming over to us, he took Paul's belt, tied his own hands and feet with it and said, "The Holy Spirit says, 'In this way the Jews of Jerusalem will bind the owner of this belt and will hand him over to the Gentiles.' " |
| Acts 28:25 | They disagreed among themselves and began to leave after Paul had made this final statement: "The Holy Spirit spoke the truth to your forefathers when he said through Isaiah the prophet…" |

## Appendix Three

### "Spirit" References in Paul

| | |
|---|---|
| Rom 1:4 | … and who through the Spirit of holiness was declared with power to be the Son of God by his resurrection from the dead: Jesus Christ our Lord. |
| Rom 2:29 | No, a man is a Jew if he is one inwardly; and circumcision is circumcision of the heart, by the Spirit, not by the written code. Such a man's praise is not from men, but from God. |
| Rom 5:5 | And hope does not disappoint us, because God has poured out his love into our hearts by the Holy Spirit, whom he has given us. |
| Rom 7:6 | But now, by dying to what once bound us, we have been released from the law so that we serve in the new way of the Spirit, and not in the old way of the written code. |
| Rom 8:2 | … because through Christ Jesus the law of the Spirit of life set me free from the law of sin and death. |
| Rom 8:4 | … in order that the righteous requirements of the law might be fully met in us, who do not live according to the sinful nature but according to the Spirit. |
| Rom 8:5 | Those who live according to the sinful nature have their minds set on what that nature desires; but those who live in accordance with the Spirit have their minds set on what the Spirit desires. |
| Rom 8:6 | The mind of sinful man is death, but the mind controlled by the Spirit is life and peace… |
| Rom 8:9 | You, however, are controlled not by the sinful nature but by the Spirit, if the Spirit of God lives in you. And if anyone does not have the Spirit of Christ, he does not belong to Christ. |
| Rom 8:11 | And if the Spirit of him who raised Jesus from the dead is living in you, he who raised Christ from the dead will also give life to your mortal bodies through his Spirit, who lives in you. |
| Rom 8:13 | For if you live according to the sinful nature, you will die; but if by the Spirit you put to death the misdeeds of the body, you will live, |
| Rom 8:14 | because those who are led by the Spirit of God are sons of God. |

| | |
|---|---|
| Rom 8:15 | For you did not receive a spirit that makes you a slave again to fear, but you received the Spirit of sonship. And by him we cry, "Abba, Father." |
| Rom 8:16 | The Spirit himself testifies with our spirit that we are God's children. |
| Rom 8:23 | Not only so, but we ourselves, who have the firstfruits of the Spirit, groan inwardly as we wait eagerly for our adoption as sons, the redemption of our bodies. |
| Rom 8:26 | In the same way, the Spirit helps us in our weakness. We do not know what we ought to pray for, but the Spirit himself intercedes for us with groans that words cannot express. |
| Rom 8:27 | And he who searches our hearts knows the mind of the Spirit, because the Spirit intercedes for the saints in accordance with God's will. |
| Rom 9:1 | I speak the truth in Christ—I am not lying, my conscience confirms it in the Holy Spirit… |
| Rom 14:17 | For the kingdom of God is not a matter of eating and drinking, but of righteousness, peace and joy in the Holy Spirit, |
| Rom 15:13 | May the God of hope fill you with all joy and peace as you trust in him, so that you may overflow with hope by the power of the Holy Spirit. |
| Rom 15:16 | …. to be a minister of Christ Jesus to the Gentiles with the priestly duty of proclaiming the gospel of God, so that the Gentiles might become an offering acceptable to God, sanctified by the Holy Spirit. |
| Rom 15:19 | … by the power of signs and miracles, through the power of the Spirit. So from Jerusalem all the way around to Illyricum, I have fully proclaimed the gospel of Christ. |
| Rom 15:30 | I urge you, brothers, by our Lord Jesus Christ and by the love of the Spirit, to join me in my struggle by praying to God for me. |
| 1 Cor 2:4 | My message and my preaching were not with wise and persuasive words, but with a demonstration of the Spirit's power, |
| 1 Cor 2:10 | … but God has revealed it to us by his Spirit. The Spirit searches all things, even the deep things of God. |
| 1 Cor 2:11 | For who among men knows the thoughts of a man except the man's spirit within him? In the same way no one knows the thoughts of God except the Spirit of God. |
| 1 Cor 2:12 | We have not received the spirit of the world but the Spirit who is from God, that we may understand what God has freely given us. |
| 1 Cor 2:13 | This is what we speak, not in words taught us by human wisdom but in words taught by the Spirit, expressing spiritual truths in spiritual words. |
| 1 Cor 2:14 | The man without the Spirit does not accept the things that come from the Spirit of God, for they are foolishness to him, and he cannot understand them, because they are spiritually discerned. |

| | |
|---|---|
| 1 Cor 3:16 | Don't you know that you yourselves are God's temple and that God's Spirit lives in you? |
| 1 Cor 6:11 | And that is what some of you were. But you were washed, you were sanctified, you were justified in the name of the Lord Jesus Christ and by the Spirit of our God. |
| 1 Cor 6:19 | Do you not know that your body is a temple of the Holy Spirit, who is in you, whom you have received from God? You are not your own… |
| 1 Cor 7:40 | In my judgment, she is happier if she stays as she is—and I think that I too have the Spirit of God. |
| 1 Cor 12:3 | Therefore I tell you that no one who is speaking by the Spirit of God says, "Jesus be cursed," and no one can say, "Jesus is Lord," except by the Holy Spirit. |
| 1 Cor 12:4 | There are different kinds of gifts, but the same Spirit. |
| 1 Cor 12:7 | Now to each one the manifestation of the Spirit is given for the common good. |
| 1 Cor 12:8 | To one there is given through the Spirit the message of wisdom, to another the message of knowledge by means of the same Spirit, |
| 1 Cor 12:9 | to another faith by the same Spirit, to another gifts of healing by that one Spirit… |
| 1 Cor 12:11 | All these are the work of one and the same Spirit, and he gives them to each one, just as he determines. |
| 1 Cor 12:13 | For we were all baptized by one Spirit into one body—whether Jews or Greeks, slave or free—and we were all given the one Spirit to drink. |
| 2 Cor 1:22 | … set his seal of ownership on us, and put his Spirit in our hearts as a deposit, guaranteeing what is to come. |
| 2 Cor 3:3 | You show that you are a letter from Christ, the result of our ministry, written not with ink but with the Spirit of the living God, not on tablets of stone but on tablets of human hearts. |
| 2 Cor 3:6 | He has made us competent as ministers of a new covenant—not of the letter but of the Spirit; for the letter kills, but the Spirit gives life. |
| 2 Cor 3:8 | … will not the ministry of the Spirit be even more glorious? |
| 2 Cor 3:17 | Now the Lord is the Spirit, and where the Spirit of the Lord is, there is freedom. |
| 2 Cor 3:18 | And we, who with unveiled faces all reflect the Lord's glory, are being transformed into his likeness with ever-increasing glory, which comes from the Lord, who is the Spirit. |
| 2 Cor 5:5 | Now it is God who has made us for this very purpose and has given us the Spirit as a deposit, guaranteeing what is to come. |
| 2 Cor 6:6 | … in purity, understanding, patience and kindness; in the Holy Spirit and in sincere love… |
| 2 Cor 11:4 | For if someone comes to you and preaches a Jesus other than the Jesus we preached, or if you receive a different spirit from the one |

|            | you received, or a different gospel from the one you accepted, you put up with it easily enough. |
|------------|--------------------------------------------------------------------------------------------------|
| 2 Cor 13:14 | May the grace of the Lord Jesus Christ, and the love of God, and the fellowship of the Holy Spirit be with you all. |
| Gal 3:2 | I would like to learn just one thing from you: Did you receive the Spirit by observing the law, or by believing what you heard? |
| Gal 3:3 | Are you so foolish? After beginning with the Spirit, are you now trying to attain your goal by human effort? |
| Gal 3:5 | Does God give you his Spirit and work miracles among you because you observe the law, or because you believe what you heard? |
| Gal 3:14 | He redeemed us in order that the blessing given to Abraham might come to the Gentiles through Christ Jesus, so that by faith we might receive the promise of the Spirit. |
| Gal 4:6 | Because you are sons, God sent the Spirit of his Son into our hearts, the Spirit who calls out, "Abba, Father." |
| Gal 4:29 | At that time the son born in the ordinary way persecuted the son born by the power of the Spirit. It is the same now. |
| Gal 5:5 | But by faith we eagerly await through the Spirit the righteousness for which we hope. |
| Gal 5:16 | So I say, live by the Spirit, and you will not gratify the desires of the sinful nature. |
| Gal 5:17 | For the sinful nature desires what is contrary to the Spirit, and the Spirit what is contrary to the sinful nature. They are in conflict with each other, so that you do not do what you want. |
| Gal 5:18 | But if you are led by the Spirit, you are not under law. |
| Gal 5:22 | But the fruit of the Spirit is love, joy, peace, patience, kindness, goodness, faithfulness… |
| Gal 5:25 | Since we live by the Spirit, let us keep in step with the Spirit. |
| Gal 6:8 | The one who sows to please his sinful nature, from that nature will reap destruction; the one who sows to please the Spirit, from the Spirit will reap eternal life. |
| Eph 1:13 | And you also were included in Christ when you heard the word of truth, the gospel of your salvation. Having believed, you were marked in him with a seal, the promised Holy Spirit… |
| Eph 1:17 | I keep asking that the God of our Lord Jesus Christ, the glorious Father, may give you the Spirit of wisdom and Rev, so that you may know him better. |
| Eph 2:18 | For through him we both have access to the Father by one Spirit. |
| Eph 2:22 | And in him you too are being built together to become a dwelling in which God lives by his Spirit. |
| Eph 3:5 | … which was not made known to men in other generations as it has now been revealed by the Spirit to God's holy apostles and prophets. |
| Eph 3:16 | I pray that out of his glorious riches he may strengthen you with power through his Spirit in your inner being… |

| | |
|---|---|
| Eph 4:3 | Make every effort to keep the unity of the Spirit through the bond of peace. |
| Eph 4:4 | There is one body and one Spirit—just as you were called to one hope when you were called… |
| Eph 4:30 | And do not grieve the Holy Spirit of God, with whom you were sealed for the day of redemption. |
| Eph 5:18 | Do not get drunk on wine, which leads to debauchery. Instead, be filled with the Spirit. |
| Eph 6:17 | Take the helmet of salvation and the sword of the Spirit, which is the word of God. |
| Eph 6:18 | And pray in the Spirit on all occasions with all kinds of prayers and requests. With this in mind, be alert and always keep on praying for all the saints. |
| Phil 1:19 | Yes, and I will continue to rejoice, for I know that through your prayers and the help given by the Spirit of Jesus Christ, what has happened to me will turn out for my deliverance. |
| Phil 2:1 | If you have any encouragement from being united with Christ, if any comfort from his love, if any fellowship with the Spirit, if any tenderness and compassion… |
| Phil 3:3 | For it is we who are the circumcision, we who worship by the Spirit of God, who glory in Christ Jesus, and who put no confidence in the flesh… |
| Col 1:8 | … and who also told us of your love in the Spirit. |
| 1 Thess 1:5 | … because our gospel came to you not simply with words, but also with power, with the Holy Spirit and with deep conviction. You know how we lived among you for your sake. |
| 1 Thess 1:6 | You became imitators of us and of the Lord; in spite of severe suffering, you welcomed the message with the joy given by the Holy Spirit. |
| 1 Thess 4:8 | Therefore, he who rejects this instruction does not reject man but God, who gives you his Holy Spirit. |
| 1 Thess 5:19 | Do not put out the Spirit's fire… |
| 2 Thess 2:13 | But we ought always to thank God for you, brothers loved by the Lord, because from the beginning God chose you to be saved through the sanctifying work of the Spirit and through belief in the truth. |
| 1 Tim 3:16 | Beyond all question, the mystery of godliness is great: He appeared in a body, was vindicated by the Spirit, was seen by angels, was preached among the nations, was believed on in the world, was taken up in glory. |
| 1 Tim 4:1 | The Spirit clearly says that in later times some will abandon the faith and follow deceiving spirits and things taught by demons. |
| 2 Tim 1:14 | Guard the good deposit that was entrusted to you—guard it with the help of the Holy Spirit who lives in us. |
| Titus 3:5 | … he saved us, not because of righteous things we had done, but because of his mercy. He saved us through the washing of rebirth and renewal by the Holy Spirit… |

## Appendix Four

### "Spirit" References in John

| | |
|---|---|
| John 1:32 | Then John gave this testimony: "I saw the Spirit come down from heaven as a dove and remain on him. |
| John 1:33 | I would not have known him, except that the one who sent me to baptize with water told me, 'The man on whom you see the Spirit come down and remain is he who will baptize with the Holy Spirit.' |
| John 3:5 | Jesus answered, "I tell you the truth, no one can enter the kingdom of God unless he is born of water and the Spirit. |
| John 3:6 | Flesh gives birth to flesh, but the Spirit gives birth to spirit. |
| John 3:8 | The wind blows wherever it pleases. You hear its sound, but you cannot tell where it comes from or where it is going. So it is with everyone born of the Spirit. |
| John 3:34 | For the one whom God has sent speaks the words of God, for God gives the Spirit without limit. |
| John 4:23 | Yet a time is coming and has now come when the true worshipers will worship the Father in spirit and truth, for they are the kind of worshipers the Father seeks. |
| John 4:24 | God is spirit, and his worshipers must worship in spirit and in truth." |
| John 6:63 | The Spirit gives life; the flesh counts for nothing. The words I have spoken to you are spirit and they are life. |
| John 7:39 | By this he meant the Spirit, whom those who believed in him were later to receive. Up to that time the Spirit had not been given, since Jesus had not yet been glorified. |
| John 14:16 | And I will ask the Father, and he will give you another Counselor to be with you forever— |
| John 14:17 | the Spirit of truth. The world cannot accept him, because it neither sees him nor knows him. But you know him, for he lives with you and will be in you. |
| John 14:26 | But the Counselor, the Holy Spirit, whom the Father will send in my name, will teach you all things and will remind you of everything I have said to you. |
| John 15:26 | "When the Counselor comes, whom I will send to you from the Father, the Spirit of truth who goes out from the Father, he will testify about me. |
| John 16:7 | But I tell you the truth: It is for your good that I am going away. Unless I go away, the Counselor will not come to you; but if I go, I will send him to you. |
| John 16:8 | When he comes, he will convict the world of guilt[a] in regard to sin and righteousness and judgment: |
| John 16:9 | in regard to sin, because men do not believe in me; |
| John 16:10 | in regard to righteousness, because I am going to the Father, where you can see me no longer; |

| | |
|---|---|
| John 16:11 | and in regard to judgment, because the prince of this world now stands condemned. |
| John 16:13 | But when he, the Spirit of truth, comes, he will guide you into all truth. He will not speak on his own; he will speak only what he hears, and he will tell you what is yet to come. |
| John 16:14 | He will bring glory to me by taking from what is mine and making it known to you. |
| John 16:15 | All that belongs to the Father is mine. That is why I said the Spirit will take from what is mine and make it known to you. |
| John 20:22 | And with that he breathed on them and said, "Receive the Holy Spirit. |

# Bibliography

## Commentaries on John

Beasley-Murray, George R. *John.* Word Biblical Commentary, Vol. 36. Waco, TX: Word, 1987.

Brown, Raymond E. *The Gospel According to John XIII-XXI.* The Anchor Bible, Vol. 29a. New York: Doubleday, 1970.

Burge, Gary M. *The Anointed Community: the Holy Spirit in the Johannine Tradition.* Grand Rapids: William B. Eerdmans, 1987.

Carson, D. A. *The Gospel According to John.* The Pillar New Testament Commentary. Grand Rapids: William B. Eerdmans, 1991.

-----. *The Farewell Discourse and Final Prayer of Jesus: An Exposition of John 14-17.* Grand Rapids: Baker, 1980.

Köstenberger, Andreas J. *John.* Baker Exegetical Commentary on the New Testament. Grand Rapids: Baker Academic, 2004.

Morris, Leon. *The Gospel According to John.* The New International Commentary on the New Testament. Grand Rapids: Wm. B. Eerdmans, 1971.

Ridderbos, Herman N. *The Gospel According to John: A Theological Commentary.* Translated by John Vriend. Grand Rapids: William B. Eerdmans, 1997.

Segovia, Fernando F. *The Farewell of the Word: The Johannine Call to Abide.* Minneapolis: Fortress, 1991.

Smith, D. Moody. *The Theology of the Gospel of John.* New Testament Theology Series. Cambridge: Cambridge University Press, 1995.

Williamson Jr., Lamar. *Preaching the Gospel of John: Proclaiming the Living Word.* Louisville: Westminster John Knox, 2004.

## Works on the Holy Spirit

Boatman, Russell. *What the Bible Says about the Holy Spirit.* Joplin, MO: College Press, 1989.

Bruner, Fredrick Dale. *A Theology of the Holy Spirit.* Grand Rapids: William B. Eerdmans, 1970.

Fee, Gordon. *God's Empowering Presence: The Holy Spirit in the Letters of Paul.* Peabody, MA: Hendrickson, 1994.

-----. *Paul, the Spirit, and the People of God.* Peabody, MA: Hendrickson, 1996.

Floyd, Harvey. *Is the Holy Spirit for Me? A Search for the Meaning of the Spirit in Today's Church.* Nashville: 20th Century Christian, 1981.

Foster, Richard. *Streams of Living Water.* New York: HarperOne, 2001.

Johnson, Ashley S. *The Holy Spirit and the Human Mind.* Knoxville, TN, 1903.

Keener, Craig. *Gift and Giver: The Holy Spirit for Today.* Grand Rapids: Baker, 2001.

Nouwen, Henri. *Life of the Beloved.* New York: Crossroads, 2002.

Pinnock, Clark H. *Flame of Love: A Theology of the Holy Spirit.* Downers Grove, IL: InterVarsity, 1996.

Richardson, Robert. *A Scriptural View of the Office of the Holy Spirit.* 1872.

## Works on the Trinity

Allen, C. Leonard. *Participating in God's Life: Two Crossroads for Churches of Christ.* Abilene, TX: Leafwood, 2002.

Cunningham, David. *These Three Are One: The Practice of Trinitarian Theology*. Oxford: Blackwell, 1998.

Grenz, Stanley J. *The Social God and the Relational Self: A Trinitarian Theology of the Imago Dei*. Louisville: Westminster John Knox Press, 2001.

Gunton, Colin. *Father, Son, and Holy Spirit*. London: T & T Clark, 2003.

-----. *The Promise of the Trinity*. Edinburgh: T & T Clark, 1991.

Moltmann, Jürgen. *The Trinity and the Kingdom*. Translated by Margaret Kohl. Minneapolis: Fortress Press, 1993.

Seamands, Stephen. *Ministry in the Image of God: The Trinitarian Shape of Christian Service*. Downers Grove: InterVarsity Press, 2005.

Works Related to the American Restoration Movement:

Allen, C. Leonard. *Things Unseen: Churches of Christ in (and after) the Modern Age*. Abilene, TX: Leafwood, 2004.

Brooks, Pat. "Alexander Campbell, the Holy Spirit, and the New Birth." *Restoration Quarterly* 31 (1989), 149-164.

Campbell, Alexander. *A Compend of Alexander Campbell's Theology*. Edited by Royal Humbert. St. Louis, MO: Bethany Press, 1961. See Chapter 6, "The Holy Spirit," 122-125.

Hughes, Richard T. *Reviving the Ancient Faith: The Story of Churches of Christ in America*. 2nd Edition. Abilene, TX: Abilene Christian University Press, 2008.

Hughes, Richard T. and C. Leonard Allen. *Illusions of Innocence: Protestant Primitivism in America, 1630-1875*. Chicago: University of Chicago Press, 1988.

Nance, David W. "Restoration Writers on the Indwelling of the Holy Spirit from 1843 to 1867." M.A. Thesis, Harding Graduate School of Religion, 1991.

Olbricht, Thomas H. "Alexander Campbell's View of the Holy Spirit." *Restoration Quarterly* 6 (1961), 1-11.

Shelly, Rubel and Randall J. Harris. *The Second Incarnation: A Theology for the 21st Century Church*. Abilene, TX: Abilene Christian University Press,

Woodroof, Tim. *A Church that Flies: A New Call to Restoration in the Churches of Christ*. Abilene, TX: Leafwood, 2000.

Web Sites

*Holy Spirit in General:*
www.spirithome.com
www.carm.org/christianity/christian-doctrine/holy-spirit

*Spiritual Gifts (Assessment):*
http://archive.elca.org/evangelizingchurch/assessments/spiritgifts.html
www.kodachrome.org/spiritgift/
www.churchgrowth.org/cgi-cg/gifts.cgi

*Spiritual Gifts (Information):*
http://preceptaustin.org/spiritual_gifts_chart.htm
www.intothyword.org/pages.asp?pageid=53503
www.spirithome.com/gifts-sp.html

# Endnotes

## Chapter Three

1  1500 years later, the Apostle Paul connects this "radiance" to the ministry of the Spirit (2 Cor 3:7-18). Playing with the words "face" and "glory," Paul talks about how the Spirit changes faces: God put his glory (by the Spirit?) on the face of Christ (4:6); the Spirit puts God's glory on the face of believers (3:18); and (presumably) the Spirit set God's glory on Moses' face (3:7), even though the Israelites could not bear it.

## Chapter Four

1  Forgive the hyperbole. The Spirit was not *actually* irresistible. There are several instances in Acts where people lie to, test, ignore, deny, argue with, and close their hearts to the Holy Spirit. (Acts 5:3, 9; 7:51; 8:18-19; 10:14; 28:25ff)

2  No pun or allusion intended.

## Chapter Five

1  The indwelling Spirit becomes the basis, for instance, of Paul's teaching about our being "marked" by the Spirit, who is God's brand on our lives. ("Having believed, you were marked in him with a seal, the promised Holy Spirit ... until the redemption of those who are God's possession"—Eph 1:13-14; see also 2 Cor 1:21-22 and Gal 4:6). The indwelling Spirit is the primary reason Paul can urge his churches to live with assurance, hope, confidence, and boldness—the Spirit "in" us being a constant source of assurance about who we are and whose we are, a constant "testimony" to our status before God. ("The Spirit himself testifies with our spirit that we are God's children. Now if we are children, then we are heirs—heirs of God and co-heirs with Christ"—Rom 8:15-17; see also 2 Cor 1:22; 5:5). Paul can even speak of the Spirit "living in" the church. "You are being built together to become a dwelling in which God lives by his Spirit," he tells the Ephesians (2:22). He expresses the same idea to the Corinthians: "Don't you know that you yourselves are God's temple and that God's Spirit lives in you [plural]?" (1 Cor 3:16).

2  Our Restoration forefathers, with a few exceptions, limited knowledge and experience of God to the five senses. The writings of Campbell and his protégés are full of arguments for "sensory" learning and against any other sort. No other doctrine is so tainted by their Lockean, Enlightenment assumptions. See Alexander Campbell, "The Whole Work of the Holy Spirit in the Salvation of Men," *Millennial Harbinger* 2 (July 1831), 289ff; Thomas H. Olbricht, "The Rationalism of the Restoration," *Restoration Quarterly* 11 (1968), 77-88; C. Leonard Allen, "Unearthing the 'Dirt Philosophy': Baconianism, Faith, and the Spirit," in *Things Unseen: Churches of Christ in (and after) the Modern Age* (Abilene, TX: Leafwood Publishers, 2004), 71-98.

3  Don't confuse this "washing," by the way, with the symbol of baptism. Baptism may point to this and foreshadow this. But water washing can never accomplish what God's Spirit does in our hearts and characters. To confuse the two, to conflate the two, makes no more sense than confusing a wedding ring with love and commitment.

Chapter Six

1   John 2:1-11; 4:46-54; 5:1-9; 6:5-13, 19-21; 9:1-7; 11:1-44. Even the traditional seven signs do not exhaust the miraculous element in John. Jesus consistently reads the hearts and lives of people he meets in this Gospel: Nathaniel (1:48); Nicodemus (3:3); the woman at the well (4:16); and the crowds (6:43). He also, and mysteriously, avoids being stoned to death and evades arrest—even though the authorities try their hardest. (See 5:18; 7:30-32, 45-46; 8:20, 59; 10:31-33, 39).

2   All of these statements refer to the same handful of incidents: blasphemy against the Spirit; the Spirit providing words when the disciples are arrested; David speaking by inspiration of the Spirit; etc.

3   William Shakespeare; *Romeo and Juliet.*

4   Contemporary English Version; Worldwide English Version

5   New Living Translation; New Revised Standard Version; Today's New International Version

6   King James Version; American Standard Version; Wycliffe New Testament

7   New International Version; Holman's Christian Standard Version

8   New American Standard Bible, English Standard Version; New King James Version; New Century Version

9   The Message; New International Readers Version

10  Amplified Bible

11  Amplified Bible

12  "In John 14-16 no such function of the Spirit as advocate of the disciples and defender before God is mentioned." Herman Ridderbos, *The Gospel According to John: A Theological Commentary* (Grand Rapids: William B. Eerdmans, 1997), 500. "The actual function of the Spirit-Paraclete as set forth in chapters 14-16 is not so much to represent the disciples before the divine tribunal ... as to represent Jesus to his disciples left behind on earth." D. Moody Smith, *The Theology of the Gospel of John* (Cambridge: Cambridge University Press, 1995), 140. There *is* that statement about the *Paraclete* working to "convict the world of guilt"—John 16:8. But it is the world's own conscience, rather than a law court, where a verdict of "Guilty" is demanded. And the usual task of a *Paraclete*—even in court contexts—is *defense* rather than prosecution. Legal images certainly arise in other texts. But they should not color our understanding of the word here.

13  "The consensus is that in John 14-16 *parakletos* does not have the meaning in Greek and Hellenistic usage of advocate, professional legal adviser, defender, or representative before a court." Ridderbos, *John*, 500.

14  D. A. Carson, *The Gospel According to John* (Grand Rapids: William B. Eerdmans, 1991), 499.

15  "For the specific use and meaning of the name "Paraclete" in John 14-16 we are dependent on the texts themselves and cannot base our conclusions on representations and figures in other sources." Ridderbos, John, 503.

16  Ridderbos, *John*, 503.

17  Andreas Köstenberger, *John* (Grand Rapids: Baker Academic, 2004), 446.

## Chapter Eight

1  Herman Ridderbos, *The Gospel According to John: A Theological Commentary* (Grand Rapids: William B. Eerdmans, 1997), 503.

2  "The implication of v 16 is that Jesus has performed the role of a Paraclete during his earthly ministry, and after his departure he will ask the Father to send another Paraclete to perform a like ministry for his disciples." George Beasley-Murray *John* (Waco, TX: Word Books, Publisher, 1987), 256. "Nevertheless 'another Paraclete' in the context of Jesus' departure implies that the disciples already have one, the one who is departing." D. A. Carson, *The Gospel According to John* (Grand Rapids: William B. Eerdmans, 1991), 500. "Clearly, therefore, John presents the Spirit-Paraclete as the successor of Jesus who carries on his revelatory work, sustaining the disciples after the rupture represented by Jesus' death." D. Moody Smith, *The Theology of the Gospel of John* (Cambridge: Cambridge University Press, 1995), 143.

3  Jesus refers to the Spirit as the "Spirit of truth" three times in this Final Discourse.

4  "Jesus' identification with the Spirit, the 'other *paracletos*,' is so strong that he can say that *he himself* will return to his followers in the person of the Spirit." Andreas Köstenberger, *John* (Grand Rapids: Baker Academic, 2004), 434. "John presents the Paraclete as the Holy Spirit in a special role, namely, as the personal presence of Jesus in the Christian while Jesus is with the Father. ... Virtually everything that has been said about the Paraclete has been said elsewhere in the Gospel about Jesus. ... Thus, the one whom John calls 'another Paraclete' is another Jesus. ... the Paraclete is the presence of Jesus when Jesus is absent. Jesus' promises to dwell within his disciples are fulfilled in the Paraclete. ... [The Paraclete is] the continued post-resurrectional presence of Jesus with his disciples..." Raymond Brown, *The Gospel According to John XIII-XX,* (New York: Doubleday, 1970), 1139-1141. "In the person of the Paraclete, Jesus is present within and among all believers." Lamar Williamson, Jr., *Preaching the Gospel of John: Proclaiming the Living Word* (Louisville: Westminster John Knox Press, 2004), 189. "The actual function of the Spirit-Paraclete as set forth in chapters 14-16 is not so much to represent the disciples before the divine tribunal (as in John 2:1) as to represent Jesus to his disciples left behind on earth. The Spirit-Paraclete speaks to the question of how Jesus will continue with his disciples or church during his physical absence from them." Smith, *Theology of John*, 140.

5  "It is obvious that Jesus is speaking of a more continued presence than was possible in the brief period of post-resurrectional appearances—not only the words 'I shall not leave you orphans' but the whole tone of his remarks imply permanency." Raymond Brown, *John*, 645-646. "Though 'yet a little while' in 14:19 and 'on that day' in 14:20 at first blush may appear to refer to Jesus' resurrection appearances, Jesus' promise in 14:18 not to leave his disciples as orphans is hardly satisfied by his resurrection appearances, which were temporary in nature, and more likely refers to the permanent replacement of his presence with the Spirit." Kostenberger, *John*, 434.

6  "This understanding of the coming again of Jesus Christ transforms the meaning of the expression 'on that day' in the Fourth Gospel.... [John is] referring to the time when believers will live on the strength of Jesus' presence as the Paraclete." Williamson, Jr., *Preaching John*, 189.

7    Jesus "lives," but the proof of that is not his walking out of the tomb so much as his walking into disciples' lives through the ministry of the Spirit. And the disciples "live," not only because Jesus was raised from the dead but because he makes the Spirit available to them—his presence in Spirit form.

8    "It would be inaccurate to represent the Fourth Gospel as merging the resurrection of Jesus, the coming of the Spirit, and the return of Jesus into one event, for the evangelist can obviously distinguish among them. Yet the fundamental theological reality to which they point is the same, namely, Jesus' continued presence with his disciples after the death that terminates his physically mediated relationship with them." Smith, *Theology of John*, 141. "One can see that in 14:15-17 it is the Paraclete/Advocate/Spirit who will come to be with the disciples forever. In 14:18-21 it is Jesus who will come to live in the disciples and reveal himself to them. In 14:23-24 it is the Father who will come with Jesus to make a dwelling place within the disciples. All of these indewellings are thought of as accomplished through and in the Paraclete, who is the presence of Jesus while Jesus is absent ..." Williamson, Jr., *Preaching John*, 190.

9    In fairness, we must admit that Jesus is not speaking here with mathematical precision. His language is enigmatic, riddled. He hints rather than specifies, intrigues rather than defines. Still, it is clearly the *Paraclete* he is offering his disciples ... and *himself* in the form of the *Paraclete*.

## Chapter Nine

1    "The need for this among the disciples was acute, as is evident from the questions that they asked Jesus during this farewell, which prove their incomprehension." Herman Ridderbos, *The Gospel According to John: A Theological Commentary* (Grand Rapids: William B. Eerdmans, 1997), 510.

2    In the High Priestly Prayer that immediately follows the Final Discourse (John 17), mission continues to be the point. Jesus speaks of his own mission (17:1-4) and refers repeatedly to the transfer of that mission to the Twelve: "I gave them the words you gave me and they accepted them" (17:8) ... "I have given them your word and the world has hated them" (17:14) ... "As you sent me into the world, I have sent them into the world" (17:18) ... "those who believe in me *through their message*" (17:20) ... "to let the world know" (17:23).

3    You also see evidence of this hand-off in Matthew's Great Commission: "Go and make disciples of all nations" (Matt 28:19). You hear it in Mark's version: "Go into all the world and preach" (Mark 16:15). There are echoes of it in Luke's "Repentance and forgiveness of sins will be preached in [my] name to all nations" (Luke 24:47—where Jesus hastens to add, "You are witnesses of these things"). And, of course, there is Luke's additional memory of commissioning captured in Acts: "You will be my witnesses in Jerusalem, and in all Judea and Samaria, and to the ends of the earth" (Acts 1:8).

4    "In the NT, the experience of the Spirit is never insular. It pushes the Christian community out into the world. Therefore an important corollary of NT pneumatology is mission and witness.... The community did not merely enjoy tranquil reflection or the satisfaction of spiritual enthusiasm; its life was intimately involved with history. Its word of testimony became flesh and actively engaged the

surrounding world." Gary Burge, *The Anointed Community: the Holy Spirit in the Johannine Tradition* (Grand Rapids: William B. Eerdmans, 1987), 198-199.

5   "The work that the Spirit is sent out to do as the other Paraclete remains the work of Jesus; the work is being continued by the Spirit, but Jesus, in his heavenly mode of existence and position of power, is and remains the great sponsor of that work." Ridderbos, *John*, 510.

6   "In John's Gospel, the disciples are shown to fail, throughout Jesus' ministry, in their understanding of Jesus. One of the Spirit's principle tasks, after Jesus is glorified, is to remind the disciples of Jesus' teaching and thus, in the new situation after the resurrection, to help them grasp its significance and thus to teach them what it meant." D. A. Carson, *The Gospel According to John* (Grand Rapids: William B. Eerdmans, 1991), 505. "[The Spirit] not only enables them to *recall* these things but to perceive their significance, and so he *teaches* the disciples to grasp the revelation of God brought by Jesus in its richness and profundity. Two observations accordingly are in place regarding this saying about the Paraclete: first, it is clear that the Spirit brings no new revelation; his task is to point to that which Jesus brought and to enable the disciples to understand it; second ... his role as representative of Jesus and his task of recalling and interpreting the revelation brought by Jesus make very clear the personal nature of the Spirit." George Beasley-Murray, *John* (Waco, TX: Word, 1987), 261. "Therefore, the statement about 'teaching all things' is explained by 'and bring to your remembrance all that I have said to you,' which obviously relates not just to the disciples' capacity to remember but also to the process of learning to understand that which lay hidden, as an undiscovered treasure, in their memories and traditions concerning Jesus." Ridderbos, *John*, 510-511.

7   "Contrary to what is sometimes claimed for the 'all things' taught by the Spirit, Jesus is not suggesting that the Spirit has something to say that is new or distinct from his own teachings, or that they involve hidden revelations and secret mysteries 'that could never be imagined on the basis of Jesus' teaching during his ministry.'" D. Moody Smith, *The Theology of the Gospel of John* (Cambridge: Cambridge University Press, 1995), 141. The Spirit's teaching is not *other* than Jesus' or *different* from Jesus'. It is, rather, an *extension* of Jesus' teaching to the new world of the resurrection and the new conditions of the future.

## Chapter Ten

1   "The Paraclete passage in xv 26-27 not only looks forward to the passages that follow, but is also related to what has just been said by Jesus, for the coming of the Paraclete gives a profound explanation of why the world treats Jesus' disciples the same way it treated him. The Paraclete represents Jesus' presence among men ... and in hating the disciples who are the dwelling place of the Paraclete, the world is striking at Jesus' continued presence on earth." Raymond Brown, *The Gospel According to John XIII-XXI* (New York: Doubleday, 1970), 698-699.

2   "The Spirit's task is to 'bear witness' concerning Jesus ... His witness therefore is not here conceived of as that of an advocate, speaking in defense of *the disciples* ... nor is it that of a prosecuting attorney, giving evidence *against* the world ... The witness of the Spirit, conjoined with that of the disciples, is to bring to light the

truth of the revelation of Jesus in his word and dead, and death and resurrection." George Beasley-Murray, *John* (Waco, TX: Word, 1987), 276-277.

3    "[The disciples'] witness is linked with that of the Holy Spirit. It is the same Christ to whom they bear witness and it is the same salvation of which they bear witness. At the same time it is *their* witness. They cannot simply relax and leave it all to the Spirit. They have a particular function in bearing witness in that they were with Jesus from the very beginning. There is a responsibility resting on all Christians to bear their witness to the facts of saving race. They cannot evade this." Leon Morris, *The Gospel According to John* (Grand Rapids: Wm. B. Eerdmans, 1971), 684.

4    See Acts 4:29-31; 1:8; 6:9b-10; Luke 12:11-12; 21:14-5; 24:46-48

5    "Although the Spirit may bear witness to the world apart from Christians, it would be out of step with these chapters to think that Christians are thought of as those who bear witness apart from the Spirit. Whether we think of the Spirit's help in the crisis of acute persecution … or in the context of sustained, faithful witness …, the community's witness is to be empowered by the Paraclete himself." D. A. Carson, *The Gospel According to John* (Grand Rapids: William B. Eerdmans, 1991), 530.

6    "When, after all the negative things he has said, Jesus now promises the coming of the Paraclete as the one who will bear witness to him, this is naturally intended to reassure the disciples that in the enormous opposition they encounter in the world they will not stand alone. The Paraclete's witness to Jesus is the assistance that the Spirit will give the disciples in the great controversy between the church and the world…" Herman Ridderbos, *The Gospel According to John: A Theological Commentary* (Grand Rapids: William B. Eerdmans, 1997), 526.

7    The "careers" of the various Apostles, of course, are speculative, depending on an uncertain mix of tradition, legend, and later embellishment. What is important for our purposes is not the accuracy of the details but the certainty of the Apostolic commitment to witness to the dying and rising Jesus, a commitment that led them to risk everything and (in the end) give everything to be true to their mission.

## Chapter Eleven

1    Robert Louis Stevenson, *The Celestial Surgeon*.

2    "The thought is not that Jesus and the Holy Spirit cannot, for unarticulated metaphysical reasons, simultaneously minister to God's people, or any other such strange notion. Rather the thought is eschatological. The many biblical promises that the Spirit will characterize the age of the kingdom of God … breed anticipation. But this saving reign of God cannot be fully inaugurated until Jesus has died, risen from the dead, and been exalted to his Father's right hand, returned to the glory he enjoyed with the Father before the world began." D. A. Carson, *The Gospel According to John* (Grand Rapids: William B. Eerdmans, 1991), 533-534.

3    The disciples who remained on the plain while Jesus was transfigured on the mountain, for instance, had to wait for Jesus to rejoin them before knowing what to do about a demon-possessed boy (Matt 17:1-21).

4    Matt 15:15-20 (Compare Luke 24:45 where the resurrected Jesus has the power to "open their minds.")

5    "The verb [convict] occurs eighteen times in the New Testament … Arguably, in every instance the verb has to do with showing someone his sin, usually as a summons to repentance." Carson, _John_, 534.

"[W]e should take the words to mean also that the Spirit brings the world's guilt home to itself. The Spirit convicts the individual sinner's conscience. Otherwise men would never be convicted of their sin." Leon Morris, _The Gospel According to John_ (Grand Rapids: Wm. B. Eerdmans, 1971), 698.

6    "In common with other New Testament usages, [convict] means 'to convict [the world]' in the personal sense, i.e., not arguing the case of the world's objective guilt before God at the final Great Assize, but shaming the world and convincing it of its own guilt, thus calling it to repentance." Carson, _John_, 536.

7    I am indebted to D. A. Carson for his cogent and convincing work on this passage.

8    "Just as Jesus forced a division in the world (15:20) by showing that what it does is evil …, so the Paraclete continues this work." Carson, _John_, 537. "In being the moving force behind this [convicting work] the Paraclete is simply continuing the work of Jesus who himself bore evidence against the world that what it does is evil." Raymond Brown, _The Gospel According to John XIII-XXI_ (New York: Doubleday, 1970), 712.

9    "It might be objected that it is passing strange to speak of convicting the world of _righteousness_ at all…. Within the Fourth Gospel, this reading of 'righteousness' is eminently appropriate." Carson, _John_, 538.

## Chapter Twelve

1    "O unbelieving and perverse generation," Jesus replied, "how long shall I stay with you and put up with you?" (Lk 9:41—a comment directed at the Twelve when they failed to cast out a demon.) "Don't you understand this parable? How then will you understand any parable?" (Mark 4:13—again, expressed to the disciples on their failure to grasp what Jesus was telling them.)

2    "This fifth and final Paraclete passage (vv. 12-15) is a suitable climax to the series, since it focuses on the completion of the revelation of Jesus Christ." D. A. Carson, _The Gospel According to John_ (Grand Rapids: William B. Eerdmans, 1991), 539.

3    "Despite his words of consolation and his promise to "come back" so that they can see him again, Jesus cannot unpack for them the full meaning of these events; that would be too much for them…. Only the overpowering surprise of seeing him again after his resurrection will explain the riddle—partly in the light of the Scriptures (cf. 20:9) and above all through the assistance of the Spirit." Herman Ridderbos, _The Gospel According to John: A Theological Commentary_ (Grand Rapids: William B. Eerdmans, 1997), 535.

4    "We are to understand that Jesus is the nodal point of revelation, God's culminating self-disclosure, God's final self-expression, God's 'Word' (1:1, 14)…. That does not mean he himself provides all the details his followers will need; it does mean that 'extra' bits the Holy Spirit provides after he is sent by Christ Jesus,

consequent upon Jesus' death/exaltation, are nothing more than the filling out of the revelation nodally present in Jesus himself." Carson, *John*, 539.

5   "More likely vs. 12 means that only after Jesus' resurrection will there be full understanding of what happened and was said during the ministry, a theme that is familiar in John.... It is unlikely that in Johannine thought there was any concept of further revelation after their ministry of Jesus, for Jesus is *the* revelation of the Father, the Word of God." Raymond Brown, *The Gospel According to John XIII-XXI* (New York: Doubleday & Company, Inc., 1970), 714. "The Paraclete's guidance along the way of all truth involves more than a deeper intellectual understanding of what Jesus has said—it involves a way of life in conformity with Jesus' teaching ..." Brown, *John*, 715. "In any case the emphasis is on the term "all": the truth has been made known by Jesus to the disciples, but their grasp of it has been limited; the task of the Paraclete will be to lead them that they may comprehend the depths and heights of the revelation as yet unperceived by them." George Beasley-Murray, *John* (Waco, TX: Word, 1987), 283.

6   "Jesus brings the truth, and makes it present through his coming into the world; the Spirit-Paraclete opens up this truth and creates the entrance into it for the believers." Porsch as quoted by Beasley-Murray, *John*, 283.

7   Brown, *John*, 716.

## Chapter Fourteen

1   "Jesus' valuation of what is for his disciples' 'good', indeed, for our good, ought to temper longings of the 'Oh-if-only-I-could-have-been-in-Galilee-when-Jesus-was-there!' sort. That same Jesus insists it is better to be alive now, after the coming of the Spirit." D. A. Carson, *The Gospel According to John* (Grand Rapids: William B. Eerdmans, 1991), 534.

## Chapter Fifteen

1   That's what much of this letter does, by the way—point to ideas that are essential for Christian faith: Jesus came in the flesh; we have to live obediently, we have to love each other.

2   Again, personal morality is very much on John's mind in this letter: walking in darkness, confessing sin, obeying commands, living like Jesus.

## Chapter Sixteen

1   It is interesting to notice that this interpretation of Acts 8:14-17 must be driven by our view of water baptism and its effects. There is nothing in this passage that links "receiving the Holy Spirit" with a full and miraculous experience of the Spirit. These believers do not speak in tongues or prophesy when Peter and John lay hands on them. They simply "receive" the Spirit. But our understanding of baptism requires us to see the miraculous here. They already *had* the Spirit because they had already been baptized "in the name of the Lord Jesus." Thus, this "reception of the Spirit" must refer to a second and miraculous experience of the Spirit. To help matters out, we went to Acts 19:1-7—where apostolic hands *do* result in the Spirit "coming on" disciples with accompanying tongues and prophecies—and simply

conflated the two passages—Acts 8 is just another instance of what happened in Acts 19.

2   An example of our teaching on this point can be found in a tract by V. E. Howard, *The Indwelling of the Holy Spirit* (West Monroe, LA: Central Printers and Publishers, 1970), 6-8:

"Miracles and healings have ceased because the means of securing miraculous power to perform miracles have ceased. The New Testament reveals two means of bestowing miraculous power upon men chosen by God. One: The baptism of the Holy Spirit (Acts 2:4, 43). Two: The laying on hands of the Apostles (Acts 8:14-18; 19:1-7).

According to Acts 1:2, 26; 2:4, 14, 43, the Apostles received the baptism of the Holy Spirit. In Acts 10:44, 45, it is revealed that a special miraculous "gift of the Holy Spirit" was "poured out" upon Cornelius and his household. Paul, as a special chosen Apostle, was endowed with the Holy Spirit and was divinely guided by the Spirit (Galatians 1:11, 12). This last occurrence of the baptism of the Holy Spirit, which we have record of, was about the year of a.d. 33. Some twenty-three years later the Apostle Peter wrote about water baptism which saves (1 Pet. 3:20, 21). The Holy Spirit, through Paul, declared there is "one baptism" (Eph. 4:5). Obviously, that is water baptism.... We must, therefore, scripturally conclude that there is no baptism of the Holy Spirit now as a source for miraculous works....

The Apostles have been dead more than nineteen hundred years now. The last persons upon whom the Apostles laid their hands and conferred miraculous power have been dead now about nineteen hundred years. When the last Apostle died and the last person upon whom the Apostles laid their hands died, miracles by power of the Holy Spirit ceased."

3   Note Ananias' statement that he had been sent to Saul so that he might "be filled with the Holy Spirit."

4   Elders of the church laid hands on Timothy and conveyed a "gift."

5   Paul warns his protégée not to be hasty in laying on hands. Perhaps this refers to ordination of church leaders. But the language is certainly consistent with the impartation of spiritual gifts.

6   See Matt 5:48; 19:21; Rom 12:2; 1 Cor 2:6; 13:10; 14:20; Eph 4:13; Phil 3:15; Col 1:28; 4:12; Heb 5:14; 9:11; Jas 1:4, 17, 25; 3:2; 1 John 4:18.

7   Just a few quotes to give the gist:

"As all the influence which my spirit has exerted on other spirits, at home or abroad, has been by ... my written or spoken word; so believe I that all the influence of God's good Spirit now felt in the way of conviction or consolation in the four quarters of the globe is by the Word, written, read and heard, which is called the living oracles." (Alexander Campbell, *Millennial Harbinger*, vol 6, 356)

"Every single step in the divine plan, from the time the sinner decides to become a child of God until he sweeps through the gates into the heavenly realm—every step is effected by God's word! There is no such thing as the Spirit of God operating away or distinct from the written word." (N. B. Hardeman, *Hardeman-Bogard Debate*, 80).

"The only spiritual instruction, guidance, or influence possible to man is to be gained through coming to the word of God and taking it into the heart as the seed of the kingdom, treasuring it there, and guiding our feelings, thoughts, purposes, and lives by its sacred teaching. In this way the Spirit that dwells in the word, introduced into our hearts, infects pervades and molds our feelings, thoughts, purposes, and lives." (David Lipscomb, *Salvation from Sin*, 93)

"The word of God is the 'sword of the Spirit' (Heb. 4:12.) It is the instrument which the Spirit uses to accomplish his mission. To illustrate: A man uses an axe to chop wood. The energy is inherent in the man; but, it is transmitted through the axe to the timber, and the axe is the means by which the energy resident in the man is applied to the wood. Similarly, the Holy Spirit, in both conversion and sanctification, operates on human hearts; but, he does so through the medium of the word which is his instrument. And, as there is not direct impact between the man and the wood, neither is there direct impact between the Spirit and the human heart; the influence is wrought by means of the word, 'the sword of the Spirit.'" Guy N. Woods, *How the Holy Spirit Dwells in the Christian* (Shreveport, LA: Lambert Book House, 1971), 12.

## Chapter Seventeen

1  In the literal sense of without ("un-") an indwelling Spirit ("inspirited").

2  Deists typically accept the existence of God and his creative work at the foundations of the world, but reject supernatural events (prophecy, miracles) and tend to assert that God does not interfere with human life and the laws of the universe.

3  1 Cor 3:16-17; 2 Cor 6:16; Eph 2:21-22

4  Read the howls that greeted the publication of Shelly and Harris' *Second Incarnation* to get a sense of where many in our movement stand on the issue of the Spirit indwelling the church. Rubel Shelly and Randall J. Harris, *The Second Incarnation: A Theology for the 21st Century Church* (Abilene, TX: ACU Press, ).

5  Acts 13:2; 20:28; Rom 12:8

# A Study Guide and Workbook for
# A SPIRIT FOR THE REST OF US

## by Tim Woodroof

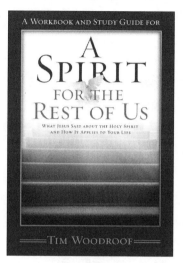

$6.99 paper
ISBN 978-0-89112-636-2

## For use in classes, small groups, and personal study

WORKBOOK INCLUDES:

1. Reflection questions for each of the 18 chapters
2. Personal inductive Bible studies
3. Small group studies
4. "Disciplines" for inviting the Spirit
5. Prayers and personal devotions

1-877-816-4455 toll free
www.leafwoodpublishers.com

# A Spirit for the Rest of Us
## Conversations about the Spirit for You and Your Church

This ten week series serves as a guide for congregations ready to discuss the Spirit and his work in our world today. Does the Spirit have a role to play in our lives and in our churches? If so, what does that look like? What does the promise of the *Paraclete* mean for you and me?

Series includes:
- Program Manual
- Sermon Outlines
- Sermon Handouts
- PowerPoint Slides
- Worship Plans
- Publicity Package

www.lookpress.com
(800) 863-5665
1730 Coachman's Court
Brentwood, TN  37027